eBooks for Elementary School

# eBooks for Elementary School

Terence W. Cavanaugh

LIBRARIES UNLIMITED

AN IMPRINT OF ABC-CLIO, LLC
Santa Barbara, California • Denver, Colorado • Oxford, England

Copyright © 2015 by Terence W. Cavanaugh

All rights reserved. No part of this publication may be reproduced, stored in a retrieval system, or transmitted, in any form or by any means, electronic, mechanical, photocopying, recording, or otherwise, except for the inclusion of brief quotations in a review, without prior permission in writing from the publisher.

**Library of Congress Cataloging-in-Publication Data**

Cavanaugh, Terence W.
  eBooks for elementary school / Terence W. Cavanaugh.
    pages cm
  Includes bibliographical references and index.
  ISBN 978-1-61069-849-8 (pbk.) — ISBN 978-1-61069-850-4 (ebook)
1. Electronic books. 2. Children's electronic books. 3. Libraries—Special collections—Electronic books. 4. School children—Books and reading—United States. 5. Electronic book readers. I. Title.
Z1033.E43C383   2015
070.5′73—dc 3          2014037205

ISBN: 978-1-61069-849-8
EISBN: 978-1-61069-850-4

19  18  17  16  15      1  2  3  4  5

This book is also available on the World Wide Web as an eBook.
Visit www.abc-clio.com for details.

Libraries Unlimited
An Imprint of ABC-CLIO, LLC

ABC-CLIO, LLC
130 Cremona Drive, P.O. Box 1911
Santa Barbara, California 93116-1911

This book is printed on acid-free paper ∞

Manufactured in the United States of America

# Contents

Introduction .................................................................................ix

**PART I: eBOOK TECHNOLOGY** ............................................................. 1

**Chapter 1: Why Use eBooks in the Classroom?** ............................................. 3
   Defining eBooks................................................................... 3
   Advantages of eBooks............................................................. 4
   eBooks Versus Traditional Books.................................................. 7
   eBooks and Standards ............................................................ 8
   Availability of eBooks............................................................ 9
   Conclusion....................................................................... 10
   Online Resources ................................................................ 10

**Chapter 2: The eBook Platform: Hardware and Software** ................................. 11
   The eBook TRIO.................................................................. 11
   eBook Software Determines File Type ........................................... 12
   The Main eBook Choices ........................................................ 14
   Conclusion....................................................................... 20
   Online Resources ................................................................ 21

**Chapter 3: eBook File Formats** .......................................................... 25
   Types of eBook File Formats..................................................... 25
   Flash and Web Format .......................................................... 30
   eBook Apps (Apple and Android)................................................. 31
   Presentation eBooks ............................................................ 33
   Audiobook File Formats ......................................................... 34
   Conclusion....................................................................... 35
   Resources ....................................................................... 35

**PART II: eBOOK SOURCES** ............................................................... 41

**Chapter 4: Getting Free eBooks** ......................................................... 43
   Picture Books and Emergent Readers............................................ 44
   Fiction, Including Short Stories, Chapter Books, and Novels..................... 53
   Nonfiction ....................................................................... 57

General Library Collections with Children's or YA Sections . . . . . . . . . . . . . . . . . . . . . . . . . . 59
Coloring Books, Comics, and eMagazines . . . . . . . . . . . . . . . . . . . . . . . . . . . . . . . . . . . 61

## Chapter 5: eBook Stores and eBook Borrowing . . . . . . . . . . . . . . . . . . . . . . . . . . . . . . . . . . . . 65
eBook Stores. . . . . . . . . . . . . . . . . . . . . . . . . . . . . . . . . . . . . . . . . . . . . . . . . . . . . . . . . . . . 65
eBook Borrowing: Public Libraries and Lending Clubs . . . . . . . . . . . . . . . . . . . . . . . . . . 69
eBook Lending Clubs. . . . . . . . . . . . . . . . . . . . . . . . . . . . . . . . . . . . . . . . . . . . . . . . . . . . 71

## Chapter 6: Converting and Cataloging Your eBook Collection . . . . . . . . . . . . . . . . . . . . . . . 75
Converting eBook Formats . . . . . . . . . . . . . . . . . . . . . . . . . . . . . . . . . . . . . . . . . . . . . . . 75
Converting Audiobooks . . . . . . . . . . . . . . . . . . . . . . . . . . . . . . . . . . . . . . . . . . . . . . . . . 76
Cataloging Your Collection. . . . . . . . . . . . . . . . . . . . . . . . . . . . . . . . . . . . . . . . . . . . . . . 77
Classroom Activities with the Class Catalog. . . . . . . . . . . . . . . . . . . . . . . . . . . . . . . . . 78
Conclusion. . . . . . . . . . . . . . . . . . . . . . . . . . . . . . . . . . . . . . . . . . . . . . . . . . . . . . . . . . . . 79
Online Resources. . . . . . . . . . . . . . . . . . . . . . . . . . . . . . . . . . . . . . . . . . . . . . . . . . . . . . 79

## PART III: CREATING eBOOKS. . . . . . . . . . . . . . . . . . . . . . . . . . . . . . . . . . . . . . . . . . . . . . . . . . . . 83

## Chapter 7: Creating eBooks as a Classroom Project . . . . . . . . . . . . . . . . . . . . . . . . . . . . . . . 85
eBook Creation. . . . . . . . . . . . . . . . . . . . . . . . . . . . . . . . . . . . . . . . . . . . . . . . . . . . . . . . 87
Sample Lesson Plan: Fairytale eBooks . . . . . . . . . . . . . . . . . . . . . . . . . . . . . . . . . . . . . 89
Online Resources. . . . . . . . . . . . . . . . . . . . . . . . . . . . . . . . . . . . . . . . . . . . . . . . . . . . . . 92

## Chapter 8: Online Tools for Creating Picture eBooks . . . . . . . . . . . . . . . . . . . . . . . . . . . . . . 93
Storybird . . . . . . . . . . . . . . . . . . . . . . . . . . . . . . . . . . . . . . . . . . . . . . . . . . . . . . . . . . . . . 94
CAST UDL Book Builder. . . . . . . . . . . . . . . . . . . . . . . . . . . . . . . . . . . . . . . . . . . . . . . . . 97
Creating Comics . . . . . . . . . . . . . . . . . . . . . . . . . . . . . . . . . . . . . . . . . . . . . . . . . . . . . 101
Online Resources. . . . . . . . . . . . . . . . . . . . . . . . . . . . . . . . . . . . . . . . . . . . . . . . . . . . . 102

## Chapter 9: Creating eBooks with Productivity and Other Software . . . . . . . . . . . . . . . . . 107
Creating Text (TXT) eBooks. . . . . . . . . . . . . . . . . . . . . . . . . . . . . . . . . . . . . . . . . . . . . 107
Creating Adobe Reader (PDF) eBooks. . . . . . . . . . . . . . . . . . . . . . . . . . . . . . . . . . . . . 108
Creating eBooks for Kindle or Nook Readers. . . . . . . . . . . . . . . . . . . . . . . . . . . . . . . 108
More Word Processing Tools . . . . . . . . . . . . . . . . . . . . . . . . . . . . . . . . . . . . . . . . . . . 110
PowerPoint and Other Presentation Tools . . . . . . . . . . . . . . . . . . . . . . . . . . . . . . . . 110
Creating Audiobooks. . . . . . . . . . . . . . . . . . . . . . . . . . . . . . . . . . . . . . . . . . . . . . . . . . 115
Creating eBooks with iPads . . . . . . . . . . . . . . . . . . . . . . . . . . . . . . . . . . . . . . . . . . . . 116
Publishing Your eBook . . . . . . . . . . . . . . . . . . . . . . . . . . . . . . . . . . . . . . . . . . . . . . . . 117
Online Resources. . . . . . . . . . . . . . . . . . . . . . . . . . . . . . . . . . . . . . . . . . . . . . . . . . . . . 117

## PART IV: INTEGRATING eBOOKS INTO THE CLASSROOM . . . . . . . . . . . . . . . . . . . . . . . . . . . 121

## Chapter 10: eBooks in the Classroom and School. . . . . . . . . . . . . . . . . . . . . . . . . . . . . . . . 123
eBooks, Literacy, and Reading. . . . . . . . . . . . . . . . . . . . . . . . . . . . . . . . . . . . . . . . . . 124
Integrating Technology. . . . . . . . . . . . . . . . . . . . . . . . . . . . . . . . . . . . . . . . . . . . . . . . 124
Book Cards . . . . . . . . . . . . . . . . . . . . . . . . . . . . . . . . . . . . . . . . . . . . . . . . . . . . . . . . . 130
Assessing with eBooks . . . . . . . . . . . . . . . . . . . . . . . . . . . . . . . . . . . . . . . . . . . . . . . . 132
Online Resources. . . . . . . . . . . . . . . . . . . . . . . . . . . . . . . . . . . . . . . . . . . . . . . . . . . . . 134

**Chapter 11: Picture eBooks and Content Area Reading** ............................. **137**
*Co-written by Gigi David and Katrina W. Hall*
   eBooks in Content Areas ............................................. 138
   Picture eBooks ..................................................... 138
   Mathematics ....................................................... 139
   Science ........................................................... 140
   Social Studies ..................................................... 141
   Visual Art and Music ............................................... 142
   Foreign Language .................................................. 145
   A Little Research Goes a Long Way .................................. 145
   Online Resources .................................................. 145

**Chapter 12: eBooks and Struggling Readers** ................................. **151**
*Co-written by Lunetta Williams and Andrea Thoermer*
   Struggling Readers ................................................ 152
   Adapting Text ..................................................... 152
   Reading Aloud .................................................... 154
   Building Background Knowledge ..................................... 156
   Using Songs ...................................................... 157
   Using Poetry and Nursery Rhymes ................................... 158
   Setting Up a Readers Theater ...................................... 159
   Providing Wide Access to Books .................................... 160
   Online Resources .................................................. 161

**Chapter 13: Gifted Students and Advanced Readers** .......................... **167**
*Co-written by Christine Weber*
   Characteristics of Gifted Readers .................................. 168
   Differentiating Instruction ........................................ 169
   Using eBooks with Gifted Readers ................................... 170
   Next Steps ........................................................ 172
   Where to Start? ................................................... 173
   Online Resources .................................................. 173
   Print Resources ................................................... 175

**Chapter 14: eBooks and ESL / ELL Students** ................................. **177**
*Co-written by Jin-Suk Byun*
   The ELL Student ................................................... 178
   Educational Applications .......................................... 178
   The Connection between Spoken and Written Language .................. 179
   Text-Enhancing Functions .......................................... 180
   On-Demand Referencing ............................................. 181
   Promote Interaction in the Classroom ............................... 182
   More Sites to Come ................................................ 183
   Online Resources .................................................. 183

**Chapter 15: Students with Special Needs** .................................................. **187**
   Accommodations Provided by eBooks .................................................. 188
   Sample Accommodation ..................................................................... 194
   Obtaining eBooks for Students with Special Needs ............................... 195
   Achieving Success with eBooks ......................................................... 197
   Online Resources ............................................................................... 197

**Appendix A: eBook Formats List** ............................................................ 201

Index ......................................................................................................... 205

# Introduction

Schools no longer need to take a "wait and see" attitude concerning eBook technology, as was the case in the past. Instead, we can explore the tremendous possibilities that eBooks offer to anyone with an interest in education. When thinking about integrating eBooks into your classroom, think AND, not OR. We don't have to make a shift to fully digital books. Instead we can start integrating them in the classroom and home with print books - eBooks AND paper books, not eBooks OR paper books.

In reading this book, I hope that you will learn to apply eBooks in creating interactive educational activities and find helpful materials to support reading instruction, literacy, standards, and reading in the content areas. Numerous strategies have been developed for integrating eBooks into reading instruction and remediation. eBooks can help with a variety of reading problems, including print disabilities. Educators can easily locate eBooks to support reading in all content areas or even use eBook software to create their own eBooks.

## THE GOAL OF THIS BOOK

The goal of this book is to provide information and instruction on how library media specialists, teachers, students, and parents can expand and enhance the student reading experience through the use of technology. This book can help you

- develop a functional understanding of eBook technology, including hardware, software, and content,
- understand, demonstrate, and describe the features of eBook technologies that make them effective teaching tools and resources,
- become aware of standards relating to reading and technology,
- reflect on the potential of technology to empower students, teachers, librarians, media specialists, and parents,
- understand ways to apply eBooks as reading and writing tools,
- gain new techniques for using eBooks in the classroom,
- integrate eBooks into a variety of educational settings by providing sample eBook lessons, activities, assessments, and applications for a range of grade levels,

- discover the advantages and costs of using various eBook technology,
- discover online sources of eBooks, such as online libraries and bookstores, and eBook software,
- create educational and professional resources using eBook technology and other software applications,
- use eBook technology to help learners with various abilities, language backgrounds, and special needs.

## WEBSITES MENTIONED IN THIS BOOK

Throughout the book, you will find links to online resources. To make it easier to navigate to resources with long web addresses (URLs), I have included shortcut links in <brackets>. For example, look at this resource:

>Newbery Honor Books and Medal Winners (http://digital.library.upenn.edu/women/_collections/newbery/newbery.html) <http://goo.gl/rds1P>

Here, you only need to type in the shorter URL in brackets to reach that address, or **http://goo.gl/rds1P**.

Because the Internet is constantly changing, some web addresses may have moved or become inactive by the time you read this. If you find that a link is not functioning, try shortening the actual URL (this is called backtracking) by dropping off slashed sections of the address, or do a keyword search for the title or topic.

The Internet contains a wide range of materials, some of which may not be appropriate for certain students. Instructors should always visit websites before allowing student access, to make sure that the content is appropriate. For example, some collection sites mentioned in this book contain public domain books with content inappropriate for elementary school children.

# Part I

# eBOOK TECHNOLOGY

"Do not wait: the time will never be 'just right.' Start where you stand, and work whatever tools you may have at your command and better tools will be found as you go along."
—Napoleon Hill, *Think and Grow Rich* (1938, p. 127)

Ebooks were first described in Robert A. Heinlein's science fiction classic *Space Cadet* (Bryant, 2003; Heinlein, 1948). But perhaps the most famous fictional eBook is the namesake of Douglas Adams' 1979 *Hitchhiker's Guide to the Galaxy*, which is described this way:

Robert Heinlein's 1948 classic *Space Cadet* (First Edition), the first book with a description of an electronic book, sits beside a Kindle and a NOOK Color displaying the eBook

"It's a sort of electronic book. It tells you everything you need to know about anything. That's its job" (Adams, 1981).

Today's students are technology savvy, with 53% of all two- to four-year-olds and 90% of all five- to eight-year-olds in the United States having used a computer (Common Sense Media, 2011). A study of children in the European Union, North America, Australia/New Zealand, and Japan found that 69% of two- to five-year-olds are able to operate a computer mouse, which is particularly impressive when you consider that only 11% of that age group can tie their own shoelaces (AVG, 2011). Children want to read eBooks and have said that they would read more if they had access to eBook devices (Scholastic, 2010).

Do we have to wait until every child has his or her own electronic book device to begin using eBooks? As Napoleon Hill counsels above, there is no need to wait. We can begin using eBooks with elementary students right now. At little or no cost, we can start integrating eBooks into education by using the technology available in most classrooms today. Yes, there are dedicated eBook reading devices, such as the popular NOOK or Kindle. But eBook reading software is also widely available on a variety of familiar devices—from laptop, desktop, and tablet computers, to game devices, calculators, MP3 players, and smartphones.

However, the sheer variety and ever-evolving nature of eBook devices, software, and content formats complicates things. As you will see, there is a great deal of overlap between the three core elements that comprise an eBook: hardware, software, and content. Part I of this book, Ebook Technology, will help you become better acquainted with eBook technology and terminology.

Part I consists of three chapters. Chapter 1 explains what an eBook is. I make the case for using eBooks in the classroom, describing their advantages over print books. Chapter 2 describes the eBook platform, with a look at the numerous hardware and software options that can make up an eBook. Chapter 3 explores eBook file formats—some of them might surprise you.

# Chapter 1

# Why Use eBooks in the Classroom?

Teachers, students, and books are the foundations of schools. Whenever I give a presentation on technology and reading, I start by asking the group to define "book." Usually, most people in the group say that a book is an item consisting of a number of pages (made of paper) with words on them. Then I show them an audiobook on tape or on CD and ask if this is also a book. Everyone usually agrees that it is. Next, I show them a child's CD storybook, such as *Arthur's Teacher Trouble*, and ask them if this is a book. Again, they agree that it is. But when I show my smartphone running an app and put forth the same question, they are not sure.

Books have gone beyond the limits of paper and ink. The ever-changing world of technology has broadened the scope of what can be considered an eBook. A book can now be ink on paper, digital ink on a screen, an audio file, a streaming video, and even refreshable Braille.

## DEFINING EBOOKS

Before I define eBooks, I would like to point out how the definition of a book is changing. I recently looked up "book" in a "dictionary." Actually, I used Dictionary.com, because no one in the front office actually had a physical dictionary anymore. Dictionary.com defined a book as "a written or printed work of fiction or nonfiction, usually on sheets of paper fastened or bound together within covers."

Compare this to how the online *American Heritage Dictionary* defined "book" just 13 years ago as "a set of written, printed, or blank pages fastened along one side and encased between protective covers; a printed or written literary work" (www.bartleby.com/61/2/B0390200.html).

**FIGURE 1.1** Collection of various forms of eBooks

The main point to notice is the inclusion of "usually" in dictionary.com's definition. This acknowledges that books no longer need covers, binding, paper, or ink.

You may think of an eBook as just a fancy specialized digital display pad like the Kindle or NOOK. That would fit with Dictionary.com's definition of an eBook as "1. a portable electronic device used to download and read books or magazines that are in digital form; 2. a book in digital form." But my definition of an eBook expands on that—at its most basic, an eBook is any material presenting text through a digital method. That definition of eBook means that your stereo, playing audiobooks on CD, would also be an eBook device or reader (see Figure 1.1).

I love books, and by that I mean that I love books in all forms, be they print (on paper), audio, or digital (you can see my own book collection at www.librarything.com/catalog/tcavanau). I believe that for the near future, at least, we will be reading from a variety of print display options. I see value in expanding the definition of a book rather than keeping it narrow.

## eBook Formats

A wide variety of eBook options are available. Although most people think of eBooks as print books displayed on computer devices, other formats also exist. One variety of eBook that most people are familiar with is audiobooks—books on tape or CD. The audiobook format has expanded to books on MP3 that can be either streamed directly from the Internet or read on digital devices. While not commonly thought of as an eBook option, most television programs and movies are close-captioned, providing subtitles of what is being said (see chapter 2 for more on these options).

Though these audio and visual formats have important uses, for the most part this book will focus on print-based eBook formats that can be read on a desktop computer or handheld device, such as EPUB books, PDFs, and web-based books.

## ADVANTAGES OF EBOOKS

eBooks offer students, teachers, schools, and parents an enhanced tool for teaching reading, the integration of reading into other subjects such as math or social studies, and a hook to attract more children to read. They also offer an important health advantage.

# Students

Do eBooks make a difference as an educational tool? Maybe you have been saying to yourself, "I should not get an eBook device. What could I do with it? I cannot use it with my students. Sure, it might be good for older students, but not for elementary children." If you have been thinking along these lines, then be reassured. Studies are already showing that eBook devices can be wonderful tools to help elementary students read and learn, so these tools should not be limited to middle- and high-school students.

A recent study found that 25% of children ages 6 to 11 had already been reading books on digital devices. More importantly is the eBook motivation factor—about 63% of 9- to 11-year-olds were interested in reading on electronic devices (such as Kindle or iPad). One third said they would read more for fun if they could do it on a digital device (Scholastic, 2010). Another study of elementary children using mobile devices (such as iPhones) found that two-thirds of younger children had already used such a device, most often in the backseat of the family car. That project also found that children who used the reading applications based on PBS KIDS programs had a vocabulary gain of over 30% (Chiong and Schuler, 2010). Another study of fourth graders found that there were no statistically significant differences in reading comprehension between eBooks and print books (Arme, 2006).

Young students find technology attractive and fun. Although the electronic book or eBook is a relatively recent book format, that "recent" aspect generally applies only to adults. Children of today have seen eBooks all their lives. To them, eBooks have always existed, just as electronics such as computers and cell phones have always been a part of their lives. To them these tools are not new or special; they have always been around.

Whenever I visit a school campus, I like to watch what happens with students outside the classroom. For example, what happens when elementary school children leave school in the afternoon? Focusing on technology, I notice that some students get into vehicles that have DVDs playing on monitors. Other children play on their handheld gaming devices or talk on their cell phones. A recent study found that 31% of 8- to 10-year-olds have their own cell phones (Rideout, V. J., Foehr, U. G., and Roberts, D. F., 2010).

Computer and handheld technology use is common among elementary students today, with 90% of 5- to 8-year-olds having used a computer regularly, with 22% using a computer at least once a day, and 46% using computers at least once a week (*Common Sense Media*, 2011).

I introduced eBooks to my nephew when he was in Grade 3. He is (and has always been) very interested in animals, and he had just finished reading a print copy of *Doctor Dolittle*. He had checked it out from his school library, but the library didn't have the other titles in the series. So, we went to his computer and quickly downloaded and installed an eBook program. We then went to an online library and downloaded another volume in the *Doctor Dolittle* series (all for free).

I showed him how to start the program, select a book from the downloaded books, and turn the pages. I also showed him how he could have the computer read the book aloud.

**FIGURE 1.2** My nephew reading a *Doctor Dolittle* eBook on his home desktop computer

In moments, he had restarted the program, selected the *Doctor Dolittle* book he wanted, pressed the play (read aloud) button, and was entranced watching the screen as it highlighted the text and read it aloud (see Figure 1.2). He was so focused on his reading that when he was called to dinner, his reply was "Not yet, I want to get through chapter three first."

The children of today embrace technology in ways that previous generations may have a hard time understanding. Reading and interacting with words on a screen is something children have experienced all their lives.

## Teachers

Where do teachers stand? A study of the reading habits of teachers (90% were elementary teachers) found that after trying eBook devices, 83% of the teachers strongly agreed that they enjoyed reading books, up from the pre-survey score of 72%. Using eBook devices also changed the teachers' perceptions about reading books on a device. At the beginning of the study, only 27% "somewhat agreed" that they liked to read books on a device. However, after using an eBook device, 50% of the teachers agreed that they liked to read books this way (Manarino-Leggett, 2010).

As always, students will continue to learn to read and improve their skills. But how we teach reading and the tools we use are changing. As educators, we need to recognize the advantages, options, scaffolds, and supports that these digital tools present, from a child reading an eBook for enjoyment, to a student using an eBook as a scaffold to improve reading ability, to a student exploring a content area.

## Schools

Children seem to be naturally attracted to technology, and we should use that interest to pique their interest in learning. One way to do this is with eBooks. After all, the technology is now available in schools. According to the U.S. National Center for Education Statistics, nearly all public schools in the United States have had access to the Internet since 2005 (USDOE-NCES, 2006). Most schools have some form of computer access in every classroom.

The time is right for schools to start incorporating eBooks into their classrooms and library collections. In the United States, there is a federal push to switch to digital textbooks (FCC and USDOE, 2012). Some states have already started the process in their public schools. For example, Florida has passed legislation (FL Statute SB, 2012) for all K–12 public schools to adopt digital textbooks by the 2015–16 school year. More than 20 other states have legislation concerning electronic books for schools. Today, educators need to integrate new technologies, such as smartphones and laptops, into teaching, and this hardware enables reading of eBooks.

## Parents

Many homes already have access to technology, and parents are supportive of the concept of using technology for school books and reading. In fact, 67% of parents said they would purchase a mobile device for their child to use for schoolwork if the school allowed it. Furthermore, 61% said they liked the idea of students using technology, such as mobile devices, to access online textbooks (Project Tomorrow, 2011).

**FIGURE 1.3** Between 4th and 6th grade the average bookbag weight goes from 5 to over 18 pounds

In today's information-based society, technology surrounds everyone, including elementary children, and younger. Because eBooks are available in schools and in students' homes, it's time to start incorporating this book format into education.

## Health Concerns

Another reason for using eBooks is a weighty one (see Figure 1.3). The next time you have a chance, borrow a student's book bag to see how much it weighs. Paper books are heavy, and students are carrying too much information on their backs. Researchers from *Consumer Reports* visited three sample schools and found that students in Grades 2 and 4 are carrying about 5 pounds in their backpacks. Once students reach Grade 6, their backpacks weigh and average of 18.4 pounds (*Consumer Reports*, 2008). Considering that the average textbook weighs 3.5 pounds, a student with homework in just three subjects would carry 10.5 pounds of textbooks plus the backpack itself, along with notebooks, pencils, lunch box, and cell phone.

According to the American Chiropractic Association, children should never carry more than 10% of their body weight. Overweight backpacks can result in back pain, poor posture, and other health concerns (ACA, 2005). Considering the size and weight of elementary school students, the weight of their backpacks may be too much. A 100-pound student should not be carrying more than 10 pounds in total. eBook devices offer us the ability to add text content without adding much weight. For example, a Kindle can carry several thousand books in its half-pound weight.

## EBOOKS VERSUS TRADITIONAL BOOKS

eBooks have benefits that paper books lack. On most eBook devices or program, you can control the look of the text by changing the font style and size—a useful adaptation for younger students, students with special needs, or indeed any reader.

> ***Ergonomic Concerns***
>
> Although eBook devices can provide ergonomic benefits for children because they are typically lighter than even a single paper book, they do have potential downsides. It is always a good idea to reinforce positive posture and reading habits in early readers, whether reading a paper or eBook. As with paper books, many eBook readers require adequate light to avoid eyestrain. eBooks on a computer screen or color eBook device can be incredibly immersive as they stimulate several senses. However, long periods of reading on a computer or tablet screen can cause problems. Remind students to look away occasionally from the screen and focus on other objects before returning to reading on the eBook device.

With an eBook, you may also be able to write and save notes, highlight portions of text, and even draw sketches. It is even possible to have the books read aloud to students while simultaneously providing interactive dictionaries (click on words to get definitions) and web links. Some eBook devices or programs also offer speech recognition. eBook devices can also be used for viewing images and playing educational games. These and other tools can provide scaffolding for readers that help improve student learning.

Practically speaking, in most situations using an eBook in the classroom is no different than using a printed book. Students may be reading their eBooks on devices at their desks, or they may read or listen to a book that is online or on a CD at the school's reading center.

Because the resources are digital, educators can compile onto a web page all student reading material from a variety of online sources, including picture books, fiction chapter books, and nonfiction readings. And students can access this online resource from anywhere, through the Internet.

The big difference between traditional books and eBooks? Using eBooks in the classroom requires that students have either handheld devices or access to computers.

# EBOOKS AND STANDARDS

In an effective standards-based classroom, you should see a print-rich environment. A number of standards support the use of eBooks in schools. ISTE's NETS (International Society for Technology in Education's National Education Technology Standards; www.iste.org/standards) specify that students are to "apply digital tools to gather, evaluate, and use information" (Standard 3, ISTE, 2007).

This aligns well with some of the 1996 Standards for the English Language Arts, from the National Council of Teachers of English (NCTE) and the International Reading Association (IRA) (www.ncte.org/standards/ncte-ira), which state that:

(1) Students read a wide range of print and nonprint texts to build an understanding of texts, of themselves, and of the cultures of the United States and the world; to acquire new information; to respond to the needs and demands of society and the workplace; and for personal fulfillment. Among these texts are fiction and nonfiction, classic and contemporary works.

(6) Students apply knowledge of language structure, language conventions (e.g., spelling and punctuation), media techniques, figurative language, and genre to create, critique, and discuss print and non-print texts.

(8) Students use a variety of technological and information resources (e.g., libraries, databases, computer networks, video) to gather and synthesize information and to create and communicate knowledge.

The Common Core State Standards address and promote using digital reading resources in elementary programs. For example, the Grade 2 standard for reading literature (RL.2.7) states that students "use information gained from illustrations and words in a print or digital text to demonstrate understanding of its characters, setting or plot" (CCSSO and NGA, 2010). Even the National Association for the Education of Young Children (NAEYC) supports the use of technology in achieving developmentally appropriate literacy experiences; the association believes that students should have access to resources, including computer-based software, to engage in enriching interactive literacy experiences, which could include eBooks (NAEYC, 2012; NAEYC, 2009).

## AVAILABILITY OF EBOOKS

eBook libraries are an excellent application of today's technology. Teachers, librarians, and parents can expand the collections available to students, often at no cost and using technology tools already in classrooms and libraries. One day, eBooks will most likely be tied into the school network and library, but for now, we can look at free resources that will allow educators to bring additional books to children.

Finding digital content is usually easy. Numerous online libraries and bookstores distribute freely or sell eBooks that can be used in the classroom or in libraries. Texts are available for use in virtually every content area. These books range from copyright-free texts such as classic literature to nonfiction science, current bestsellers, textbooks, and reference books. At the beginning reading level, there are electronic books that can interact with students, providing feedback and a two-way flow of information. As of this writing, more than 5 million books are available online for free.

A teacher can easily collect hundreds of texts that can be made available to students at no cost. Teachers can use free online eBook libraries and free software to create their own classroom collection of eBooks and then make them available to their students. For more on building an eBook library, see Part 2.

Instructors and students can also create their own eBooks, which can then be shared with a worldwide audience (see Part 3).

> **The Home/School Connection**
>
> Increase reading opportunities for students between home and school. Place links for selected eBooks on the school or classroom website for students and parents to access from home.

# CONCLUSION

eBook awareness and availability has been growing. The time is right for educators to start bringing eBooks into the classroom. Not long ago, some people thought that paperback or pocket books would never last or be accepted as real books, but once people started using them, they became essential. In much the same way, eBooks can be thought of as the next new format for books. Just as Gutenberg made the first modern printed book created with movable type printed on paper, we now have digital text on display screens distributed through wired and wireless networks. We have a new text medium that is integrating the possibilities of computer processing and resources, going far beyond just printing on paper and moving to the fully electronic text concept with interactive capabilities.

To encourage and support reading, educators should strive to make sure that students can select from as many tools for reading as possible, and electronic books should be one of those tools, in schools and in students' homes.

# ONLINE RESOURCES

### Corestandards.org
www.corestandards.org/the-standards
Council of Chief State School Officers and National Governors Association Common Core State Standards

### ISTE.org
www.iste.org/standards.aspx
International Society for Technology in Education Standards (Students, Teachers, and Administrators)

### NCTE.org
www.ncte.org/standards
Standards for the English Language Arts, from the National Council of Teachers of English and the International Reading Association

# Chapter 2

# The eBook Platform: Hardware and Software

If you thought that an eBook device was just a fancy specialized digital display pad like the Kindle or NOOK, then you have been misinformed. At its most basic, an eBook is any hardware presenting text through a digital method. That definition of eBook means that your stereo, playing audiobooks on CD, would also be an eBook device.

## THE EBOOK TRIO

eBooks, like many other forms of digital technology, have three different elements: hardware, software, and content. No matter which configuration you choose, all eBooks work this way: the hardware, or device, runs the eBook program (software), to display the content (book).

### Hardware

There are two types of eBook reading hardware: dedicated devices, typically called *eBook readers*, and *general-purpose devices* that can display eBook files and run a variety of software applications (see Figure 2.1).

The Kindle, Nook, and Sony Reader are examples of dedicated eBook readers. Although these book-sized devices can often perform some other basic tasks, they were made primarily to display eBook content. General-purpose devices can also display eBooks, such as desktop and laptop computers, smartphones, and tablets. Even some game consoles and handheld music and video players can display eBook content.

### Software

For most dedicated eBook readers, the eBook reading software is embedded in the device, though often it can be updated, modified, or even replaced either by the manufacturer

**FIGURE 2.1** Printed and digital book versions displaying Sir Arthur Conan Doyle's *The Lost World*

or sometimes by the user. General-purpose devices can run many versions of eBook software. The programs, or applications (apps), are generally free and often provided by the same manufacturers that produce the dedicated devices. For instance, Amazon (makers of the Kindle) offers Kindle software for Windows, Macintosh, Android, iPads, and a large variety of other devices. Barnes & Noble (Nook), Sony (Reader), Kobo (Kobo) and many others also provide versions of their software for a huge range of devices. Also, third-party developers offer software that can display (and often convert) eBook files from most of the popular formats.

The software does much more than just display the book. Today's eBook programs remember where users stopped reading, allow for multiple methods of page navigation, and allow readers to place bookmarks for rapid location return. Some also can launch an Internet browser via hyperlinks embedded in the text. Other eBook programs have on-demand dictionaries, provide text highlighting tools, allow users to write the equivalent of margin notes, and provide whole-book search features. Some eBook software programs even have a text-to-speech option that reads the book aloud. Of course, the commercial programs almost always have a slick module to entice readers to browse their shop and purchase books.

## File Format

Besides hardware and software, there is the eBook file itself. This file contains all of the book material: text, sound, pictures, Internet links, and anything else the author and publisher wish to include. Chapter 3 discusses file formats in depth.

## EBOOK SOFTWARE DETERMINES FILE TYPE

Just as the relationship between eBook hardware and software is tightly entwined, so is the relationship between the software and the eBook files. There is quite a range of eBook file options. Initially, eBooks looked similar to a word processing document. In this classic eBook file, a computer would display the text, and possibly pictures, on a monitor or other display screen as one giant page to be scrolled through. These eBooks were published in pure text or web-based text format, and were used pretty much like you'd use any word-processing document. Many "doc-style" books are still available, but because they can be difficult and unwieldy to read, they aren't popular despite almost always being free or inexpensive.

> ### *Project Gutenberg*
>
> The first system of distributing eBooks was through the Internet, from organizations such as Project Gutenberg (www.gutenberg.org). Created in 1971 by Michael Heart, Project Gutenberg maintains a public database of texts that are no longer, or never have been, copyrighted and thus now in the public domain. Project Gutenberg offers more than 39,000 eBooks for free download in multiple formats (including audio versions), with more than 300 books in the Children's Literature section and almost 200 books in the Children's Picture Books section.
>
> In addition to Project Gutenberg are numerous free online libraries of downloadable electronic texts, along with online eBook bookstores where readers can purchase and download eBooks for reading on a device or computer.

It didn't take long for eBooks to move beyond a word-processing format into a multitude of more advanced formats. These new formats, when used with their device readers, present the eBooks in a much more user-friendly style (see Figure 2.2). Book pages are displayed one at a time, much like an actual book. Some even mimic the look and sound effects of a real book as you turn each page.

It's easy to get confused about the various software programs and how they work (or don't work) with various eBook formats. We'll delve deeper into eBook formats in the next section, but it is important to know that not all formats are compatible with every device. Even so-called "open standard" formats such as EPUB files may or may not be compatible with a particular eBook software or hardware device. Others may technically work, but with limited features. For instance, you might be able to open a book with color illustrations on your grayscale Kindle or Nook, but obviously you won't see color and perhaps not even a grayscale version of the image.

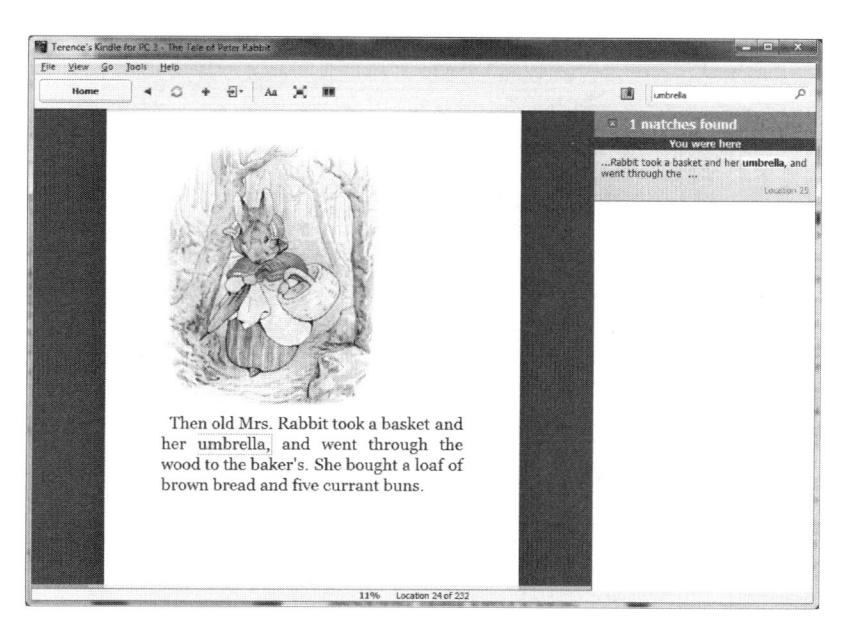

**FIGURE 2.2** Searching within a Kindle ebook *The Tale of Peter Rabbit,* using the Kindle software on a PC

# THE MAIN EBOOK CHOICES

The following are common eBook device and format choices that are appropriate for elementary classroom use. Because the three elements are entwined (hardware, software, and content file type), some of these are devices designed for eBooks; others are software for your existing computer; and still others are audio-based.

## Dedicated eBook Readers

Dedicated eBook devices, popularly called *eBook readers*, have been in the news a lot lately, from home use to their introduction into schools around the world. The next time you are in an airport waiting area, look around—I'm sure that you will spot a number of people using eBook readers while they wait for their flight. Perhaps the best-known eBook readers at the moment are the NOOKs from Barnes & Noble, the Kindles from Amazon, the Kobo, and Sony's Readers (see Figure 2.3 & Table 2.1). But those are just four platforms—there are quite a few others, such as the Bebook, Pandigital Novel, and COOLER. As of this writing, I have identified more than 70 models of eBook readers now being sold. Apple also has its own eBook software that runs on iOS devices, such as the iTouch, iPhone, and iPad.

**Storage Capacity.** The only limit on the number of books that can be stored within an eBook reader is the amount of memory available within the eBook device and the size of the eBook files. This ability to carry many books, references, and resources in a single hardware device which may weigh as little as a half-pound allows users to carry around practically an entire library's worth of books.

According to one eBook company, using the PDF format a gigabyte of storage could contain more than "200 illustrated college reference books, or 350 legal volumes, or about 2,500 600-page novels" (Munyan, 1998). Most eBook devices such as the Kindle and NOOK include 16 or 32 gigabytes of storage, and many models allow you to add as much as 32 gigabytes of additional storage space—the equivalent of a building full of books! The eBook concept allows users to have volumes of information either at their desktop or within their pocket without taking up additional space.

**FIGURE 2.3** E Ink devices include the Kindle, Sony Reader, Nook, and Kobo

**TABLE 2.1** Five Popular eBook Readers (Specialized Devices)

| | Kindle | Kindle Fire | NOOK Simple Touch | NOOK Tablet | Sony Reader (Model PRS-T2) | Kobo eReader Touch |
|---|---|---|---|---|---|---|
| Manufacturer | Amazon | Amazon | Barnes & Noble | Barnes & Noble | Sony | Kobo, Inc. |
| Display Size | 6" | 7–8.9" | 6" | 7" | 6" | 6" |
| Text Display Type | E Ink (electronic paper) | LCD | E Ink electronic paper | LCD | E Ink Pearl (electronic paper) | E Ink (electronic paper) |
| Input | Keyboard or Touch screen | Touch screen | Touch screen | Touch screen | Touch screen | Touch screen |
| Text to Speech/Audio Output | Yes | No | No | No | No | No |
| Connectivity* | USB, Wi-Fi | USB, Wi-Fi | USB, Wi-Fi | USB, Wi-Fi | USB, Wi-Fi | USB, Wi-Fi |
| eBook Formats | Kindle (AZW), MOBI, PRC; PDF, audible (audiobooks) | | ePUB, PDF | ePUB, PDF | ePub, PDF, RSS newsfeeds, JPEGs, BBeB ("BroadBand eBook," Sony's proprietary format). | EPUB, PDF, MOBI |
| Weight | 8.5 oz. | 14 oz. | 7.4 oz. | 15.8 oz. | 5.9 oz. | 7 oz. |
| Cost | $69–179 | $170–400 | $79 | $129 | $130 | $99 |
| Available as Software for Other Devices | Yes | Yes | Yes | Yes | Yes | Yes |
| Battery Life before Recharge** | 8 weeks of reading | 8 hours of reading | 8 weeks of reading | 8 hours of reading | Up to 2 months (Wi-Fi off) | 4 weeks of reading |

*Some versions of Kindle, NOOK Simple Touch, and NOOK Tablet are able to connect through a cell phone network.
**Estimated—actual battery working time may vary upon usage patterns, settings, networking, and environmental conditions. For E Ink display, 3,750 page turns equates to one week of reading for 75 minutes per day with networking turned off.

**E Ink versus LCD Displays.** eBook readers use either an LCD screen or an E Ink electronic paper display (grayscale). E Ink devices display up to 16 shades of gray and can be read in bright light, like a printed book. One big advantage of E Ink displays is very low power requirement, allowing readers such as the NOOK Simple Touch to go for more than a month on a single battery charge, depending on wireless use. The advantage of an LCD display is the color, although it will use power much more quickly and can be troublesome when reading in bright light. E Ink technology also has an advantage in screen stability—unlike LCD screens, the image doesn't need to refresh (redraw itself). E Ink screens have no flicker; however, newer LCD screens have reduced the flicker that can bother some readers during longer reading sessions.

**Free Reading Software.** While we think of the device as the reader, it also contains the software, and that software is available for other devices. For example both the Nook and the Kindle are devices, but you can also run Nook or Kindle software on Mac and PC computers, iPads, Android devices, and BlackBerry devices. The software is available at no cost to users. Because most schools already have computers that can run this software, a classroom, school, or school system can easily add eBook capability to its technology resources, simply by installing the free software programs onto existing classroom computers.

The device-specific programs have their own advantages, especially if you own both a PC and an eBook device. Most allow close synchronization between your PC and device, meaning that you might store most of your books on the PC, freeing memory on your device. Some even allow you to read a chapter on your PC, then move the file to the device and have it remember where you left off. They also tend to have easy-to-use browsing and purchasing modules for finding and buying eBook titles.

For more on applications, see "Reading on Smartphones, Tablets, and Desktop Computers" below.

## Children's eBook Devices

While the popular brands such as NOOK and Kindle are aimed primarily at adults, specialized children's eBook readers are also available (see Table 2.2). Often these are game devices that also act as eBook readers, such as VTech's V.Reader and InnoTab, LeapFrog's Leapster and LeapPad, and even the Nintendo DS Wii U GamePad.

All of these game or learning devices have eBook applications that turn the device into an eBook reader. When running a book module, the device can read the text aloud and often displays animation with sound effects. To have a game device serve as an eBook reader, the child will need the device's eBook plug-in module or will need to download a file from the device's website.

eBooks for these readers range from popular children's books such as *Fancy Nancy*, *Chicka Chicka Boom Boom*, *Olivia*, and *The Cat in the Hat*, to stories based on modern Disney films.

In addition to gaming devices are stand-alone children's eBook devices, such as LeapPad's Tag. One of the biggest success stories concerning stand-alone eBook hardware in schools

**TABLE 2.2** Children's eBook Devices

| Device | Number of Books | Cost Device* | Cost Book | Interaction | Appropriate Age Range | Teacher's Manuals |
|---|---|---|---|---|---|---|
| LeapFrog Tag | 80+ | ~$40 | $7–15 | Pen touch | 4–8 | Yes |
| LeapFrog Leapster | 20+ | ~$35 | $10–15 | Pen touch | 4–9 | Yes |
| LeapFrog LeapPad | 25+ | ~$100 | $10–15 | Touch screen | 4–9 | No |
| VTech V.Reader | 20+ | ~$60 | ~$10–20 | Keyboard | 3–7 | No |
| Fisher Price iXL Learning System | 16+ | ~$80 | ~$14–25 | Turn page | 3–7 | No |
| Nintendo DS Wii U GamePad | 120+ | $150 | $20–45 (one module has 100 books, meaning that each book is actually only 45¢) | Touch screen | No specific age range | No |

*Prices based on Amazon.com listings, 2012.

has been the associated devices and reading programs from LeapFrog, with its LeapTrack Assessment & Instructional System and LeapTrack Reading Pro Classroom Kits. The LeapFrog's Tag is one of a few devices using the children's eBook format called Talking Books. With Talking Books, a child uses a device to interact with text. The device reads the page content aloud to the child and may also allow for other kinds of interactions.

## Reading on Smartphones, Tablets, and Desktop Computers

In 2002, a serialized novel in Japan titled *Deep Love* was the first real mobile-phone-based eBook to receive a lot of attention. That eBook was distributed as downloadable text files to be read on cell phones (Steuer 2004). The *Deep Love* eBook download site accumulated more than 20 million hits within three years of the book's release. The book was then printed on paper and became a bestseller, was reproduced as a Manga (illustrated novel) series, and became a movie.

Today, smartphones such as the iPhone, BlackBerry, and Android phones, along with other devices such as the iPad, iTouch, or Galaxy Tab, can also become eBook devices. With these devices, the eBook runs as an application or "app." Many of these apps also have desktop computer versions.

One example of a book-reading app is Apple's iBooks, which can be run on an iPhone, iPad, or Macintosh. Other applications that are platform specific include Tom's eTextReader for Windows, and Mantano and Aldiko for Android devices. Each of these programs allows users to purchase and download eBook files from online bookstores as well as display books from other sources, such as free online libraries.

18   eBooks for Elementary School

Cross-platform software programs or apps provide flexibility. Rather than just the formats supported by a specific vendor, on these programs you can generally read any eBook file from Amazon, Barnes & Noble, Kobo, Sony, and iTunes. These programs usually have conversion capabilities also, so you might convert a Kindle-formatted eBook into one that will open on a Nook. Two programs that can be used on a classroom's computer, laptop, or tablet include CoolReader and FBReader.

A special kind of program is the book-specific app, which only displays a single eBook. Book-specific applications are usually purchased, although quite a few free or inexpensive ones are available (see chapter 5). These apps are their own program on the device, showing only a single book. Book-specific apps are often much more interactive. Some eBook apps even display the book in 3D using specialized glasses, such as See Here Studio's *The Wrong Side of the Bed*.

## Web eBooks

A number of children's books on the web are available through a computer's browser program, such as Internet Explorer, Safari, Firefox, and Chrome. These books often use some form of plug-in, such as Flash, to display the book, although some are available as standard web pages. Web eBooks are different in their ability to display the book though video, audio, animation, and possibly interactions. For example, using video, the PBS Kids' Between the Lions (http://pbskids.org/lions/stories/) website provides synchronized, captioned streaming Flash videos of stories for children to watch and read. The Library of Congress' Read.gov site (http://read.gov) provides more than 20 books that use a specialized interface allowing for scrolling or page-flip views (see Figure 2.4). The University of Massachusetts Amherst's Aesop's Fables site (www.umass.edu/aesop/) provides the fables in a Flash animation format for reading and watching; some also have supported audio. Google Books (books.google.com) offers more than a million books for purchase and public domain titles, including a large number of children's books. Books can be read online or downloaded as PDFs or EPUBs for offline or device reading.

Scholastic has a number of interactive stories, such as Clifford the Big Red Dog site's (www.scholastic.com/clifford/) Read & Write activities, where students can click to choose elements of the story and have them read aloud.

**FIGURE 2.4**  *The Story of the Three Little Pigs* from the Library of Congress's Read.gov site

These eBooks usually do not need additional programs installed beyond the web browser, but will often need Flash or other plug-ins updated.

## Audio Books

Just about everyone is familiar with audiobooks—most schools, libraries, and bookstores commonly have audiobooks. An audiobook is still an eBook, because it is digital or electronic information that is "displayed" with an electronic device.

Numerous studies have shown that simultaneous reading and listening increases focus, concentration, retention, and learning. Audiobooks have been found to be effective in improving children's reading proficiency, and can provide an enriching reading experience through quality narration.

Audio books also come in different formats. First came books on records, then books on tape, followed by books on discs (CD), and now even books on MP3 files. You can download audible eBooks from sources such as public or school libraries using Overdrive (www.overdrive.com), audio bookstores like Amazon's Audible (www.audible.com), and even free online collections such as Librivox (librivox.org) and Audio Books for Free (www.audiobooksforfree.com), which have MP3 book files that you can listen to on a computer, cellphone, or MP3 player.

**FIGURE 2.5** LeapFrog's Tag Reader device reads printed books aloud

Librivox is a free online audio library that allows users to download books read by volunteers. Users at librivox.org select the audio format and quality of book they want to download, from a lower quality (smaller file) to higher quality (larger file) MP3 or OGG format.

As a side note, most eBook readers will also play audiobooks.

## CD/DVD eBooks or Electronic Storybooks

Electronic storybooks on CD or DVD are usually self-running discs that have their own special display program. It doesn't need to be installed on the computer (see Figure 2.5) and can also often run in regular CD or DVD players. The first notable electronic book of this type was created in 1990, with Discus' "The Tale of Peter Rabbit" made for the Macintosh. Since then, thousands of such electronic children's books have been made and sold for all kinds of computers. These eBooks can be divided into a few main types—print-first and electronic-first. Print-first are printed books first, which are then transferred into electronic books, usually with some value-added material. Electronic-first books are created and distributed initially in a digital version.

The enhanced quality of these eBooks involves special features not available in paper-based versions. For example, look at the modern children's classic *Stellaluna*, a wonderful story with vibrant illustrations. *Stellaluna* has won numerous awards, including American Bookseller's Book of the Year Award, Keyston to Reading Book Award, and SCC Literature for Young People Award. The CD storybook version of *Stellaluna*, by Living Books, provides all the text and images from the book, but also adds more pictures, information about bat science, extra text material, quizzes, and extension activities. Another example is the children's favorite *Chicka Chicka Boom Boom* where the CD version not only can play as an audiobook narrated by Ray Charles in a CD player, it can display the story on a computer, plays games with children, and even allows children to sing with the song and hear their own voice with the playback. Today, these electronic storybooks are on the decline as storybook apps for handheld devices and subscription services become more popular.

## Captioned Television Programs and DVDs

Although you might not think of television programs or movies as eBooks, with one simple menu choice, text can be displayed and a "book" appears. Research has indicated that turning on the captioning or subtitle feature can help students improve their reading while they are watching television (NCI 2004, Feinberg 2003).

Not only are most television programs captioned, most DVD and Blu-ray titles have the ability to display captions or subtitles, sometimes in a number of languages, while playing a video. Closed-caption decoders have been built into all U.S. televisions that are 13 inches or larger since 1993, so this is a technology virtually available to all. Because today's students have grown up with television as a constant companion, they are usually not reluctant to read from the TV. This type of reading has been found to have a motivational quality that is appealing to students, even those who have been difficult to teach using traditional methods.

If you want to engage in silent reading with closed captioning, simply turn down the sound. In one school where I taught, we played videos with the sound off and the captioning on. If you looked in the classrooms, you would have seen a group of students sitting around the television, reading the captioned program, while others read from books and magazines. Research has found that using the closed-caption feature can help not only students with print disabilities, but also regular students, second-language learners, and even adults improve their reading ability.

# CONCLUSION

There are a lot of options when considering technology-supported reading. The eBook devices discussed in this book are not all of them by any means. Other technology can be used to read eBooks, from a computer's word processing or presentation software, to devices such as graphing calculators, iPods, and even a set-top device that works with broadband cable called TVtextbook. If you take a moment to look around your school or home, you might find that you may already have an eBook reading device.

## ONLINE RESOURCES

### Aesop's Fables
www.umass.edu/aesop/
University of Massachusetts Amherst project website that delivers the fables in animated and audio-supported formats

### Aldiko Book Reader
www.aldiko.com/
Ereader program for Android platform devices

### Android Market
https://market.android.com/
Site to purchase or get free eBook apps to download to your device

### Audible
www.audible.com
Amazon's download and subscription audiobook store

### AudioBooksForFree.com
www.audiobooksforfree.com
Online audio library

### Between the Lions
http://pbskids.org/lions/stories/
PBS Kids website with eBooks associated with the TV program

### Clifford the Big Red Dog
www.scholastic.com/clifford/
Scholastic website with associated activities

### CoolReader
http://sourceforge.net/projects/crengine/
Cross-platform ereader program

### FBReader
www.fbreader.org/
Cross-platform ereader program

### iBooks

www.apple.com/ipad/built-in-apps/ibooks.html
Ereader for Apple products

### Internet Public Library

www.ipl.org/div/reading/
Online eBook library

### iTunes

http://itunes.apple.com/us/genre/ios/id36?mt=8
iTunes App Store to purchase or get free eBook applications
www.fisher-price.com/fp.aspx?st=10&e=ixl
Fisher Price game, eBook, and learning device for children

### Kindle

www.amazon.com
Amazon's eBook reader and bookstore

### Kobo

www.kobobooks.com
Kobo's eBook reader and bookstore

### LeapFrog

www.leapfrog.com
Leapster and Tag eBooks for children

### Librivox

www.librivox.org
Free audiobook library

### Mantano Reader

www.mantano.com/en/products/android-reader/
Ereader program for Android platform devices

### Microsoft Reader

www.microsoft.com/reader
Ereader program from Microsoft for Windows

### National Captioning Institute

www.ncicap.org
Nonprofit corporation researching captioning for deaf and hard-of-hearing people, as well as others who can benefit from the service

### Nintendo DS

www.nintendo.com/ds
Handheld gaming device that can also be used as an eBook reader

### NOOK

www.barnesandnoble.com/nook/
Barnes & Noble eBook reader and bookstore

### Overdrive

www.overdrive.com
Online eBook service that works with libraries

### Project Gutenberg

www.gutenberg.net
Online eBook library

### Read.gov

http://read.gov
The Library of Congress's classic books online site

### Scholastic Storia

http://store.scholastic.com/
Ereader program for desktops and portables for books from Scholastic

### Sony Reader

http://store.sony.com
Sony ereader device and bookstore

### Tom's eTextReader

www.fellnersoft.at/eTR.htm
Ereader program for Windows

### TVtextbook

www.tvtextbook.tv
Interactive reading and math skills education through TV broadband

### VTech's V.Reader and InnoTab

www.vtechkids.com/
VTech eBook reader for children

### Worldreader

www.worldreader.org
Nonprofit organization providing eBook readers to schools in developing countries

# Chapter 3

# eBook File Formats

After you have a device and software to display eBooks, you'll need eBook files. Each eBook contains files with text, pictures, and other information.

eBooks come several file formats, and not all formats work with all devices. Some formats are proprietary, such as Amazon's AZW, and will only work with specific devices or software, while others, such as EPUB, will work across a number of devices and programs.

The capabilities of software for readers and the programs for creating eBooks are constantly being improved. Initially, with Project Gutenberg (the first real online library, www.gutenberg.org), an eBook file was a single HTML web page or text file that was read by scrolling with a browser or any word-processing program. Today, Project Gutenberg distributes books in a variety of formats including reading online in a HTML format, or downloading the eBook in HTML, EPUB, AZW, PDF, and TXT. Some books are even available as audio files (MP3).

## TYPES OF EBOOK FILE FORMATS

As of this writing there are more than 30 eBook file formats. Some are platform or device specific; others cross platforms. Most people will only encounter a few eBook formats, which can be read using either common computer applications, such as web browsers or word processors, or freely available eBook programs (see Table 3.1).

**HTML and TXT.** The two oldest eBook formats are HTML (or HTM) and text (TXT). eBooks in these formats are ready for reading using web browsers, word processors, and some eBook programs (see Figure 3.1). Using a web browser's capabilities, readers can adjust text styles, size, and colors. With HTML or text, readers can search for terms within the book, and copy and paste selected text to other programs.

**PDF.** Adobe Portable Document Format (PDF) eBooks are accessible to most operating systems, including Apple, Windows, Android, and Linux, for viewing and printing using the Adobe Reader program (see Figure 3.3). The PDF format allows for page navigation, multiple

**TABLE 3.1** eBook Format Comparison

This table presents a comparison of the format capabilities of five major eBook formats using the default reader without add-ons.

| | Web (HTML) | Text (TXT) | EPUB | Amazon Kindle (AZW) | Adobe Reader (PDF) |
|---|---|---|---|---|---|
| **Default Reading Software** | Any Internet browser | Any text reader or word processor | Most ereader programs | Kindle software | Adobe Reader software |
| Works on desktop or noteBook computer device (PC, Mac, Linux) | Yes | Yes | Yes | Yes | Yes |
| Works on portable device (eBook reader, smartphone, tablet) | Yes | Yes | Yes | Yes | Yes |
| Printing | Yes | Yes | Yes, unless blocked by publisher. | No | Yes, unless blocked by publisher. |
| Word/text search? | Yes | Yes | Yes | Yes | Yes |
| Bookmarking | No | No | Yes | Yes | No |
| Highlighting | No (unless you use an outside program) | No (but some word processors will allow) | Yes | Yes | Yes |
| Note-taking | No | No | Yes (if allowed by software application) | Yes | Yes |
| Text-to-speech | No | No | Yes | Yes, unless blocked by publisher | Yes |
| Synchronized highlighting with "read" text | No | No | No | Yes | No |
| Adjustable text size | Yes | Yes | Yes | Yes | No (only zoom) |
| Display pictures and art | Yes | No | Yes | Yes | Yes |
| Interactive dictionary | No | No | Yes | Yes | No |
| Remember where last stopped | No | No | Yes | Yes | No |
| Display | Scroll | Scroll | Page at a time | Page at a time | Page at a time |
| Two-page display | No | No | No | No | Yes |

viewing options, adding bookmarks, and searching. With the Read Out Loud Text-to-Speech Tool, it can even read the document aloud. Most people are already familiar with the Adobe Portable Document Format as it is a common format for documents found online.

**AZW or MOBI.** Amazon's Kindle format (AZW or MOBI) is a proprietary format based on the Mobipocket format (MOBI). The Kindle software that reads AZW formatted books will also read a number of other formats, including MOBI, TXT, PDF, DOC, and even MP3 and Audible books. The Kindle software is available at no cost for a variety of desktops, laptops, tablets, and smartphone platforms (www.amazon.com/kindle).

**EPUB.** The EPUB format is the open standard for eBooks. It has been gaining in popularity and is the most widely supported eBook format. EPUB eBooks can be read with the Kobo device and software, Apple's iBooks program, Barnes & Noble's Nook software and devices, the Sony Reader device and software, the Cool-er device, the I-River Story eBook reader, and a large number of other eBook devices and software programs.

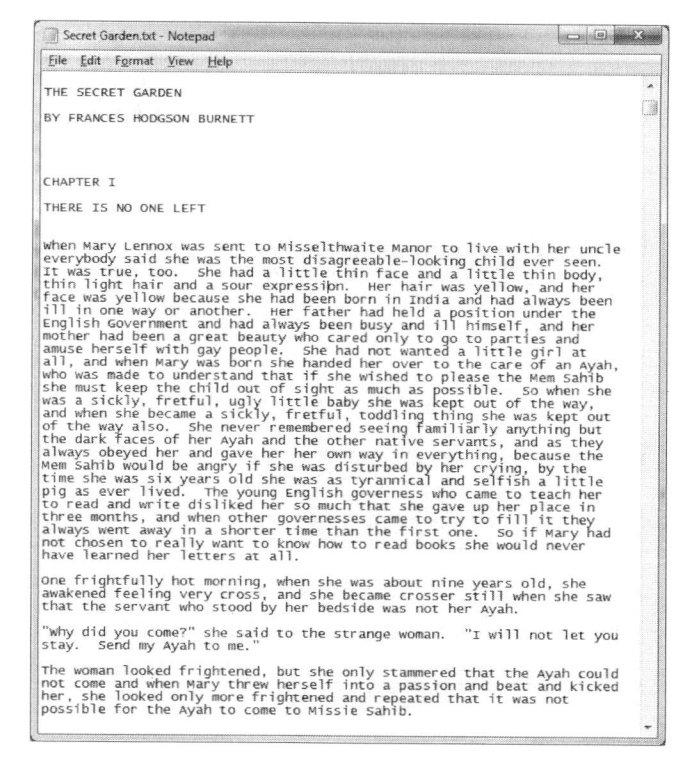

**FIGURE 3.1** Pure text (.TXT) of the eBook *The Secret Garden*, downloaded from Project Gutenberg, being read with Microsoft's Notepad

---

### *Copyright and Public Domain*

A copyright provides a set of exclusive rights to an intellectual property, such as a book, movie, or recording. The copyright protects the particular work created. Copyrights are granted by government agencies for a limited period of time. The Internet, of course, crosses over government borders, which can cause confusion when dealing with eBook rights around the world.

Once a work's copyright has expired, or if the creator did not desire a copyright, that work becomes part of the public domain. Works in the public domain are ones in which no person or other legal entity can establish or maintain proprietary interests. A recent option concerning copyright is Creative Commons, which may only reserve some (not all) rights, and may allow for free distribution and reproduction. All works created and published in the United States before 1923 are considered part of the public domain and may be accessed and used freely.

Although a work may be public domain within the United States, other nations set different copyright rules. For example, in Australia books such as *Animal Farm* and *1984* are in the public domain, but their use is still restricted under copyright in the U.S.

**TABLE 3.2** Software and Devices

|  | Web (HTML) | Text (TXT) | EPUB | Amazon Kindle (AZW) | Adobe Reader (PDF) |
|---|---|---|---|---|---|
| Browser | Yes | Yes | No | No | Yes |
| Kindle | Yes | Yes | No | Yes | Yes |
| Nook | No | Yes | Yes | No | Yes |
| Sony Reader | No | Yes | Yes | No | Yes |
| Kobo eReader | No | Yes | Yes | No | Yes |
| Apple iOS devices | Yes | Yes | Yes | Yes | Yes |

Different formats may provide different options of what you can do with the eBook file depending on the device and the format. If the program or device you are using to read an eBook file is limited, then so too would your options of what you can do with the book. For example the Nook program when reading EPUB books has a rapid navigation system allowing readers easy access through the eBook. Many of these eBook reader programs (see Chapter 2) are available on a variety of operating systems (Mac, PC, Linux) for desktop and laptop computers as well as tablets and smartphones. The more advanced programs create their own annotation file for each eBook. This annotation files will store a variety of information about the book being read, such as where readers have stopped and when the eBook was last accessed. Additionally eBook devices may allow readers to annotate the text that they are reading with tools such as bookmarks, highlights, and margin notes, this information will also be contained in the eBook's annotation file. The ereader programs will also allow readers to search within the eBook file's text for specific words (or for some ereaders across all books in the device), and most also have interactive dictionary look-up features.

---

### *Digital Rights Management*

If you purchase an eBook, or even if you are only dealing with free ones, you will hear about Digital Rights Management, or DRM. DRM is a controlling technology used by the hardware manufacturers, publishers, and copyright holders to put limits on the use of the digital content and devices. For example, an eBook's DRM can restrict whether you can convert an eBook to a different format, give or loan the book, or even have the software read the book aloud.

DRM adds considerable complexity to the already complex issue of eBook file formats. Although EPUB and MOBI formats are standardized formats used by a variety of eBook readers and software applications, the formats can also include proprietary DRM software. What this means is that even when a device is capable of displaying the open-source EPUB format, a book's DRM may not allow it. For instance, an eBook retailer may choose to sell its EPUB titles to be read only on NOOK devices and software applications. Virtually every leading eBook device manufacturer with its own eBook store uses DRM to limit at least some of its titles to its proprietary EPUB format.

Besides the big five formats (HTML, TXT, EPUB, AZW, and PDF), there are a number of other formats, some with specific uses.

**DAISY.** The DAISY (Digital Accessible Information SYstem) eBook format is designed for people who have vision disabilities. DAISY books are digital talking books with features for navigation and synchronization along with being able to be used with a refreshable Braille display.

**CBR and CBZ.** Comic book reading programs such as Comical (http://comical.sourceforge.net/) can read CBR or CBZ formats, displaying the compressed JPG-scanned comic book pages.

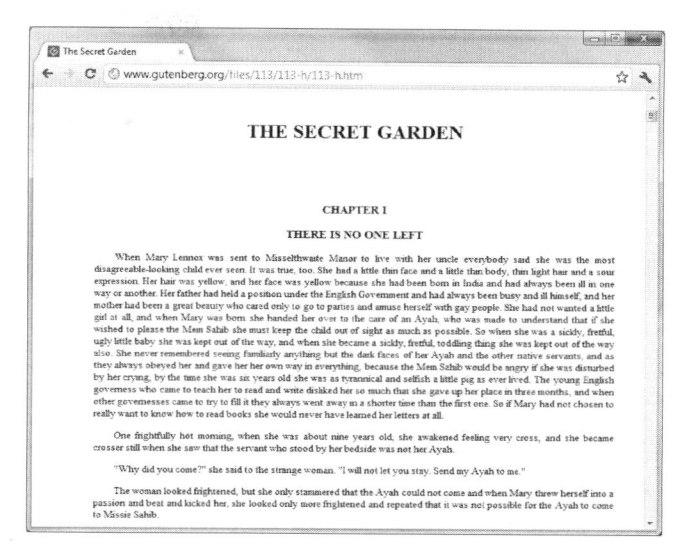

**FIGURE 3.2** HTML/XML or web eBook of *The Secret Garden*, downloaded from Project Gutenberg, being read with Google Chrome browser

**LIT.** Microsoft created its own eBook format (LIT) in 2000 and offered its own eBook reading program, Microsoft Reader. Although Microsoft stopped supporting the LIT platform in 2012, eBooks in the LIT format are still available from a number of eBook stores and free online libraries.

**POD.** The POD eBook is a print-on-demand eBook. With POD, while the book can be read online, it can also be printed and bound. The Internet Archive's Bookmobile (http://archive.org/texts/bookmobile.php) used the Million Book Collection (www.ulib.org) and POD technology to visit schools and allow users to access, download, print, and bind titles from more than one million public domain books available online. The Bookmobile used a network of computers connected to a server to access the eBook files, and then used a high-speed printer to make the printed copies, with another printer to make covers. The books were then assembled using a binding machine. My StoryMaker (www.carnegielibrary.org/kids/storymaker/) allows children to create a picture book from existing options and then print it out on their own printer. Other sites such as Storybird (http://storybird.com), Mixbook (www.mixbook.com/edu), TikaTok (www.tikatok.com), and Storyjumper (http://storyjumper.com), allow children to create their own stories online, and then share and read other stories online. If they wish, they can even have their story professionally bound and shipped as an actual book (see creating eBooks in Part III).

**Moon Shell, DPG.** A different format is used with the Moon Books Project (http://moonbooks.net). The Moon Book Project uses software called Moon Shell for the Nintendo DS or Windows computer. The Moon Shell program displays eBooks in the DPG format. The website offers more than 50 free books in DPG format. Moon Books also has another reader called Comic Book DS, just for reading comics.

**Story Mouse.** Story Mouse (www.thestorymouse.com/) is a children's eBook application for the iPad or other iOS device that displays eBooks with audio, illustrations, and text. The free app comes with one free story; other stories can be purchased through iTunes.

**CAST UDL.** CAST UDL Book Builder (http://bookbuilder.cast.org/library.php) hosts a public library of books created by individuals that have used CAST's own program. The books are readable in a web browser running Java. The CAST books can be read aloud using the Texthelp feature, and can have accommodations and interactions built into the books.

# FLASH AND WEB FORMAT

A number of children's eBooks are freely available in the Flash format. Others are available through subscription.

Flash (SWF), created by Adobe, is a common format for websites that use animation, interaction, or video. For example, if you watch a YouTube video, you are most likely watching it in Flash format. Just about every browser has the plug-ins necessary to be able to play Flash objects (an exception at this time is Apple's iOS devices like the iPad and iTouch). Usually, most people will access Flash eBooks on a computer connected to the Internet.

## Free Flash Books

Websites that offer free Flash books include:

**FIGURE 3.3** The Screen Actors Guild Foundation's website Storyline Online delivers eBooks using Flash video

**Screen Actors Guild Foundation** (http://www.storylineonline.net). Online books delivered through video are read by celebrities (see Figure 3.7).

**University of Massachusetts** (www.umass.edu/aesop/contents.html). This Aesop's Fables site provides the classic stories with audio and animation.

**Clifford's Interactive Storybooks** (http://teacher.scholastic.com/clifford1/). Scholastic's four interactive stories about Clifford the Big Red Dog in Flash format allow readers to select story elements and have the story read aloud.

**RIF Reading Planet** (www
.rif.org/kids/reading
planet/bookzone/read
_aloud_stories.htm). On-
line stories in Flash format at this Reading Is
Fundamental site inclu-
de fiction, non-fiction,
and story songs to read
or sing along to.

**Read.gov.** The Library of
Congress offers Kids
(http://read.gov/kids/)
and Teens (http://read
.gov/teens/) sections
that allow users to read
classic children's books

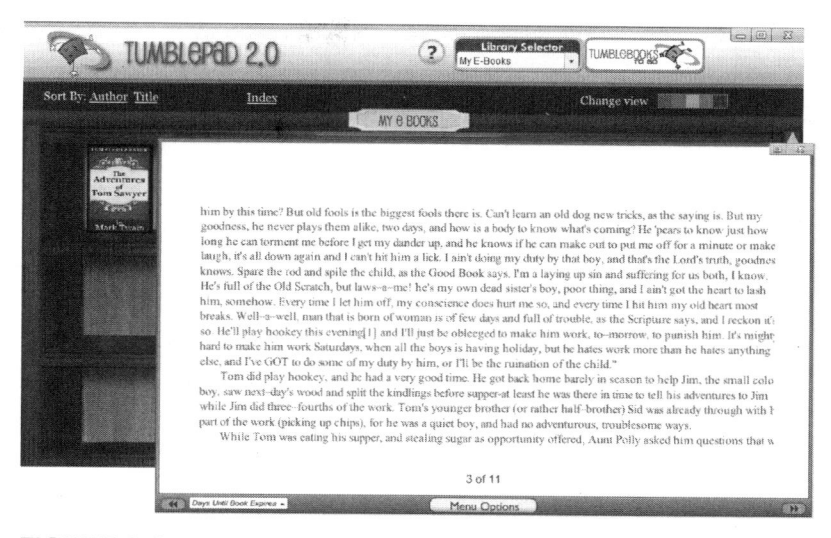

**FIGURE 3.4** Tumblebooks' Tumblepad bookshelf and eBook reader displaying *the Adventures of Tom Sawyer*

online in HTML or Flash format, displaying the picture books in Flash so that readers can click on the pages to turn them and zoom in on page elements. These books are also downloadable in PDF format.

## Subscription Services

Tumblebooks (www.tumblebooks.com), a division of Tumbleweed Press Inc., has an online subscription library that provides access to more than 200 Tumblebook titles, many of which also have extra materials, such as quizzes, games, lesson plans, and worksheets. Tumblebooks also has an additional collection of 200 chapter books with adjustable online text and audio narration with synchronized highlighting. The Tumblebooks animated talking books will play on any computer browser that can accept the Flash plug-in and use the free TumblePad software (see Figure 3.4).

Other children's book subscription services that use an animated Flash format include Disney Digital Books (http://disneydigitalbooks.go.com/), Sesame Street eBooks (http://ebooks.sesamestreet.org), and Scholastic's BookFLIX (http://teacher.scholastic.com/products/bookflix), which offers fiction and nonfiction for Grades PK–3.

## EBOOK APPS (APPLE AND ANDROID)

Android and Apple (iOS) devices can run eBook applications (apps) for children. These apps are available from the respective app stores: Google Play for Android-based devices and the Apple Store for Apple devices (see Figure 3.5). Yes, these devices were designed for adults. But with their full-color screens, interactive touch surfaces, and motion sensors, these

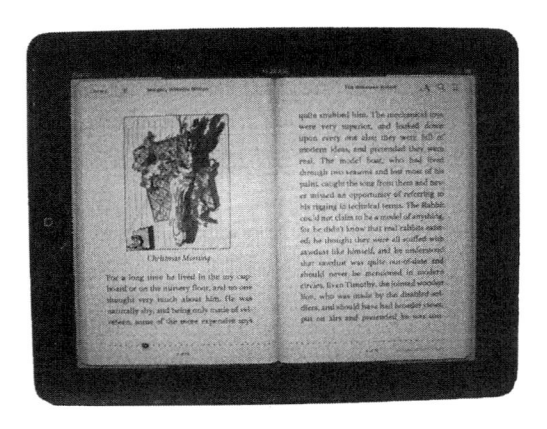

**FIGURE 3.5** iPad's eBook software program iBook displays text from *The Velveteen Rabbit* in EPUB format

devices are tailor-made for apps aimed at children. Some apps are a single interactive book, and others either create or access entire libraries. Quite a few of these apps are affordable (either very inexpensive or even free.)

## Library Apps

Apple or Android users can access entire libraries with apps. For example, the International Children's Digital Library (free) has an Apple app that links to a library of children's literature with more than 4,000 books, mostly picture books, in 54 languages. The free app Read Me Stories—Children's Books (Apple) or Read Me Stories: Kids Books (Android) provides a different talking picture book every day. iStoryBooks for Android devices provides access to a collection of free interactive storybooks with pictures, text, and audio.

The free iBooks app for Apple devices provides a bookshelf for users to manage their books. Thousands of books are available for free to add, including children's books from picture books to chapter books. For Android devices, the Google Books app gives readers access to a million free books.

The free Kindle app for both Apple and Android platforms gives access to 16,000 public domain classics at no charge, such as *Anne of Green Gables*, *The Secret Garden*, *The Jungle Book*, *Little Women*, and *White Fang*. Barnes & Noble's NOOK app also offers free public domain books.

Scholastic's free Storia app—for Windows, iPad, and Android devices—allows users to purchase books from Scholastic.

## Audiobook Library Apps

Applications are available that provide access audio book libraries, too. Cross Forward Consulting's Audiobooks ($0.99) for Apple devices or Traveling Classics' Audiobooks for Android both allow users to listen to more than 2,500 public domain titles. If you are looking for more current books, for an Apple device you might try Tales2Go, a subscription service that costs $3/month or $25/year. Its selections range from modern classics such as *Stellaluna* and *Curious George Rides a Bike* to popular series and characters such as *Diary of a Wimpy Kid* and *How to Train Your Dragon*.

## Individual Book Apps

Individual book apps are single-title, stand-alone books designed around illustrated children's literature. These apps feature interactive and multimedia features.

There are apps for novels, resource books, graphic novels, comic books, chapter books, picture books, and more. For young students, some apps have taken the flip-book or pop-up book concept to new levels. Examples of highly interactive Apple eBook apps include *Alice* (from the publisher Atomic Antelope) and *The Fantastic Flying Books of Mr. Morris Lessmore* (from Moonbot Books). These books are quite beautiful and interactive. In Alice, readers can pick up items and move them around, and tip the iPad to make Alice shrink or grow (Alice Lite is free; the full version is $9). In *The Fantastic Flying Books of Mr. Morris Lessmore*, readers can play music on a keyboard that appears within the story ($4.99). Booktrack has a collection of book apps. Its free downloads include *The Ugly Duckling*, *Riki-Tiki-Tavi*, and a Sherlock Holmes story. Booktrack's take on the electronic book includes a music soundtrack, background sounds, and sound effects as a reader progresses—the software calculates the reading speed and adjusts the sounds accordingly.

**FIGURE 3.6** Smartphone eBook app for the Android OS for StoryChimes' Rumblestiltskin illustrated by Anca Delia Budeanu

Grimm's *Rumpelstiltskin* is an app that creates a modern version of a traditional pop-up book, so while there are no actual paper flaps to pull or push, readers can move things around, poke characters, and even change some aspects of the scene on their device. Another interesting adaptation on the concept of the digital book is *The Wrong Side of the Bed* (2D and 3D). This eBook can be read right-side up or upside down as a regular flat book or in 3D (using red/cyan glasses) on the iPad or iPhone.

## PRESENTATION EBOOKS

A number of eBooks available were created and are shown using presentation software, such as PowerPoint, Open Office, or LibreOffice. These books are in the PPT or PPS formats. These eBooks are also sometimes called Talking Books, because people have added their own audio recordings using the presentation software to accompany the text and images.

Most of the eBooks in this format are designed for beginning readers or children with special needs. You can download the presentation eBook file (usually PowerPoint PPT or PPS), and then use your computer's presentation software, such as PowerPoint or PowerPoint Viewer, to display the book to the whole class, a small group, or even a single student who can read and listen to the book at his or her own pace.

To find these books, teachers can visit the Adapted Books and Materials collection (http://goo.gl/r14U8) of the New York City school system, and download books from the more than 70 eBooks available to use with his or her students (see Figure 3.7). Also for beginning readers, teachers can visit the Tar Heel Reader site (http://tarheelreader.org).

34  eBooks for Elementary School

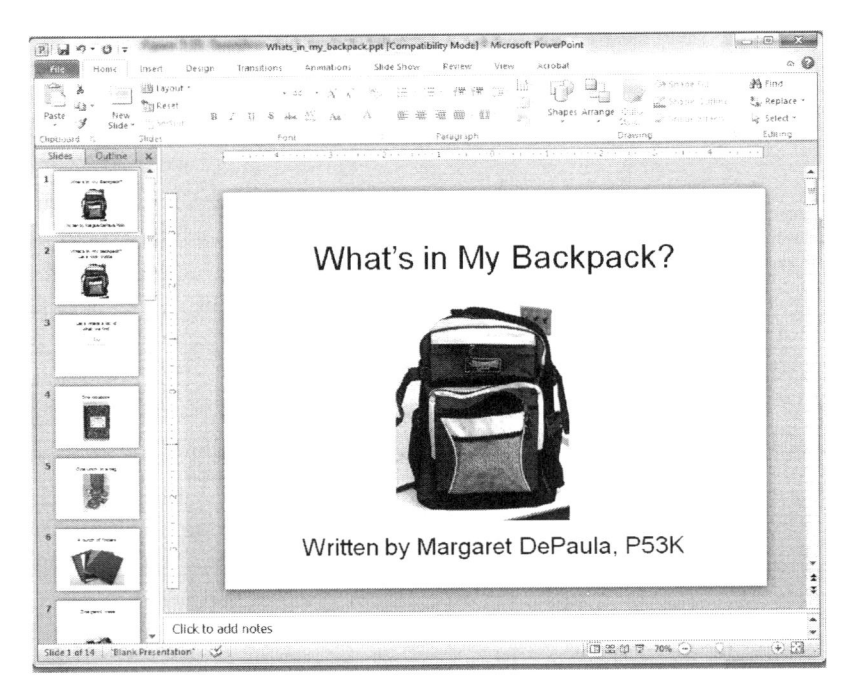

Teachers and students can also create their own presentation eBooks, as the students at the Priory Woods School did (http://goo.gl/7oWTF). See chapter 9 for more on creating your own presentation eBooks.

**FIGURE 3.7**  The eBook *What's in My Backpack* by Margaret DePaula is available in PowerPoint and Acrobat Reader formats from the New York City Department of Education's Adapted Books

## AUDIOBOOK FILE FORMATS

The computers in most schools will already have the necessary software to play audiobook CDs. Audiobook files can be played using software such as Windows Media Player or iTunes, or on portable players such as iPods or MP3 players, depending on the file format.

Quite a few websites offer downloads of audiobooks that you can use with your students. Most free download sites offer the audiobooks as MP3 files, but another common format includes OGG. OGG is a compressed audio file about the same size as an MP3, but with slightly better quality. Some audiobooks may also be available as an M4B file. The M4B format is actually the same as Apple's M4A audio format; it allows iTunes software to recognize that the file is an audiobook and enables bookmarking.

Websites that offer audiobooks in multiple formats include the free audiobook libraries LibriVox (librivox.org) and Project Gutenberg (www.gutenberg.org), which both offer audiobooks in MP3, M4B, and OOG file formats. Books Should Be Free (http://www.booksshouldbefree.com) (see Figure 3.8) offers books in iTunes podcast, M4B, and MP3 formats, along with text formats (EPUB, MOBI, HTM, TXT). LibriVox has audio versions of classics, including the Doctor Dolittle and Oz books, and about fifty others for children read by volunteers.

Other audiobook sources, such as Florida's Lit2Go (http://etc.usf.edu/lit2go/) and the AudioBooksForFree.com (www.audiobooksforfree.com) sites, only have audiobooks in the MP3 format.

Another format is that of Amazon's Audible (www.audible.com), an online audiobook store where you can purchase individual titles or subscribe and get multiple titles per year. Audible uses its own proprietary AA format.

Keep in mind that some sites offer their audiobooks in different quality levels, which change the sound quality. A lower number, such as 8 Kb/second, means lower quality, but also uses less file space. A higher number, such as 32 Kb/second, is a higher quality file, uses more file space, and will take longer to download.

**FIGURE 3.8** Books Should Be Free audiobook collection from public domain texts (www.booksshouldbefree.com)

## CONCLUSION

To decide which format is the most appropriate for any specific classroom situation, educators will need to evaluate their own learning environment. Think about the books available, the technology in the room (and what else may be needed), the level of the students, and the desired interactions. For example, if you wanted to use animated eBooks that read aloud to your students, you will need to have headphones for them to use, so that students don't disturb each other while reading. Try each of the big formats and experiment with some of the other formats and judge which would be best for your situation.

## RESOURCES

### Adobe Reader
www.adobe.com
eBook software program

### Android Market
http://market.android.com
Apps for Android devices

## Audible

www.audible.com
Amazon's online audiobook store for downloading audiobooks

## Between the Lions Stories

http://pbskids.org/lions/stories/
From the PBS Kids program, this site presents a collection of stories as short videos

## Audobooksforfree.com

www.audiobooksforfree.com
Collection of free lower sound quality version audiobooks

## Books Should Be Free

www.booksshouldbefree.com
Audiobook and text versions of public domain texts (M4b, MP3, EPUB, MOBI, HTM, TXT)

## Calibre

http://calibre-ebook.com/
eBook management and file conversion software

## CAST UDL Book Builder's Pubic Library

http://bookbuilder.cast.org/library.php
Online and downloadable eBooks collection

## Chrome

www.google.com/chrome
Web browser program for multiple platforms that can display web based eBooks

## Clifford's Interactive Storybooks

http://teacher.scholastic.com/clifford1/
From Scholastic, this site has four interactive stories about Clifford the Big Red Dog in flash format

## Comical

http://comical.sourceforge.net/
Multiplatform comic book reader for CBR or CBZ comic book formats

## Disney Digital Books

http://disneydigitalbooks.go.com/
eBooks subscription service from the Disney corporation

## FireFox

www.firefox.com/
Web browser program for multiple platforms that can display web based eBooks

### Internet Archive Bookmobile

www.archive.org/texts/bookmobile.php
Print on demand mobile digital library

### Internet Explorer

www.microsoft.com/downloads
Web browser program for Windows' devices that can display web based eBooks

### Kids4Classics

http://kids4classics.com/
More than 40 classic books in PDF and chapter HTM formats

### iTunes

itunes.apple.com
Applications for Apple devices and Apple music player

### LibreOffice

www.libreoffice.org
Free office application suite that includes Impress, which can show or create PowerPoint compatible files

### LibriVox

librivox.org
Public domain audiobooks read by people

### Lit2Go

http://etc.usf.edu/lit2go/
Public domain audiobooks collection from the Florida Educational Technology Clearinghouse

### Million Book Collection

www.ulib.org
Online eBook library

### Mixbook

www.mixbook.com/edu
Online digital story creation and sharing site, with the option to have books professionally printed

### Moon Books Project

http://moonbooks.net
eBook reader for Nintendo DS

### Microsoft Reader

http://www.microsoft.com/reader
eBook software program

### My StoryMaker

www.carnegielibrary.org/kids/storymaker/
Online digital story creation and sharing site, with the option to have books printed using local printer

### New York City Department of Education's Adapted Books and Materials

http://schools.nyc.gov/Offices/District75/Departments/Literacy/AdaptedBooks/default.htm or http://goo.gl/r14U8
Books in presentation format for beginning readers and special needs students

### Open Office

http://openoffice.org
Free office application suite that includes Impress, which can show or create PowerPoint compatible files

### PowerPoint

http://www.microsoft.com/powerpoint
Presentation software program sold by Microsoft, free PowerPoint Viewer available from their site

### Project Gutenberg

www.gutenberg.org
Online eBook library

### Read.gov Kids

http://read.gov/kids/
Classic children's stories presented in multiple formats

### Read.gov Teens

http://read.gov/teens/
Classic children's stories presented in multiple formats

### Rif Reading Planet

www.rif.org/kids/readingplanet/bookzone/read_aloud_stories.htm
A collection fiction, non-fiction, and story songs in flash format

### Safari

www.apple.com
Web browser program for Apple operating systems

### Scholastic's BookFLIX

http://teacher.scholastic.com/products/bookflix
Subscription service of fiction and nonfiction for grades PreK-3

### Sesame Street eBooks

http://ebooks.sesamestreet.org
eBooks subscription service from the Sesame Street

### Storybird

http://storybird.com
Online digital story creation and sharing site, with the option to have books professionally printed

### Storyjumper

http://storyjumper.com
Online digital story creation and sharing site, with the option to have books professionally printed

### Storyline Online

www.storylineonline.net/
This site sponsored by the Screen Actors Guild Foundation presents a collection of 24 books presented as streaming videos read by actors

### Storytime

www.barnesandnoble.com/storytime/
This site from Barnes & Noble has 14 books presented as video, many read by the book's author

### Talking Storybooks from Piory Woods School

www.priorywoods.middlesbrough.sch.uk/page_viewer.asp?page=Talking+Story+Books&pid=75 or http://goo.gl/7oWTF
eBook student created collection in PowerPoint format

### Tar Heel Reader

http://tarheelreader.org/
eBook collection in PowerPoint format

### The Story Mouse

www.thestorymouse.com/
Children's eBook reader application for iOS devices

### TikaTok

www.tikatok.com
Online digital story creation and sharing site, with the option to have books professionally printed

### Tom's eTextReader

http://pws.prserv.net/Fellner/Software/eTR.htm
eBook reader program for reading pure text eBooks, can also edit

### Tumble Books

www.tumblebooks.com
Online books for children

### University of Massachusetts' Aesop's Fables

www.umass.edu/aesop/contents.html
Collection of classic stories

# Part II

# eBOOK SOURCES

"Kids not only need to read a lot but they need lots of books they can read right at their fingertips. They also need access to books that entice them, attract them to reading."

—Richard L. Allington (2005)

A well-organized, extensive classroom library, which includes all genres of literature as well as high-interest reading materials such as magazines, comic books, and picture books, plays an important part in helping maintain students' interest in extending reading (Worthy, 1996, 2000). The International Reading Association (IRA, 1999) points out many reasons why it is important for students to have access to books, including higher reading rates, higher levels of comprehension, and improved fluency. The IRA states that "access to books refers to the availability of quality literature in classroom, school, community, or home libraries," (p. 2) and that school and classroom libraries should have adequate amounts of reading material for each student. The IRA provides suggestions about what those "adequate amounts" should be: students should have access to approximately seven books per student in a classroom collection (adding one book per student per year), and the school library collection should have a minimum of 20 books per student (adding two new books per student).

The Main Reading room of the U.S. Library of Congress (Photograph by Carol M. Highsmith)

Anderson (2006) has identified six major categories of children's literature: picture books, traditional literature (myths, fables, legends, fairy tales), fiction, nonfiction, biography and autobiography, and poetry. You can find all of these types of books as eBooks. However, instead of listing books by genre, I have divided the sources of eBooks into two categories: those you can get for free, and those that you can buy or borrow.

Chapter 4 explores free locations, such as online libraries or websites that let you access or download and keep books at no cost. Chapter 5 considers lending services, including public libraries and eBook-lending clubs, and pay services, such as bookstores and subscription services.

Cost is always a factor when adding books to a classroom collection, and using eBooks can help save money. Fortunately, many no- and low-cost sources for children's literature eBooks are available.

Now that you've sourced eBooks, how do you catalogue and organize them, or convert them to a format you can use? Chapter 6 discusses easy-to-use tools to convert eBooks and manage your eBook library.

# Chapter 4

# Getting Free eBooks

One of the nice things about getting started with eBooks is the initial cost requirement. If your book budgets are like the ones I have to deal with, most likely your budget hasn't gone up lately, even though the cost of books has. If a classroom teacher or school library is having trouble finding the funds to expand book collections, consider free online eBook sources. The odds are that you already have the necessary hardware and connectivity to get started, without any additional device or connection costs.

To begin using eBooks with your students, you don't need specialized eBook reader devices. If you have them, that's great, and there will be much that you can do with such mobile technology. But to start using eBooks, just about any school or classroom computer will do. Internet access for each computer would help, but if it's unavailable, you can still download eBook files to use with offline computers.

I suggest that you start with free eBook software and eBook files. More than five million free eBooks are available online. Although a majority of these books may not be appropriate for your students' age group, I'm sure that once you start looking you will find many that you can integrate into your classroom or school.

Your computers may need additional software or plug-ins to read eBooks. Depending on your school's policy or technology set-up, you may need to contact your information technology (IT) department to have their staff install, or give your computers permission to install, specialized eBook reader software such as the NOOK, Kindle, and Tumblebooks eBook programs. Even without installing any programs, you can access many eBooks using your computer's Internet browser, either for HTML books or by using a free EPUB reader plug-in. See chapter 2 for more on software.

This chapter lists more than 100 eBook sites that provide free eBooks in various formats. Don't think that free means limited; although many of the free eBooks are classics in the public domain, authors have generously shared quite a number of recent books.

Many free eBook sites offer collections by focus, format, or genre, and others offer large general collections with multiple formats. Children's Books Forever! (www.childrensbooks

forever.com) is a collection of picture books by Hans Wilhelm. Golden Gems (http://goldengems.blogspot.com/) has a lot of books by different authors, but the collection contains only Little Golden Books. Award book collections include Newbery Honor Books and Medal Winners (http://goo.gl/rds1P), which provides nine books written by women who received the Newbery Honor and Medal Award.

Some sites focus on the presentation format, such as audiobook collections and video book collections. The Screen Actor's Guild (SAG) Foundation (www.storylineonline.net) and Barnes & Noble (www.barnesandnoble.com/storytime/) both provide video versions of popular picture books being read either by the book's author or by well-known actors. Kiddie Records Weekly (www.kiddierecords.com) and the children's section of Books Should Be Free (www.booksshouldbefree.com/genre/Children) focus their collections on children's audio books.

Children's book sites with a general focus include the International Children's Digital Library (http://en.childrenslibrary.org/), which has a variety of books including picture and chapter books for children.

Then there are sites that have large, general collections for all kinds of readers. These sites are similar in design to a public library, with fiction, nonfiction, and children's books. Project Gutenberg and the Internet Archive are such repositories, and they both have extensive collections of children's books in the public domain.

The end result is that there are lots of books online that are being shared and can be used in the home, classroom, or library without additional costs.

## PICTURE BOOKS AND EMERGENT READERS

A picture book, illustrated book, or picture storybook delivers its tale in two narratives, where pictures and text work interdependently, a joining of verbal and visual arts. Most picture books are between twenty-four and forty-eight pages (Benedict & Carlise 1992). To young readers, this book length is not daunting, and can act as an important motivator. Not only can picture books be effective tools for reading, they are also often a perfect tool for illustrating all kinds of topics such as science, humanities, art, and more. For example, NASA produces two online picture books that demonstrate and teach about remote sensing through the context of a story. One of these, *The Adventures of Echo the Bat*, is also published in print format by the Government Printing Office. This is the only pop-up book (actually lift the flap) that I believe the U.S. government prints.

One of the best multicultural picture book libraries that I have found is the International Children's Digital Library (ICDL). The ICDL is a jointly funded project of the National Science Foundation and the Institute for Museum and Library Services. Within the ICDL site, users can search for books by title, topic, publication date, language, author, or even book cover color. Although international in scope, the collection includes 500 books in English, some of which have included "classics" like Jane Cowen-Fletcher's *It Takes a Village*, and the award-winning *When Sophie Gets Angry—Really Really Angry . . .* by Molly Bang. The other languages represented in the ICDL range from Arabic to Vietnamese and Maori to Russian, and a number of the books are in multiple languages, such as English and Spanish. The ICDL not only gives teachers and students more picture and chapter books, but also provides them with books with which to see the world from different viewpoints and experiences, and to access other cultures and languages.

Pearson has an interesting project with its "We Give Books" initiative (www.wegivebooks.org). This project provides a free online library of more than 200 Penguin and DK picture books for students to read. Every time students read one of the online picture books, credit is given to send physical books to other literacy campaigns.

**FIGURE 4.1** The NASA Imagers collection of online eBooks includes *The Adventures of Echo the Bat*

The following eBook sites offer picture books and easy-to-read books for younger students and emergent readers. Some of these sites also have stories for older, more fluent readers.

## Absolutely Whootie
www.storiestogrowby.com
Myths and fables from around the world, with adventures and animal tales. Also offers readers' theater scripts

## Adapted Books and Materials
http://schools.nycenet.edu/d75/academics/literacy/adaptedbooks/default.htm#titles
<http://goo.gl/2VSAQ>
More than 70 adapted books in a variety of formats including Boardmaker, PowerPoint, and PDF

## Aesop's Fables
www.umass.edu/aesop/contents.html
Thirty-eight fables in traditional and modern forms. Most in HTML, some in Flash

### Amazing Adventure Series

www.amazingadventure.com
Children's stories that can be read on the screen or read aloud. Includes two books in Flash format

### Ant Bee's Children's' Books and Stories

www.antbee.com/default.asp
Nine easy-read stories of pictures and text (HTML)

### BAB Books

www.sundhagen.com/babbooks/
More than 12 online HTML picture books

### Baldwin Library of Historical Children's Literature

http://web.uflib.ufl.edu/spec/baldwin/baldwin.html
Digitized versions of children's books published in Great Britain and the United States from the early 1700s through the current year (scanned images)

### Barnes & Noble's Storytime

www.barnesandnoble.com/storytime/
Video versions of children's stories, many read by the book's author

### Bembo's Zoo

www.bemboszoo.com
Animated site to teach children their ABCs

### Between the Lions

http://pbskids.org/lions/stories/
Flash video stories

### Blue Jellyfish Press—Afrikaans

www.bluejellyfish.com.au/
A collection of picture books designed to assist in learning Afrikaans. Each of the Parrot series contains integrated bilingual text for second-language learning

### BookBox

www.bookbox.com/free_stuffcat.php
Selected stories available free as PDF single sheets and as MP3 files

### Book-Pop

www.bookpop.com/bookpop.html
Twelve HTML picture books with the option to have the book read aloud

## byGosh.com

www.bygosh.com
Children's classic books in HTML format

## Candlelight Stories

www.candlelightstories.com/HelpOFoodMem.htm
Children's and chapter books in a variety of formats

## CBeebies Story Circle

www.bbc.co.uk/cbeebies/storycircle/
More than 80 stories and activity books for preschool children

## Children's Books Forever!

www.childrensbooksforever.com
More than 20 picture books in PDF format by Hans Wilhelm to download or read online. Various books in the collection are also available in 10 different languages

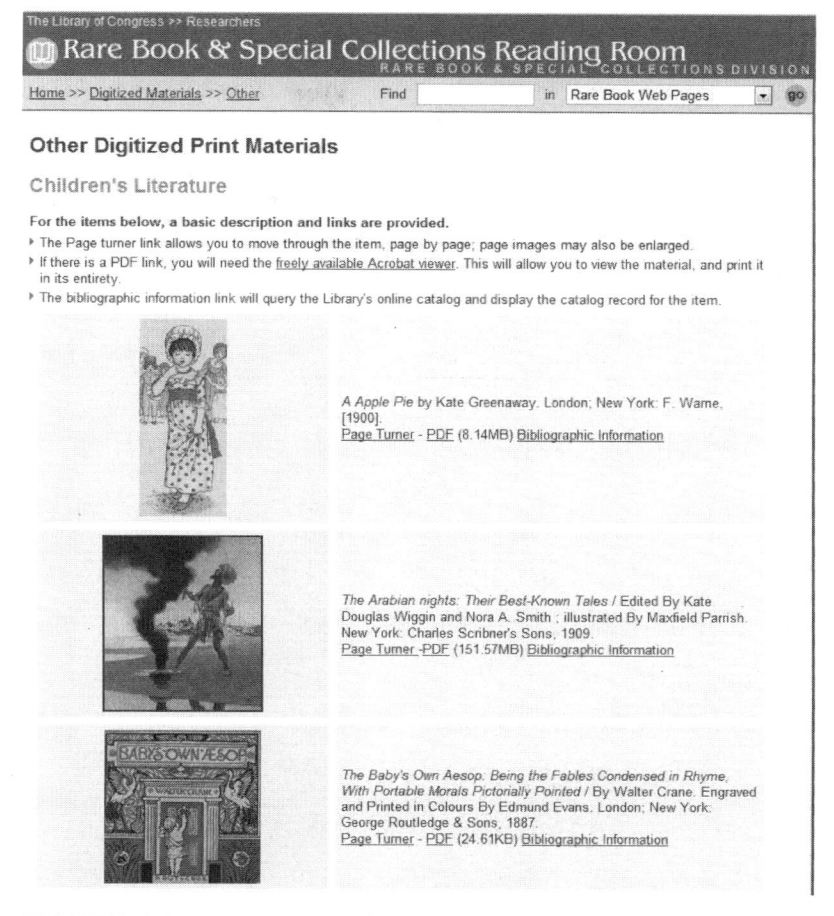

**FIGURE 4.2** Here are three of the more than 50 books in the Children's Literature from the Rare Book Room of the Library of Congress collection

## Children's Books Online: The Rosetta Project, Inc. (formerly Editec Communications' Children's Books for Free library)

www.childrensbooksonline.org
More than 1,200 antique children's books published in the 19th and early 20th centuries in HTML

## Children's Literature from the Rare Book Room of the Library of Congress

www.loc.gov/rr/rarebook/digitalcoll/digitalcoll-children.html
A large number of children's books in PDF and online page-flip formats (see Figure 4.2)

## ChildrensStories.net

www.childrensstories.net/stories.htm
Six eBooks by Elisa Gianoncelli

## Children's Storybooks Online

www.magickeys.com/books/
More than 30 illustrated children's stories in HTML

### Clifford's Interactive Storybooks

http://teacher.scholastic.com/clifford1/
Four interactive stories about Clifford the Big Red Dog in Flash format, presented by Scholastic

### Digital Gallery of World Picture Books

http://www.kodomo.go.jp/english/index.html
Collection of more than 45 Flash books from the International Library of Children's Literature/National Diet Library

### Digital Media Repository: Historic Children's Books

http://libx.bsu.edu/cdm4/browse.php?CISOROOT=/HistChldBks
Scanned PDF versions of books

### DLTK's Mini Books

www.dltk-teach.com/minibooks/
Early-reader books for printing and reading

### Dust Echoes

www.abc.net.au/dustechoes/
A collection of aboriginal stories presented as text and short movies

### GenieBooks in PowerPoint

http://www.auburn.edu/academic/education/reading_genie/bookindex.html
Decodable books for beginning readers in HTML or PPT, with books identified by phonics used

### Golden Gems

http://goldengems.blogspot.com/
Blog presenting a collection (in JPG) of Little Golden Books

### HarperCollins Children's

www.harpercollinschildrens.com/HarperChildrens/Kids/BookFinder/
HarperCollins has a special feature on its website called Browse Inside, an application allowing visitors to sample whole books from the list of HarperCollins titles online using a special Flash display. Click on the Browse Inside link to access more than 500 titles in the children's section

### Hazardous Weather Books

www.floridadisaster.org/kids/teachPlan.htm
Three early elementary Hazardous Weather Readers and Teacher Planning Guides (PDF)

## HighlightsKids.com

http://highlightskids.com/Stories/audioStories/audioStory_Top.asp
Nine animated stories with audio support

## Houghton Mifflin Company' Online Teacher Resources

www.eduplace.com/marketing/leveledbooks/sampler/content/
Fourteen leveled reading booklets (K–6) in a special web format with associated teacher information

## Inkless Tales

www.inklesstales.com/stories/
Variety of early-reader/emergent and Dolch stories

## International Children's Digital Library (ICDL)

www.icdlbooks.org
The ICDL is building an international collection that reflects both the diversity and quality of children's literature from 27 cultures in more than 40 languages (HTML)

## Internet Public Library—KidSpace

www.ipl.org/div/kidspace/
This section of IPL contains The Reading Zone, which is similar to the fiction section at a public library; includes links to online stories and information and links about favorite books and authors

## Kiddie Records Weekly

www.kiddierecords.com
Recordings in MP3 format of classic children's records from the 1940s and 1950s

## Kennedy Center's Storytime Online

www.kennedy-center.org/multimedia/storytimeonline/
Four video storybooks (in Real format)

## Kids' Corner from Wired for Books

http://wiredforbooks.org/kids.htm
Audio stories from Beatrix Potter (English, French, German, and Japanese) as well as *Alice's Adventures in Wonderland, The Frog Prince, A Christmas Carol, Grimm's Fairy Tales,* and more (Real media)

## Kiz Club

www.kizclub.com
Forty-four leveled Flash books with printable versions

## LearningPage.com

www.learningpage.com
A variety of early reader books, most in printable PDF and some in web-based formats. Free registration required

## Light Up Your Brain

http://lightupyourbrain.com/
Eighteen children's stories read aloud

## Lil' Fingers

www.lil-fingers.com/storybooks/
Storybook site for toddlers (HTML and Flash)

## Literature for Children

http://palmm.fcla.edu/juv/
More than 1,600 children's literature titles from the U.S. and UK presented by the State University Libraries of Florida

## Little Bird Tales

http://littlebirdtales.com/
Online books can be made of student artwork or photos; write and then record audio

## Lit2Go

http://etc.usf.edu/lit2go/
Online audiobook collection of classics and children's literature from Florida's Educational Technology Clearinghouse. You can browse the collection by reading level K–12

## Mighty Book Catalogue

www.mightybook.com
More than 50 children's books for ages two to preteen in HTML, including those read aloud

## Museum of Unnatural Mystery: Children's Reading Room

www.unmuseum.org/crr/
Eight online (HTML) stories for children

## NASA Books Imagers

http://science.hq.nasa.gov/kids/imagers/
Online stories *The Adventures of Echo the Bat* and *The Adventures of Amelia the Pigeon* in HTML (see Figure 4.1)

## Robin Whirlybird on her Rotorcraft Adventures

http://rotored.arc.nasa.gov
A story and activities of a girl visiting her mother's work: in English, Spanish, and Chinese (HTML)

### Our Very Own Star and Auroras! (Flash format)

http://stargazers.gsfc.nasa.gov/students/stories_fun.htm

### Online Storytime from Barnes & Noble

www.barnesandnoble.com/u/online-storytime-books-toys/379002381/
More than 15 streaming videos of popular children's books read by authors or celebrities

### PBS Kids mobile apps

http://pbskids.org/mobile/apps.html
Variety of interactive eBooks for the iPad, iPhone, and iPod Touch

### Playtime Books

www.playtime-books.com/Individual-Download-Page-Addresses/special-offer.htm
Fourteen free children's audiobooks (MP3) for download in zipped format

### Read.gov

http://read.gov/kids/
Children's book collection with picture and short books in PDF and online formats

### Reader's Theater Scripts and Plays for the Classroom

www.teachingheart.net/readerstheater.htm
Links to more than 50 scripts

### Reading A-Z

www.readinga-z.com
An online bookseller of leveled books that you print out. Sample books are available (PDF)

### Read to Me LV

www.readtomelv.com/current-books/
An online streaming video eBook site with 18+ books read by Las Vegas personalities

### RIF Reading Planet

www.rif.org/readingplanet/content/read_aloud_stories.mspx
A collection of read-aloud books that changes monthly (Flash format)

### Roy, Tale of a Singing Zebra

www.roythezebra.com/
Nine-part online guided reading story; comes with literacy worksheets and discussion sheets. Use in the classroom on your interactive whiteboard or computers

### Sebastian Swan

www.sebastianswan.org.uk/
Eight online big books (HTML)

## Snee

www.snee.com/epubkidsbooks/
Sixteen free EPUB children's picture books

## Speakaboos

www.speakaboos.com/stories/favorites
One hundred twenty stories presented as videos; includes Arthur stories read by the author

## Starfall.com

www.starfall.com
Designed for first grade, the 75 Flash reading/writing resources are also useful for pre-kindergarten, kindergarten, and second grade

## Story Book Castle

www.storybookcastle.com
Read-online stories from Aesop's Fables and Fairy Tales. The site also has a few stories with pictures, and multiple stories can be translated into other languages

## StoryJumper

www.storyjumper.com
Online tool to create and read stories with online text and images

## Storyline Online—from the Screen Actors Guild (SAG) Foundation

www.storylineonline.net
Stories read by members of the Screen Actors Guild, including modern classics such as *Stellaluna* and *The Polar Express*. Stories are read and displayed through streaming video

## StoryPlace Elementary Library

www.storyplace.org/eel/other.asp
Six stories for elementary students along with suggested readings and print-out activities

## StoryPlace PreSchool Library

www.storyplace.org/preschool/other.asp
Fifteen stories and associated books and activities for children and parents

## Storytime in the Reading Room

www.astorybeforebed.com/storytime
Collection of picture books read by the authors (Flash)

## Tikiri—Stories from Sri Lanka

www.tikiri.com/e-kathandara.html
Thirty-five books in PDF format in English and Sinhala

### We Give Books
www.wegivebooks.org
More than 200 books that can be read online, including fiction and nonfiction

### ZOOMplayhouse
http://pbskids.org/zoom/activities/playhouse/
Collection of reader's theater scripts from PBS Kids

# FICTION, INCLUDING SHORT STORIES, CHAPTER BOOKS, AND NOVELS

The following sites focus on books for students who are past the picture book stage and ready for more text, such as in short stories and chapter books. To help promote your student's interest in reading and practice, you should provide them the opportunity to choose books about a topic of interest to them. Within the following list are a variety of children's books on numerous topics and designs, including books that are text based, audio books, and even some reader's theater sites.

*Note:* Many of these sites are general sites, not focused for elementary students. Instructors should always first visit sites to make sure that the content is appropriate for their students.

### Absolutely Whootie
www.storiestogrowby.com
Myths and fables from around the world, with adventures, animal tales, and reader's theater scripts

### Baldwin Library of Historical Children's Literature
http://web.uflib.ufl.edu/spec/baldwin/baldwin.html
Digitized versions of children's books published in Great Britain and the United States from the early 1700s through the current year (scanned images)

### Booktrack
www.booktrack.com
Booktrack adds soundtracks of music and sound effects into their books for iOS and Galaxy. The site offers five free sound-enhanced eBooks for download

### Books Should Be Free—Children's Audio section
www.booksshouldbefree.com/genre/Children
More than 120 children's audio books

## British Library Online Gallery

www.bl.uk/onlinegallery/ttp/ttpbooks.html
Digitized original classics. An audio feature allows a visitor to have the book read aloud. Titles include the original version of Lewis Carroll's *Alice's Adventures Under Ground* and *Mozart's Musical Diary* with 75 audio excerpts

## byGosh.com

www.bygosh.com
Children's classic books in HTML format

## Candlelight Stories

www.candlelightstories.com/HelpOFoodMem.htm
Children's and chapter books in a variety of formats

## Children's Literature from the Rare Book Room of the Library of Congress

www.loc.gov/rr/rarebook/digitalcoll/digitalcoll-children.html
Large number of children's books in PDF and online page-flip formats

## Classics Reader

www.classicreader.com/browse/3/title/
Section for young readers of more than 200 well-loved classics

## Cyberchase

http://pbskids.org/cyberchase/web_adventures.html
Animated webisodes

## Digital Media Repository

PDF versions of historic books

**Historic Children's Books:** http://libx.bsu.edu/cdm4/browse.php?CISOROOT=/HistChldBks

**Scanned Chapbooks:** http://libx.bsu.edu/cdm4/browse.php?CISOROOT=%2Fchapbks

## Fiction Teachers Classroom Theater

www.fictionteachers.com/classroomtheater/theater.html
Fourteen reader's theater scripts (HTML)

## Grimms' Fairy Tales

www.nationalgeographic.com/grimm/
Twelve stories (four with audio options). Students can choose their reading by basic story elements or from the story list (HMTL)

## HarperCollins Children's

www.harpercollinschildrens.com/HarperChildrens/Kids/BookFinder/
HarperCollins has a special feature on its website called Browse Inside, an application allowing visitors to sample whole books from the list of HarperCollins titles online using a special Flash display. Click on the Browse Inside link to access content. There are more than 500 titles in the children's section

## Houghton Mifflin Company' Online Teacher Resources

www.eduplace.com/marketing/leveledbooks/sampler/content/index.html
Fourteen leveled reading booklets (K–6) in a special web format; also has associated teacher information

## International Children's Digital Library (ICDL)

www.icdlbooks.org
The ICDL is building an international collection that reflects both the diversity and quality of children's literature from 27 cultures in 23 languages (HTML)

## Internet Public Library – KidSpace

www.ipl.org/div/kidspace/
This section of IPL contains The Reading Zone that is similar to the fiction section at a public library. It includes links to online stories and information and links about favorite books and authors

## KidPub

www.kidpub.org
An online database of 40,000 stories written by children for children

## Kids4Classics

http://kids4classics.com/
More than 40 classic books in PDF and chapter HTM formats

## KidsWWwrite

www.kalwriters.com/kidswwwrite/
Online anthology for young authors and readers (under 16)

## Learning Island

www.learningisland.org
Online book in a printable format (PDF)

## Lit2Go

http://etc.usf.edu/lit2go/
Online audiobook collection of classics and children's literature from Florida's Educational Technology Clearinghouse. You can browse the collection by reading level, K–12

### Lokata Legends

www.aktalakota.org/index.cfm?cat=54&artid=136
Links to 17 Native American/First Nations legends or folktales. You won't see these anywhere else online. From the Acta Lakota Museum at St. Joseph's Indian School in Chamberlain, South Dakota

### Light Up Your Brain

http://lightupyourbrain.com/
Eighteen children's stories read aloud

### Literature for Children

http://palmm.fcla.edu/juv/index.shtml
A collection of 1,600 children's literature titles from the U.S. and UK presented by the State University Libraries of Florida

### Librivox

http://librivox.org
A collection of 2,000 free, public domain audio books read by volunteers

### MysteryNet's Kids Mysteries

http://kids.mysterynet.com/
Quick online reads for kids to solve mysteries. Also, the site has mysteries written by kids

### Nightmare Room

www.thenightmareroom.com
Two stories from R. L. Stine, *Dead of Night* and *Your Own Personal Nightmare* (Choose Your Own Adventure) in Flash format

### Newbery Honor Books and Medal Winners

http://digital.library.upenn.edu/women/_collections/newbery/newbery.html
<http://goo.gl/rds1P>
Eighteen books by Newbery-awarded women authors from the 1920s through the 1960s

### Read.gov

http://read.gov/teens/
Kids and teens book collection of chapter books and novels in PDF and online formats (see Figure 4.3)

### Read On—Audio Stories

www.beenleigss.eq.edu.au/requested_sites/audiostories/
More than 150 short stories in Flash format with audio

### Reader's Theater Editions

www.aaronshep.com/rt/
A collection of free scripts for reader's theater, adapted from stories by Aaron Shepard and others (search for "script")

### Read free books online

www.bookrix.com
Flash page-turn versions of books written by non-professionals. Some audio-books also available. Has a children's book section

### Reading A-Z

www.readinga-z.com
An online bookseller of leveled books that you print out. Sample books are available (PDF)

### Scripts from the Reading Lady

www.readinglady.com/index.php?name=Downloads&req=viewdownload&cid=7
More than 45 scripts in DOC and PDF formats

### Story Book Online

www.storybookonline.net
Storybook Online Network is a storytelling community for children. The website's goal is to create, develop, and disseminate original short stories for children. Content is in text, audio, animation, and video presentations

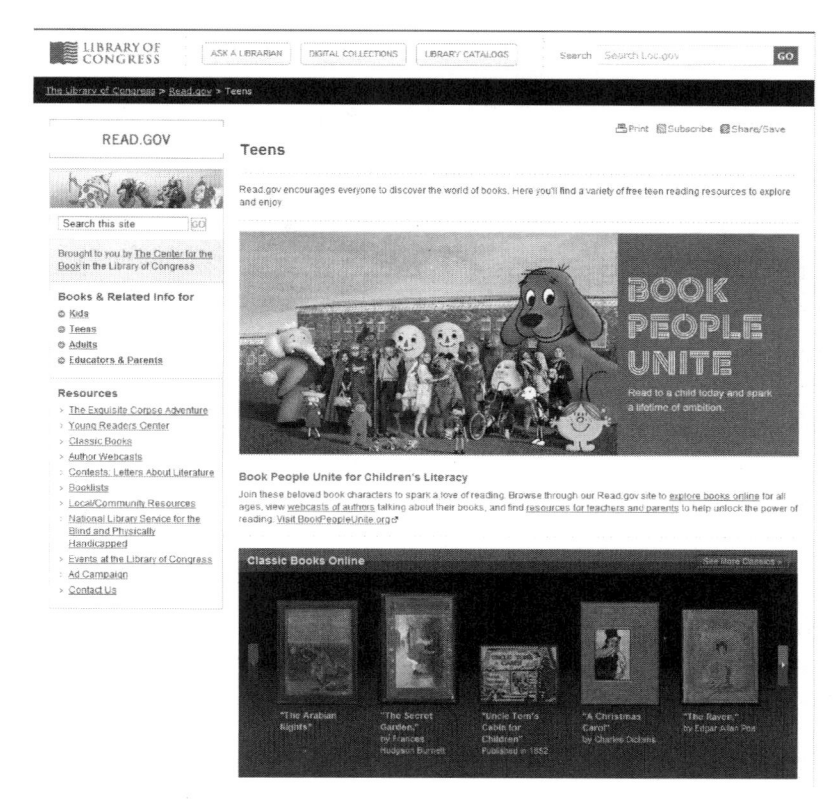

**FIGURE 4.3** Read.gov offers collections of chapter books and novels for kids and teens

# NONFICTION

Nonfiction is an important part of reading. Many children prefer nonfiction reading for pleasure. Numerous research studies have examined the use of nonfiction reading and found that students need to be exposed to a wide variety of texts to achieve proficient literacy levels. In fact, reading and understanding nonfiction text promotes abstract thinking (Kamil 1994, Boynton & Blevins 2003).

### BigUniverse (K–8)

www.biguniverse.com
This site has curriculum and tools for learning, assessment, reading, and writing development, using a vast library of online books. The site has a three-pronged approach: reading, creating, and sharing online children's books.

### CIA World Fact Book

www.cia.gov/library/publications/the-world-factbook/
An excellent online book of current geography

### Chest of Books.com

http://chestofbooks.com
Hundreds of nonfiction books across a wide range of topics, many appropriate for children

### Houghton Mifflin Company' Online Teacher Resources

www.eduplace.com/marketing/leveledbooks/sampler/content/
Fourteen leveled reading booklets (K–6) in a special web format; also has associated teacher information

### International Children's Digital Library (ICDL)

www.icdlbooks.org/
Use the "True Books" search tool.

### Internet Public Library—KidSpace

www.ipl.org/div/kidspace/
This section of IPL contains The Reading Zone that is similar to the fiction section at a public library. There are links to online stories and information and links about favorite books and authors.

### K12 Handhelds eBooks

http://k12opened.com/ebooks/
Collections of eBooks, in multiple formats, for English language arts, math, social studies, and science, for elementary and middle-school levels (see Figure 4.4).

### Learning Island

www.learningisland.org
Online book in a printable format (PDF) that can be read online

### Links Learning

www.linkslearning.org/Kids/_index.html
Nonfiction for math, reading, and science

### Listen & Read

www2.scholastic.com/browse/
collection.jsp?id=375
Short, high-interest, nonfiction stories from *Scholastic News* boost early reading skills and support differentiated reading and English language learners.

### USGS Public Interest Publications

http://pubs.er.usgs.gov/
http://goo.gl/qN9o3
More than 80 publications covering a variety of high-interest science topics

### WikiJunior

http://en.wikibooks.org/wiki/Wikijunior
Age-appropriate nonfiction books for children up to age 12

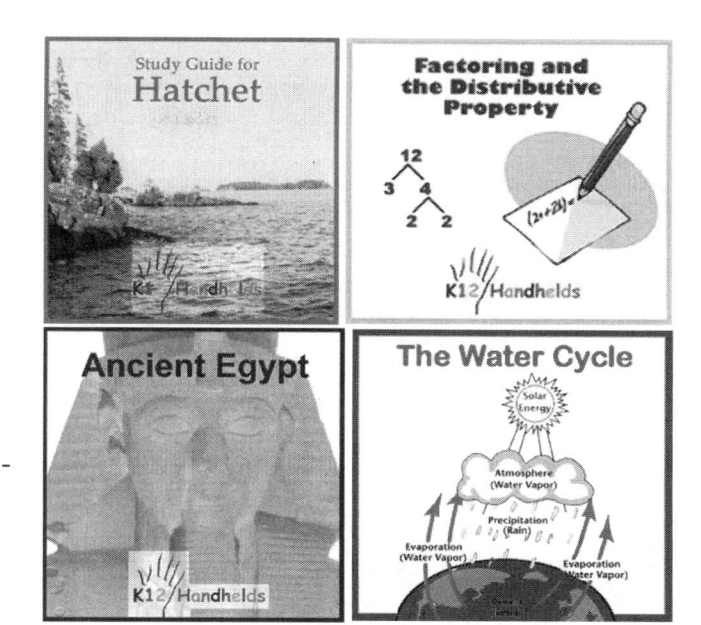

**FIGURE 4.4** K12 Handhelds eBooks offers a variety of fiction and nonfiction books

## GENERAL LIBRARY COLLECTIONS WITH CHILDREN'S OR YA SECTIONS

Just as you might use the school library or the public library down the street to access books to use in your classroom, so too can you use general online library collections. The library sites listed below have sections for children's books and young adult reading.

*Note:* These sites are general sites, not focused on elementary students, they do have children's or young adult sections. Instructors should always visit library sites first to make sure that the accessible content is appropriate for their students.

### Abacci Books

www.abacci.com/books/category.php?cid=13

### Alex Catalog of Electronic Texts

http://infomotions.com/alex/?cmd=tags&ltr=C

### Audiobooks with Annie

http://feeds.feedburner.com/LibraryLadyAudiobooks

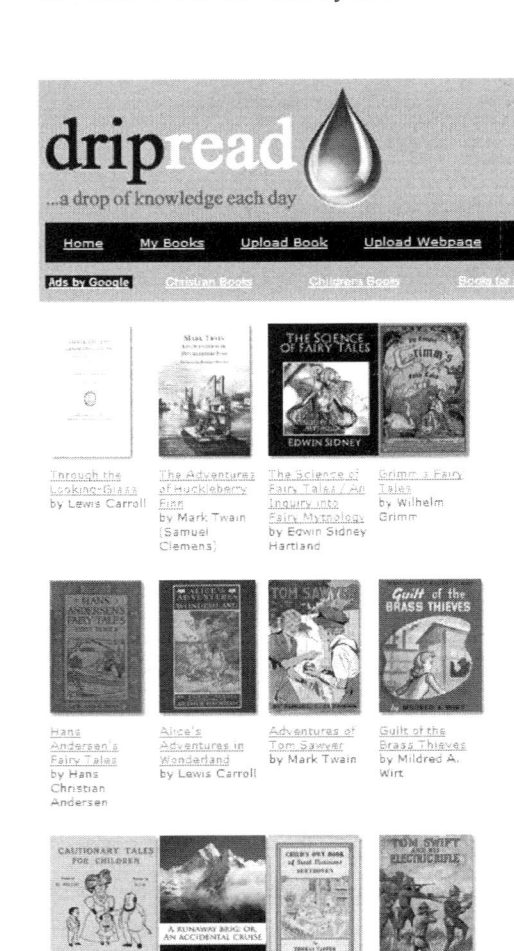

**FIGURE 4.5** Dripread is an online library that breaks up electronic books into smaller components and delivers them to your phone or email account

**Bookrix**

www.bookrix.com/library.html

**Books Should Be Free**

www.booksshouldbefree.com/genre/Children

**Classic Literature Library**

www.classic-literature.co.uk/ & http://fairy-tales.classic-literature.co.uk/

**DailyLit**

www.dailylit.com/tags/childrens

**Digitized Materials from the Rare Book & Special Collections Division**

www.loc.gov/rr/rarebook/digitalcoll/digitalcoll-children.html

**DipRead**

www.dripread.com/books/categories/childrens (see Figure 4.5)

**epubBooks - Young Readers**

www.epubbooks.com/genre/young-readers

**FeedBooks**

www.feedbooks.com/store/top?category=FBJUV000000&lang=en&range=week

**Free-books.org**

www.free-books.org/children.php

**LoudLit.org**

http://loudlit.org/

**MemoWare**

www.memoware.com
<http://goo.gl/0aQc6>

**Munseys**

www.munseys.com/detail/mode/cat/20/Children

**Open Library**

http://openlibrary.org/subjects/juvenile_literature

### Project Gutenberg
www.gutenberg.org/wiki/Category:Bookshelf

### Read Easily
www.readeasily.com/bysubject.php

### University of Virginia Library Electronic Text Center - Young Readers
http://etext.virginia.edu/subjects/Young-Readers.html

### Web-Books.com
www.web-books.com/Category.php?Category=Youth

### WikiBooks
http://en.wikibooks.org/wiki/Wikijunior

### WordiQ
www.wordiq.com/books/category/juvenile_literature/

### WOWIO
www.wowio.com/users/CategoryPage.asp?cbBrowse=34

### World eBook Library: School
www.schoollibrary.com/Main.htm
<http://goo.gl/ym3cf>

## COLORING BOOKS, COMICS, AND EMAGAZINES

When building your classroom collection, it's important that students can select texts they want to read, with the opportunity to read easy texts (Ivey 2000). This allows them to practice reading with greater fluency. A well-organized, extensive classroom library includes a variety of literature—magazines, comic books, picture books, and other high-interest reading materials—to help maintain students' interest in reading (Worthy 1996, 2000). Therefore, comic books and eMagazines should also be a part of your digital collection.

Comic books have been found to provide challenging texts (although not all of them), encourage reading, and lead to additional voluntary reading (Krashen, 1993). The reading of graphic novels goes beyond entertainment, as they promote better reading skills, improve comprehension, and complement other areas of curriculum (Frey & Fisher 2008). Being aware of how actively students read other kinds of publications, such as comics and manga, provides teachers with a deeper understanding of their students' reading abilities, interests, and skills.

eMagazines are offered by educational journal publishers and organizations. Free online content includes articles and media about current events, some of which are generated by students.

*Note:* These sites are general sites, not focused on elementary students. Instructors should always visit library sites first to make sure that the accessible content is appropriate for their students.

## Coloring Books

### Coloring.com

www.coloring.com
Free online coloring book

## Comic Books

### Action Comics

http://xroads.virginia.edu/~UG02/yeung/actioncomics/cover.html
Scans of the first issue of Action Comics (1938) introducing Superman

### BBC Buffy the Vampire Slayer EComics

www.bbc.co.uk/cult/buffy/ecomics/
More than 10 comics based on the TV series.

### Color.com

www.thecolor.com
Free online coloring book.

### Comics.com

www.unitedmedia.com/categories/index.html
More than 88 newspaper comic strips archived for the last 30 days

### Dr. Who Writers' Comics

www.bbc.co.uk/doctorwho/s4/misc/fiction/writerscomics/
Short Flash-developed comics based on the TV series

### Dark Horse

www.myspace.com/darkhorsepresents?
A MySpace site from Dark Horse comics with 140 comics for online viewing

### Digital Comic Museum

http://digitalcomicmuseum.com
Collection of free, public domain Golden Age Comics (see Figure 4.6)

## UComics.com

www.ucomics.com/comics/
More than 60 daily newspaper comic strips

# Educational Journals

### Time for Kids

www.timeforkids.com/TFK/kids/news

### Weekly Reader

www.weeklyreader.com/subcategory/74

### National Geographic Kids

http://kids.nationalgeographic.com/kids/

### Science News for Kids

www.sciencenewsforkids.org/

# Graphic Novels

### IKKI

www.sigikki.com
Thirteen manga graphic novels for reading online using a Flash player. Click on the Series button to access the different novels.

### Owly Books and Graphic Novels

www.andyrunton.com/owly/
Six comics from the Owly series

**FIGURE 4.6** Thousands of comic books in online format can be accessed at the Digital Comic Museum

I hope that this section gives you an idea of the many free possibilities that you can incorporate into your classroom reading. This list is by no means all that there is—new sites come online all the time that provide even more books that children can access without charge. Also, don't forget that special options available for students with special needs. For instance, BookShare (www.bookshare.org) is an entire digital library of more than 100,000 accessible books that are free for all U.S. students with disabilities.

# Chapter 5

# eBook Stores and eBook Borrowing

In 2010, Amazon.com announced that eBooks for Kindles outsold the online store's paperback books, with 115 Kindle-format books sold for every 100 paperbacks (Amazon.com, 2011). eBooks are becoming more and more popular every day, and sales are skyrocketing. But you do not have to decimate your school budget on purchasing eBooks. You can borrow them for free or for a small fee. You may be able to check out digital books from your local public library, or you can borrow books from an eBook lending club.

## EBOOK STORES

Although millions of free eBooks are available online, the ones that you want or need might not be free, so you might just have to buy a copy. Buying eBooks can still help stretch your book budget, because eBook versions are often available at a lower cost than their printed versions. eBooks may also be easier for parents to purchase and donate to their children's classrooms.

But before you start purchasing books, make sure to take the time to look around and see what is available free. One effective eBook search tool is Inkmesh (www.inkmesh.com), which indicates whether an author or a book is available in eBook form, if it is free, where it can be downloaded, and in what format. Inkmesh also has collated a comprehensive list of free eBooks available for a variety of platforms.

Be sure to also check the eBook stores for free eBooks—many eBook stores give away a number of eBooks, including some new ones, at no cost. For example, as of this writing, Amazon listed more than 16,000 free titles, and Barnes & Noble and Google Books had more than a million free titles for download. Even Scholastic's Storia gives you five free books when you download its player for your computer or portable device.

**FIGURE 5.1** The Kindle (left) and NOOK eBook readers

Let's start with the two of the biggest eBook stores: Barnes & Noble (EPUB format) and the Amazon Kindle store (AZW format). Both stores can be accessed with their associated eBook reader devices (NOOK and Kindle, see Figure 5.1) or through their reader software or browsers on classroom desktop computers. Using the eBook company's associated websites, you can easily purchase their eBooks, of course. But even though you are using a specific eBook reader, you can read eBooks purchased or sourced elsewhere. Usually, when you are going outside the associated bookstore, you will have to download the eBook file to your computer and then transfer the eBook file to the reader book folder on your computer or to your reading device using a USB cable. And, you may need to convert it. (See chapter 6 for more on managing and converting your eBook files.)

## Account Security

If you do plan to use eBook reader devices, you will need to take steps concerning account settings. If you are going to purchase the device for your classroom, it is probably best to buy a Wi-Fi version and not a 3G version, because the 3G (cell-phone technology) version doesn't require logging in to the school network. Most dedicated eBook devices have one-click eBook purchasing, and your account will require a credit card to make purchases, so you will need to take steps to secure that information and make sure users can't purchase books on your account.

If you are using a NOOK, you can require a password before a purchase can be completed. If you are using a Kindle, you should delete the payment information in your Amazon account and set it on the No Payment Method. Also, make sure one-click ordering is turned off. For most platforms, schools can create institutional accounts for eBook purchasing.

For school or one-to-one device use, both Kindle and NOOK have extra assistance and settings. See the *Kindle Education — Setup Guide* PDF (http://goo.gl/DdkAv) for details on

---

### *Amazon Reading Level*

Amazon provides a lot of information about each children's book it offers. The book's description usually includes the appropriate grade and age levels. Some books even have a link for text stats that provide information for the Fog, Flesch, and Flesch-Kincaid Index results, along with a word count.

setting up Kindles for the classroom or school library. For the NOOK (http://www.barnesandnoble.com/nook), look for the NOOK in Education section on the Barnes & Noble website, which provides information on using NOOKs in K–12 schools. Kobo, Sony, and other manufacturers have similar offerings.

Schools can also subscribe to a service that adds electronic books to their libraries (see Figure 5.2). Overdrive's eBooks for K12 Schools (www.overdrive.com/solutions/schools/k12/sdl/) has a collection of more than 300,000 eBooks and audiobooks that can be added to a school's or district's collection. Brain Hive (www.brainhive.com) uses a different subscription approach: your school can join free, but instead of a standard monthly or annual subscription fee, you can set up an amount in your school account, and then that amount is only charged a fee of one dollar for each book checked out.

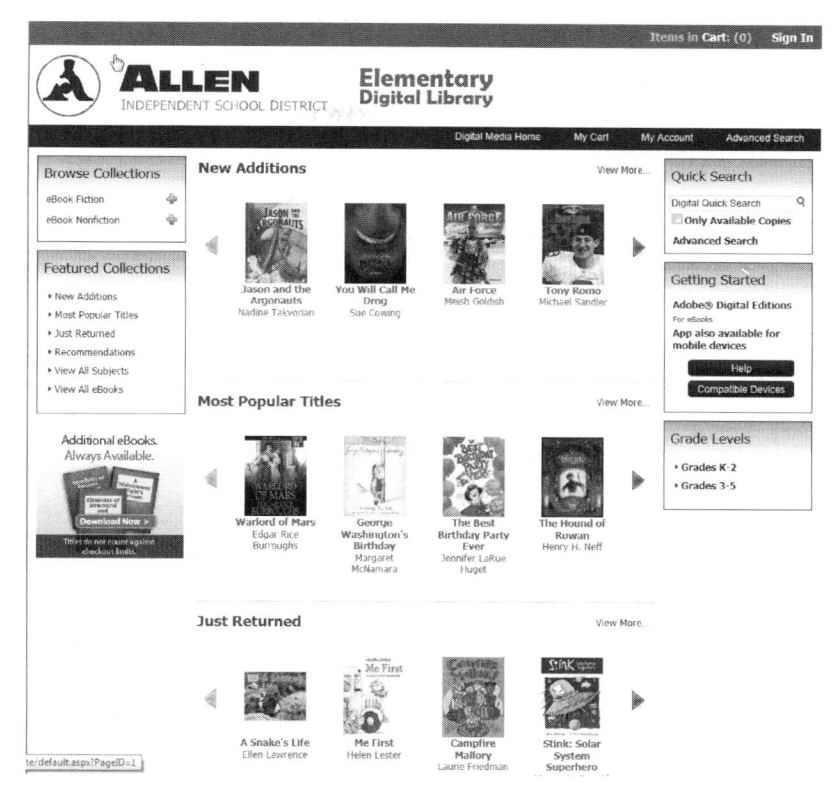

**FIGURE 5.2** Overdrive provides the Elementary Digital Library for the Allen Independent School District, Texas

## Online Bookstores

In addition to well-known names such as Scholastic, Amazon, and Barnes & Noble, other bookstores and publishers have online eBook stores. Here is a sample of general eBook stores that offer children's and young adult books.

Amazon Kindle Store: www.amazon.com
Barnes & Noble NOOK Book Store: www.barnesandnoble.com
Book Glutton: www.bookglutton.com
Diesel eBook Store: www.diesel-ebooks.com
eBooks.com: www.ebooks.com
Feedbooks: www.feedbooks.com
Fictionwise: www.fictionwise.com
Google eBookstore: http://books.google.com/ebooks
iBookstore: www.apple.com (access though iBooks)
Kobo Books: www.kobobooks.com
Powell's Books: www.powells.com/ebooks/

Reader Store: http://ebookstore.sony.com/
Sesame Street: http://ebooks.sesamestreet.org/
Scholastic's Storia: http://store.scholastic.com
Smashwords: www.smashwords.com
WOWIO: www.wowio.com

## Free eBooks from eBook Stores

Kindle Free Popular Classics (search for "free popular classics" in the Kindle Store)
www.amazon.com/s/?node=2245146011
Kindle Limited Time Offers (search for "limited time offers" in the Kindle Store)
http://goo.gl/rv4n0
Barnes & Noble (NOOK) (search for "free nook books")
http://goo.gl/sUiC8
Sony Reader Store
http://ebookstore.sony.com/category/free-ebooks
Kobo Books
www.kobobooks.com/lists/freeebooks/RYnbq2Rd7kSXf7MOhDofOQ-1.html
<http://goo.gl/FLGBX>
http://www.kobobooks.com/free_ebooks <http://goo.gl/ysXLN>
If you are using iPad, iTouch, or Android devices with your classrooms, you can purchase individual application eBooks for them. Below are a few of the affordable, quality books available from either the Apple Store or the Google Play Market. All of the books below are either free or cost less than $5

## Sample Application eBooks

*Alice for the iPad* by Atomic Antelope, lite version free, full version $8.99 (iOS)
*Animal Coloring Book,* free (Android)
*Atomic Robo #1,* free (iOS)
*The Cat in the Hat* by Dr. Seuss: $3.99–4.99 (iOS and Android)
*Colorama, Coloring Book of Bugs* by Artizia LLC, $0.99 (iOS)
*The Fantastic Flying Books* of Mr. Morris Lessmore, $4.99 (iOS)
*Freakish Animals That You Never Knew Existed*, $0.99 (iOS)
*Grimm's Rumpelstiltskin*, $2.99 (iOS)
*How It Works* magazine, free (one issue) (iOS)
*How the Grinch Stole Christmas!* by Dr. Seuss, $3.99–4.99 (iOS and Android)
*Jack and the Beanstalk* (interactive storybook), free–$3.99 (iOS and Android)
*The Lorax* by Dr. Seuss, $3.99–4.99 (iOS and Android)
*Magic Lessons* (chapter book), free (Android)
*Mystic Maggie*, free (Android)
*Oh, the Places You'll Go!* by Dr. Seuss, $3.99–4.99 (iOS and Android)
*One Fish, Two Fish, Red Fish, Blue Fish* by Dr. Seuss, $3.99 (iOS and Android)
*The Rescue of Ginger*, $0.99 (Android)
*Riki Tiki Tavi* <Booktrack>, free (iOS and Android tablets)

*Rocket Book* by Peter Newell, free at International Children's Digital Library or Google Books
*Scott Pilgrim,* free (Android)
*Slant Book* by Peter Newell, free at International Children's Digital Library or Google Books
*Story Book: The Ugly Duckling*, free (Android)
*The Tale of Peter Rabbit,* $0.99 (iOS and Android)
*Twilight: The Graphic Novel, Vol. 1*, lite version free (iOS)
*Ugly Duckling* <Booktrack>, free (iOS and Android tablets) (See Figure 5.3.)
*Winnie the Pooh* by A.A. Milne, free with iBook app ($10.99 for Android)
*The Wrong Side of the Bed* (2D and 3D) by Wallace E. Keller, $2.99 (iOS)

## EBOOK BORROWING: PUBLIC LIBRARIES AND LENDING CLUBS

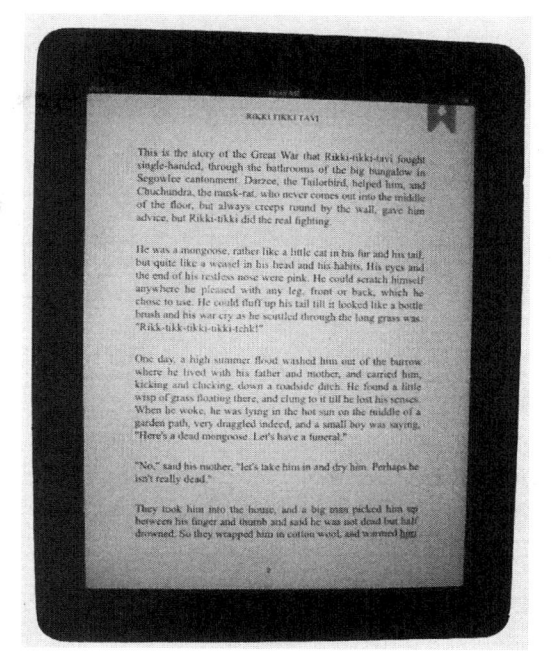

**FIGURE 5.3** Booktrack's *The Ugly Duckling* iPad App displays the text, provides ambient sound and soundtrack, and can even track the reading through highlighting, underlining, or a moving ball

If you don't want to buy books for your classroom, you might try borrowing some. Public libraries have been moving into lending digital books similar to how they lend print versions. Overdrive, a major supplier of eBooks to public libraries, reported a 200 percent increase in the circulation of eBooks in 2010 from the previous year (Overdrive 2011). eBooks accessed from a public library can be downloaded onto mobile devices such as the BlackBerry, Android, iPhone, iPad, and eBook readers, and they can be read on desktop or laptop computers.

Here are a few of the advantages of using eBook lending libraries or lending clubs (read on for more on lending clubs):

- Online lending libraries are open 24 hours a day, seven days a week.
- You don't need to travel to the library or bookstore to get more books.
- You don't have to return books; they "return" themselves.
- Because the books return themselves (always by the due date), you never pay late fees.
- There is no cost to you, your classroom, or your school book budget, yet you have increased access to books.
- Lending clubs and online libraries teach students about resources available beyond those through public libraries through the use of social-network sharing organizations.
- Students can practice library skills, such as catalog searching.

To find out if your regional public library has eBooks that you can check out for your class, visit their website and look for a link such as digital download, downloadables, or eBooks. You might also need to explore a bit; for example, with the Jacksonville Public Library site, the eBooks link is in the Resources section (see Figure 5.4). Depending on the library's subscription services, there may be only one or there might be a number of services that allow you to download eBooks and audiobooks. I would suggest that you start with Overdrive for general reading, as its collection has more than one million eBooks, audiobooks, music, and video titles for checkout. Other options that may be available at your library include the Gail Virtual Reference Library and NetLibrary (although NetLibrary has no material newer than 2004).

Next, I would suggest looking for eBook sections such as juvenile fiction or children's, and exploring them for eBooks that you would like to use in your classroom. Also, don't restrict yourself to text only. The Overdrive service also offers audiobooks that can be played on a computer. Depending on the audiobook, it can also be burned to CD, or can be downloaded to another device, such as an iPod or an eBook reader.

**FIGURE 5.4** The Jacksonville Public Library offers an Overdrive downloadable media page (http://jpl.coj.net). Credit: 2012, Overdrive, Inc.

If you find that you would like to use Overdrive with your classroom, you will need to add the library's Overdrive Media Console program to your computer. If it is your personal computer, all you need to do is click on the link for the Media Console and install the program. If you are planning on adding books in school, you will most likely need to submit a request to the IT department to have the program added to your classroom computer. You may also want the IT staff to add eBook programs (such as Adobe Digital Edition, Kindle, NOOK, Kobo, and iBooks) at the same time.

Once you have the Media Console program that lets you check out the books, try it out. Check out one book. Overdrive may offer the book for download in more than one format. For example, eBooks from Overdrive are usually in Kindle, PDF, or EPUB formats, with audiobooks either in Windows Media or MP3 formats. Once you download the eBook file, use your computer to display the book or transfer the book files to your reading device.

I used Overdrive's library search tool and found 37 different libraries using the Overdrive system in my home state. To check to see if your local library uses Overdrive, go to http://search.overdrive.com, then select the option to Search for a Library, enter your ZIP code, and see what libraries are nearby. If your local library doesn't have the digital checkout and download ability, check other regional libraries around you that may accept your district library card. Many libraries have reciprocal borrowing arrangements, and you may be able to use your library or purchase a non-resident library card.

## Library eBook Resources

### Overdrive Search

http://search.overdrive.com
Use Overdrive to find a local library that allows digital book check-out

### Overdrive Media Console

http://omc.overdrive.com
This eBook reading program allows you to check out and read Overdrive eBooks, audiobooks, and more

### Overdrive Download Station

www.overdrive.com/Software/download-station.aspx
This downloadable software turns a public PC into an audiobook download kiosk station

### Adobe Digital Editions

http://adobe.com/products/digitaleditions
This free software program can be used to download and purchase eBooks, as well as organize your collection

# EBOOK LENDING CLUBS

eBook lending clubs act like private libraries allowing NOOK or Kindle eBook users (remember, this applies to both the device and the software running on a computer) to check out and borrow books from other club members. These borrowable books are not just restricted to public domain books now available. These clubs are more like private or subscription libraries. These clubs hearkens back to the early days of libraries in the United States, when in 1731 Benjamin Franklin established a subscription library called the Library Company, which started by sharing collections owned by individuals. Today, these independent shared-subscription libraries are being developing based on eBook lending abilities.

**FIGURE 5.5** The BookLending.com service matches lenders and borrowers of Kindle eBooks (www.booklending.com). Copyright ©2012 booklending.com.

The eBook readers Kindle and NOOK both have a lending feature that will allow people to digitally share their eBooks with other readers. Using the eBook purchase site, people can loan eBook files they have purchased to others. For example Kindle eBooks can be lent to other people who have Kindles, and they can be lent to readers who don't have the device but are using the Amazon Kindle app or Kindle computer program (see Figure 5.5).

This kind of lending though does have a few limitations. First, the book's publisher is the one who decides if that version of a book can be loaned. To see if a Kindle eBook is eligible to be lent, look on the book's Amazon page for the eBook version. In the product details section, there should be a lending information item—if there is, and it lists "Enabled," then that book is lendable. To see if a NOOK eBook can be lent, check for the LendMe icon by the title in your NOOK's book list. With both of these programs, each book you own can be lent to only one person at a time, for a period of 14 days.

Besides the direct lending offered by Amazon and Barnes & Noble, independent lending club websites for Kindle and NOOK readers have been established. Some are Facebook groups. All of the lending clubs I have found so far are open and free. Readers can participate by joining the group and listing the books they want to share. Most require that you put up a book to share to others before you can check one out.

If you want to use one of the Facebook-based groups, you will need to use Facebook's private messages function to share access information to the shared eBooks. Because many schools restrict access to social networking sites such as Facebook, this may not be possible in a school setting.

With the book-sharing websites, usually when you submit a borrow request, its system attempts to match your request with a lender. When a member loans you a book, you receive an email notification that allows you to download the eBook to your eBook device or computer running the program. You then will have 14 days to read the book, after which it is automatically "returned" to the lender.

## eBook Borrowing Resources

### Multiple Formats

eBook Fling: http://ebookfling.com
Open Library: http://openlibrary.org

## Kindle-Specific

BookLending.com: www.booklending.com
Lendle: http://lendle.me
Books for My Kindle: www.booksformykindle.com

## NOOK-Specific

BooksForNooks.com: http://booksfornooks.com
Facebook: I have a NOOK and I'm willing to share books!:
https://www.facebook.com/pages/I-have-a-NOOK-and-Im-willing-to-share-books/208558169176987 <http://goo.gl/iWp5Fl>
GoodReads: http://www.goodreads.com/group/show/46224-nook-book-lending-library-club <http://goo.gl/V3wOAv>
http://www.goodreads.com/group/show/40792-kindle-lending <http://goo.gl/zpNkYB>

# Chapter 6

# Converting and Cataloging Your eBook Collection

When you start looking for free ebooks to add to your collection, you should not be limited by the books that you can find specific to the devices or programs that you have. Consider other eBook formats, even if you don't have the associated device. For example you might find free eBooks in the now-defunct .LIT format that would be great for your class. Once you have a free book, you can convert it to a format that you can use.

With so many books available, it's important to keep track of the books you have. Some great free tools are available to help you catalog your collection.

## CONVERTING EBOOK FORMATS

One great thing about the millions of eBooks freely available online is that most are in the public domain and don't restrict what you do with them or how many copies you make. With the right tools, you can download a version of *The Secret Garden* or *Puss N' Boots*, and then convert it to run on all the devices available to your class: NOOK, Kindle, or desktop computer.

Once you download a free book, you can copy it to all of your classroom devices. However, to get it to run with both NOOK and Kindle programs, you may need to convert the format.

For example, if you download the illustrated version of *The Wonderful Wizard of Oz* from Google Books, it will either be in the PDF or the EPUB format. Using Calibre (calibre-ebook.com), a free eBook conversion and management program, you can convert the downloaded EPUB file to a large number of other formats: EPUB, FB2, OEB, LIT, LRF, MOBI, HTMLZ, PDB, PML, RB, PDF, RTF, SNB, TCR, TXT, and TXTZ (see Figure 6.1).

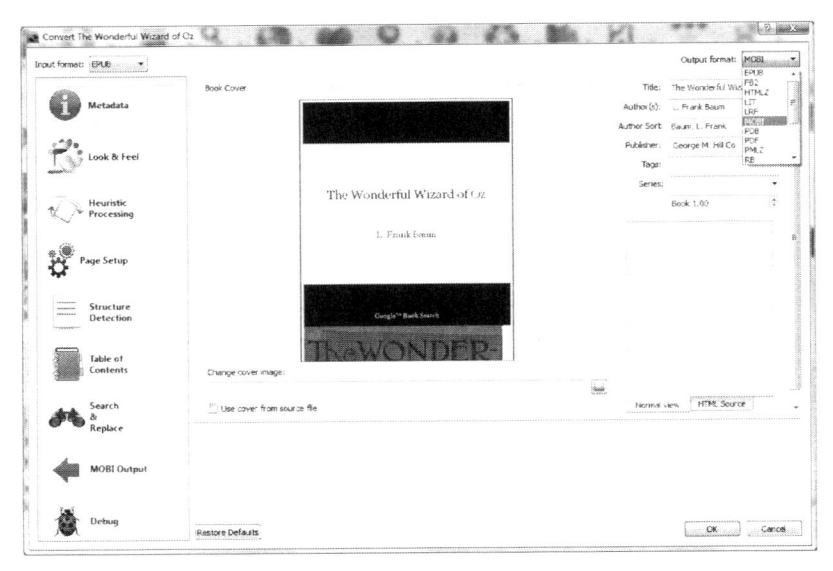

**FIGURE 6.1** The Calibre conversion window. Calibre © 2012 Kovid Goyal

Your NOOK will recognize EPUB and PDF, while the MOBI format is the appropriate format for your classroom Kindle.

Calibre is not the only eBook conversion program, but it is free and updated frequently. Others free programs are available. For example, Hamster eBook Converter (http://ebook.hamstersoft.com) allows you to convert ebook files in proprietary formats for Sony, iRiver, Amazon, Kobo, and other eBook readers so they can be read on other devices.

Some programs are format-specific: while they can take in a variety of ebook formats, they can only export a single format.

With online conversion tools, you can convert ebooks without downloading software. The online service ePubConverter.org can convert PDF or Word DOCX files to the EPUB format; ZamZar (www.zamzar.com) can convert ebooks to any of 14 different ebook formats. Online tools are useful when you are not able to install conversion programs on your computers.

Even if you don't need to convert ebooks for reading on a different device, consider converting them for student home use. eBook readers have become a popular home item, and converting some of your classroom's public domain ebooks into different formats could encourage students to download and read them at home.

## CONVERTING AUDIOBOOKS

Once you have started downloading audiobooks from free sources to use in your classroom or library, you may want to also make those books available for student checkout. You can do this by placing the audiobooks that are public domain or under the creative commons license onto portable audio players, like MP3 players and iPods for checkout, or create your own CD audiobooks to be played on a computer or CD player.

Your classroom computer should already have a program that will convert your downloaded audiobook files and burn them to a CD. Both Windows Media Player and iTunes can burn CDs. Before you start, check to see that your computer has a disc drive that can burn or write to discs, not just a player/reader drive.

A standard audio CD holds between 70 and 80 minutes of audio content. After each song is added to the burn list, your audio software will calculate how many minutes and seconds of empty space remain on the disc. The program will automatically insert two seconds between songs. Plan to have a maximum of 70 minutes of audio per disc for your audiobooks. You may need to burn additional discs for longer audiobooks. Make sure that you label all discs so they are easy to locate and store.

## CATALOGING YOUR COLLECTION

In the past, every library had large wooden boxes filled with cards with information about the contents of a book collection. Together, all of the cards were known as the library or card catalog. The information on those cards allowed users to find a book by author, title, or subject. For most schools those days are gone, and the card catalog is digital. Now that you have started collecting ebooks for your classroom, you too should have a catalog to keep track of your collection and let others know what books are available.

Before the advent of online applications, tracking your personal or classroom book collection was tedious, to say the least. Most teachers that I know didn't have any form of catalog system, or would use a hand-written notebook. Cataloging your books this way often led to frustration, because if a book went missing, it would be difficult to track down.

Today, you have access to great cataloging programs, such as the software database program Books for Mac. However, these programs can only be installed and run on a single computer. This can be a problem if you are outside your classroom and need to know how many copies of the book *Hatchet* you have for an upcoming literature circle.

The answer is an online catalog. Cataloging your classroom collection online enables you to access it from any Internet connection. It will also provide access to collaborative or social networks, where students can rate and write reviews of the books in your collection.

### Setting up Your Online Catalog

Creating your personal book catalog on one of the service providers is relatively easy. (See Online Resources at the end of this chapter for a list of services.) Once you make an account, simply enter the title or International Standard Book Number (ISBN) of a book in your collection. The service finds the rest of the information, including author, publisher, ISBN, a thumbnail image of the cover, and more. One service, LibraryThing, even provides the Lexile number in the book's details section. These services all let you view or print your catalog instantly, sorted by author, title, or tag (keywords).

Many of the services will catalog more than books, and can track video and music collections as well.

78   eBooks for Elementary School

**FIGURE 6.2**   A LibraryThing collection displays the covers of books in the collection

When browsing your collection, you are not limited to text only—your collection can be displayed with book covers, which is helpful because many students pick books based on covers. Your virtual bookshelf can be shared with others online or in the classroom. Students can browse all available titles, not just books physically on the class bookshelf. You can also create display cards to place with your paper books for students to browse (see chapter 10.)

To get started, you might want to try LibraryThing (see Figure 6.2), which allows you to catalog your first 200 books for free. (A $25 lifetime membership allows you to catalog an unlimited number of books without having to view any advertising.) You can then use the tags or the private comments section to identify books you have loaned out, including when you loaned them and to whom. Tagging is when you add keywords to help categorize a book. For instance, if you use the tag "borrowed," you can run a search on that keyword and see where those books are.

You can visit my personal LibraryThing catalog at www.librarything.com/catalog/tcavanau.

## CLASSROOM ACTIVITIES WITH THE CLASS CATALOG

You can also take cataloging to another level, turning it into a classroom tool or resource that students actively use. One method is to use the online catalog as a reading list resource for students; another is to make a book wish list for your classroom. You can create an account for your class with you as the account holder, which is useful when integrating the catalog into student activities.

### Personal Tags

Providing tags is one way your students can participate with the class catalog. Personal tags could include statements like "really scary," or the book's Lexile or reading level. For example, the tag "books in Florida" describes a story element (setting) for the book *Because of Winn*

*Dixie*. Or a character can be tagged, such as "Alex Rider" from the book *Snakehead* from the series by Anthony Horowitz.

On some cataloging sites, the tags are displayed as a tag cloud, a collection of tags people have used. The more popular tags are the largest (see Figure 6.3). Clicking on a tag will either lead to the user name of its creator and in turn to that person's other book choices, or to a list of books that have that tag attached to them.

**FIGURE 6.3** Tag cloud for *Misty's Twilight* by Marguerite Henry on the LibraryThing book catalog

## Student Book Ratings and Reviews

Most catalog services provide a method for rating books. For an activity, students can rate books by using a scoring star system, or write reviews to be published with the catalog. For homework, students can use the book catalog to investigate what others have written, do author studies, or use it as a tool for book selections for literature circles.

# CONCLUSION

Millions of free ebooks are available online and you do not have to limit yourself to the hardware or software that you have in your classroom. There are tools available to convert one format that you cannot read on your class devices to one that you can. For example, the popular conversion tool, Calibre, can covert more than a dozen different formats into something your computer can use (such as PDF or ePub). Audiobooks can also be converted into a format your equipment and use, for example, converting MP3 files to CD audio files so you can copy them onto discs. With your greatly expanded ebook collection, you will need to organize it so you can keep track of where the titles in your library are and students can view possible reading choices. Several online book-cataloging services are discussed.

# ONLINE RESOURCES

The following is a list of book cataloging tools and services.

## eBook Conversion Tools

### Calibre

http://calibre-ebook.com/
This free, open-source library management application for Windows, Mac, or Linux includes ebook conversion tools, library management, and an ebook viewer

### Hamster eBook Converter

http://ebook.hamstersoft.com
A free Windows-based ebook conversion software program that allows you to convert ebook files in proprietary formats for Sony, iRiver, Amazon, Kobo, and other eBook readers so they can be read on other devices

### ePubConverter.org

www.epubconverter.org
This online ebook conversion service can convert PDF or Word DOCX files to the ePub format

### ZamZar

www.zamzar.com
This online ebook conversion tool can convert ebooks into 14 different ebook formats

## Online Book Cataloging Services

### All Consuming

www.allconsuming.net
This online catalog for books, music, movies, and more includes a social aspect, with suggestions from other members

### aNobii

www.anobii.com
This site allows you to shelve and show off your book collection, as well as share suggestions about books

### BookBump

www.bookbump.com
The BookBump system offers intuitive book management and allows users to find others who share similar tastes in books

### BookJetty

www.bookjetty.com
This online program allows you to catalog your books and share them with friends via Facebook and Twitter. You can check a title's availability at more than 300 local libraries in 11 countries

### GoodReads

www.goodreads.com
This social website allows you to recommend favorite authors and titles and read recommendations from others

### LibraryThing

www.librarything.com
This library-quality catalog for personal book collections includes data from 700 libraries around the world. It allows you to connect with 1.5 million book lovers to exchange opinions, recommendations, and reviews

### Shelfari

www.shelfari.com
This community-powered encyclopedia for book lovers can be used to create catalogs, discover new books, and exchange opinions. It includes best-seller lists such as those from *New York Times* and Amazon

## Additional Resources

### Author's LibraryThing Catalog

www.librarything.com/catalog/tcavanau
The author keeps a personal catalog at LibraryThing

### Books for Mac

www.macupdate.com/app/mac/12713/books
This Mac program stores, sorts, and searches a "virtual card catalog" for a personal library

# Part III

# CREATING eBOOKS

"If you would not be forgotten, as soon as you are dead and rotten, either write things worth reading, or do things worth the writing."

—Benjamin Franklin (1706–90)

As we have seen, eBooks can play a major role in students' learning to read and improving their reading skills. Digital books also can be used as part of the writing process. Kamil (2003) found that students' written communication improved in quality through their use of computers. These technologies have been found to be effective and motivating to many students and are often a central part of their lives outside of school. And, as literacy expert Jeff Wilhelm (2000) suggests, "If our students are not reading and composing with various electronic technologies, then they are illiterate…right now…" (p. 4).

Students can write and create their own eBooks individually or in group projects. It is especially motivating for students to create their eBooks for an authentic audience. For example,

Student Maggie Brengle reads a book on a tablet in the reading corner

you could ask older students to create eBooks for students in earlier grades. Creating with technology can provide students with an expanded audience, allowing them to share their work with their immediate classmates, their family, or the world at large by posting their ebooks on the Internet.

Chapter 7 introduces the idea of guiding students in creating their own digital books as part of their classwork. This chapter includes a sample lesson plan for integrating eBook creation technology into the classroom. Chapter 8 presents information on how to create eBooks using online tools. Then, in chapter 9, we discuss using standard productivity tools, such as word processors and presentation software, to create eBooks.

# Chapter 7

# Creating eBooks as a Classroom Project

Guiding students in creating their own digital books can be easily incorporated into your curriculum. Included in this chapter is a sample lesson plan for integrating eBook creation into the classroom.

After the lesson is over, student-created eBooks can be added to the classroom's digital library or become part of a student's portfolio. The eBooks can even be shared digitally with the school, home, or with the world if the student's work is published through a class or school website. Remember to get student permission before you begin sharing their work outside of the school.

Creating their own eBooks provides students with experiences that will meet a number of different standards, including national standards from the International Society for Technology in Education, the International Reading Association, the National Council of Teachers of English, and the Common Core State Standards. See the box on the next page for the specific standards that creating eBooks can meet.

As an educator, you too can create eBooks as a source of books for the classroom or school. You may decide to create eBooks for a variety of reasons. Ease of distribution, engaging interactions, compact size, and helpful reading supports may all be reasons to change what was print material into eBook files. To learn more about creating eBooks with accommodations for special needs students, see chapter 15. For more on adapting texts for emergent readers, see chapter 12.

Creating eBooks can meet the following standards.

**ISTE NETS for Students (NETS·S)** (www.iste.org/standards/nets-for-students/nets-student-standards-2007.aspx) <http://goo.gl/IvntA>

1. Creativity and Innovation:

    Students demonstrate creative thinking, construct knowledge, and develop innovative products and processes using technology.

    b. create original works as a means of personal or group expression.

2. Communication and Collaboration

    Students use digital media and environments to communicate and work collaboratively, including at a distance to support individual learning and contribute to the learning of others.

    a. interact, collaborate, and publish with peers, experts, or others employing a variety of digital environments and media.

    b. communicate information and ideas effectively to multiple audiences using a variety of media and formats.

6. Technology Operations and Concepts

    Students demonstrate a sound understanding of technology concepts, systems and operations.

    b. select and use applications effectively and productively.

**NCTE/IRA Standards for the English Language Arts** (www.ncte.org/standards)

5. Students employ a wide range of strategies as they write and use different writing process elements appropriately to communicate with different audiences for a variety of purposes.

8. Students use a variety of technological and information resources to gather and synthesize information and to create and communicate knowledge.

**Common Core Standards: Writing** (www.corestandards.org/the-standards/english-language-arts-standards/writing/grade-5/ http://goo.gl/l7Aq5>)

Production and Distribution of Writing

W.K.6 (Kindergarten): With guidance and support from adults, explore a variety of digital tools to produce and publish writing, including in collaboration with peers.

W.5.6 (Grade 5): With some guidance and support from adults, use technology, including the Internet, to produce and publish writing as well as to interact and collaborate with others; demonstrate sufficient command of keyboarding skills to type a minimum of two pages in a single sitting.

**AASL Standards for the 21st-Century Learner** (http://www.ala.org/aasl/standards-guidelines/learning-standards <http://goo.gl/W57hU>)

1.2.3 Skills: Demonstrate creativity by using multiple resources and formats.

2.2.4 Dispositions in Action: Demonstrate personal productivity by completing products to express learning.

3.3.5 Responsibilities: Contribute to the exchange of ideas within and beyond the learning community.

4.4.5 Self-Assessment Strategies: Develop personal criteria for gauging how effectively own ideas are expressed.

# EBOOK CREATION

With today's technology and our students' tech abilities, it is important to allow them to "construct content rather than just consuming it" (Milne, 2006), and eBook creation offers such an opportunity.

When students are learning about the writing process, they can create their own eBooks as class assignments. One useful website is Writer's Workshop by TeachersFirst, an interdisciplinary writing technique that builds students' writing abilities. Using Writer's Workshop, an educator can make the writing process a meaningful part of the classroom curriculum as students create a story or write about a topic (see Table 7.1).

In the Writer's Workshop process, students choose their topics, then create and complete works, and then share their creations. Story planning, editing, revising, and the mechanics of grammar are all components of the Writer's Workshop. An educator can even incorporate a computer into the Author's Chair component of the Writer's Workshop by having the computer read the book aloud using a text-to-speech program.

An example of one class creating and sharing their eBooks can be seen at the website Stories for the Heart, where an elementary class learning about the writing process created eBooks for themselves and younger students (http://www.globalschoolnet.org/gsncf/narrative_view.cfm?pID=3967).

With younger students, you might start by having them craft the artwork for a familiar story. Each student in a class can be given the text from a storybook page to work with. They can either draw an illustration, or act out the page of the story—perhaps with simple

88  eBooks for Elementary School

**TABLE 7.1** The Writer's Workshop stages applied to creating an eBook (from TeachersFirst.com)

| Writing Stage | Writing Actions |
| --- | --- |
| Pre-Write | • thinking of ideas to write about;<br>• planning and organizing of concepts;<br>• brainstorming story or content;<br>• researching information. |
| Write/Draft | • getting ideas down;<br>• developing sentences;<br>• organizing their writing;<br>• writing coherently. |
| Proof/Revise | • proof reading developed material;<br>• editing for content;<br>• spelling, punctuation, and capitalization. |
| Share | • sharing and publishing the written product as an Ebook. |

costuming—and then have their image digitally photographed to be included in the created eBook.

You can see samples of interactive storybook development with the Uncle Wow books *How Santa Got His Elves* and *This Is Mrs. Dot*, now available for sale from Amazon <http://goo.gl/MeKA5>. These books were illustrated by students at the Gig Harbor Academy (see Figure 7.1).

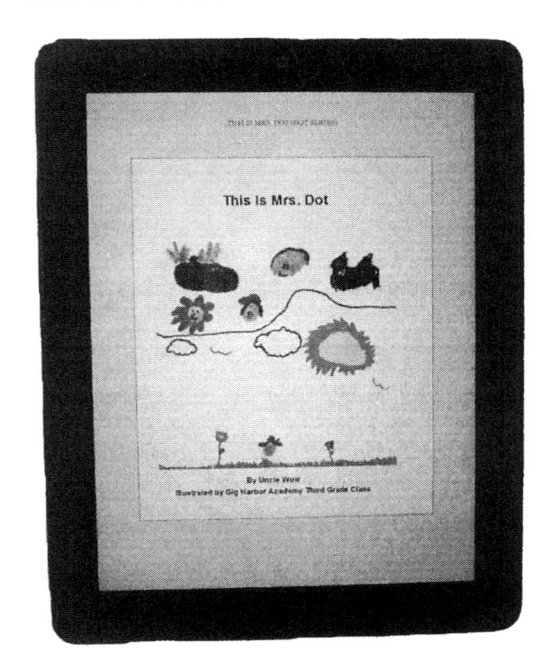

**FIGURE 7.1** This iPad is running a Kindle application displaying the Uncle Wow story *This Is Mrs. Dot,* illustrated by third-grade students

Another option is for the teacher or librarian to write a short story for the students to illustrate. Or, the educator and the children can take turns writing the text as it is being developed. (In the earlier grades, the teacher may write more than the students.) This interactive writing can be accomplished as a whole class or a small-group activity, with the teacher and the students sharing the responsibility in developing the material. As studies have shown, social interaction is an important part of learning, and students are often motivated by social interaction with their peers in their performance (Oblinger, 2005; Vygotsky, 1978; Gardner, 1993). Additionally, such collaboration decreases the amount of work that an individual student does for the project, making such an assignment much less intimidating for the student.

In higher grades, students can work independently or cooperatively developing a story, and then creating or finding artwork to fit. Sites such as Storybird allow students to select images to work from. The images then become the writing starts for each page as the students put their stories together (see chapter 8 for more on Storybird).

# SAMPLE LESSON PLAN: FAIRYTALE EBOOKS

The following sample lesson plan provides a general idea on how eBook creation can be incorporated into a reading or language arts class. As part of a unit on fairytales, students begin by reading a variety of texts and exploring that genre. Then, in cooperative groups, students either write or adapt their own fairytales. Included with the lesson plan is a sample rubric that can be used to evaluate different aspects of the students' eBook creation projects.

| Lesson Title | **Fairytale Story Writing (eBook)** |
| --- | --- |
| Time Allotment | Three to five class sessions |
| Subject | Reading/language arts |
| Cross-curricular Connection | Technology |
| Grade Level(s) | Elementary (fourth grade) |
| State Standards | LA.4.4.1.1: The student will write narratives based on real or imagined ideas, events, or observations that include characters, setting, plot, sensory details, a logical sequence of events, and a context to enable the reader to imagine the world of the event or experience; |
| *These standards were selected from the Florida Sunshine State Standards for Reading/ Language Arts* | LA.4.4.1.2: The student will write a variety of expressive forms (e.g., short story, poetry, skit, song lyrics) that employ figurative language (e.g., simile, metaphor, onomatopoeia, personification), rhythm, dialogue, characterization, plot, and/or appropriate format. |
| | LA.4.5.2.5: The student will make formal and informal oral presentations for a variety of purposes, audiences, and occasions, demonstrating appropriate language choices, body language, eye contact, gestures, and appropriate use of available technologies. |
| NETS•S Alignment | 1. Creativity and Innovation<br>　　b. create original works as a means of personal or group expression.<br>2. Communication and Collaboration<br>　　a. interact, collaborate, and publish with peers, experts, or others employing a variety of digital environments and media.<br>6. Technology Operations and Concepts<br>　　a. understand and use technology systems. |
| Activity Focus | *Opening activity - "hook"*    *Central focus of lesson*<br>☑ Part of an existing lesson   ☑ Assessment activity<br>☐ Research tool for students   ☑ Enrichment activity<br>☐ Remediation activity<br>☐ Other (describe): |
| Technology Equipment Needs | ☑ Classroom computer and projector    ☑ Computer Lab<br>☑ Internet access    ☑ Student computers<br>☐ VCR/DVD    ☐ Overhead projector<br>☑ Other (describe): Scanner or digital camera – to capture student drawings for inclusion<br>☑ Software (list): Presentation software |

*(Continued)*

| | |
|---|---|
| **Lesson Title** | **Fairytale Story Writing (eBook)** |
| Goal/Objective | Students will create a fairytale based on prior knowledge in small groups using eBook technologies. |
| Description | Cumulative activity as unit on fairytales.<br>Online book list of sites with fairytales for early exploration:<br>• Storybook Castle (http://www.storybookcastle.com/tales/)<br>• Digital Media Repository (http://libx.bsu.edu/cdm4/browse.php?CISOROOT=/HistChldBks)<br>• Rare Books & Special Collections Reading Room (http://www.loc.gov/rr/rarebook/digitalcoll/digitalcoll-children.html)<br>• Library of Congress Read.gov's Classic Books (http://www.read.gov/books/) (see Figure 7.2)<br>• Children's Books Online: the Rosetta Project (www.childrensbooksonline.org)<br>After reading/reviewing a number of fairytales, students working collaboratively will use familiar storylines, characters, and settings from traditional fairytales to create their own versions using the writing process. Stories can be a continuation of the existing story, a story focused on a different character from the story, or a story placed into a different setting.<br><br>Working together, students are to develop the story and the associated images and assemble them into a final eBook using the Google Documents Presentation tool, PowerPoint, or other similar presentation software.<br><br>When completed, students will present their eBook to the class using the presentation software and projector. |
| Alignment with Technology Continuum | ☑ *Awareness – Technology centered. Instruction is about or controlled by technology.*<br>   ☐ Technology is used separate from learning goals (reward).<br>☑ *Exploration - Technology supplements instruction by providing extension or enrichment.*<br>   ☑ The teacher predetermined experiences with technology.<br>   ☐ Technology is used for drill and practice.<br>   ☐ Student work requires little analysis or creativity.<br>   ☐ Technology is not necessary to achieve the learning objective.<br>☑ *Infusion - teacher centered/ directed; technology use is adapted to fit with traditional goals and tasks.*<br>   ☑ Productivity tools are used to augment the lesson.<br>   ☑ Productivity tools, software, and the Internet are used to modify traditional assignments given in the past.<br>   ☑ Technology skills are learned within the content (primary emphasis is on learning content.)<br>   ☐ Technology is an alternative means not essential to lesson goal.<br>   ☑ Technology provides a means for displaying student work tied to specific content goals.<br>   ☑ Technology provides adaptations in activities or assessments for special populations.<br>☑ *Integration - student centered/constructivist instruction; technologies are used for collaborative, project-based instruction.* |

*(Continued)*

| Lesson Title | **Fairytale Story Writing (eBook)** |
|---|---|
| | ☑ Technology engages students in high-level cognitive tasks |
| | ☐ Students use complex thinking tools, such as simulations, modeling, mapping, or video production. |
| | ☐ The learning activity would not be possible without technology. |
| | ☐ Technology use maximizes student involvement. |
| | ☑ Technology use promotes collaboration. |
| | ☑ Technology optimizes opportunities to demonstrate mastery of learning outcomes. |
| | ☑ *Expansion and refinement – constructivist instruction in which students and teachers are facilitators, learners, and researchers; technologies support self-directed, collaborative learning.* |
| | ☑ Technology extends the classroom beyond the school. |
| | ☐ Students select appropriate technology and initiate use. |
| | ☐ Technology is a tool for authentic problem solving. |
| | ☐ Technology is seamlessly used by students for their own inquiries, problem solving, and product development. |
| | ☑ Students seek ways to incorporate new uses of the technology into learning and acquire new skills as needed. |
| Assessment Strategies | At the end of the activity, students' stories will be evaluated for design, structure, content, and appropriateness.<br>Student presentations will be evaluated using a rubric. |

# Rubric for eBook Creation Project

| | 0 | 1 | 2 | 3 | Score |
|---|---|---|---|---|---|
| Illustrations | Did not use images | Number and quality of images not appropriate; some images off topic or missing. | Number and quality of images is appropriate for story. | Use of images is exceptional. Images fully enhance the quality of the eBook. | |
| Writing Mechanics (Capitalization, Punctuation, Spelling) | Many errors in writing | Few mechanical errors | Only 1 or 2 errors | No errors | |
| Organization | Minimal | Demonstrates some of the story organization elements. | Clear sense of story organization elements. | Demonstrates exceptional organization. | |
| Cooperative Group Work | Impeded group or created repeated disruptions of work. | Made some contributions to the group/project's success. | Was an effective contributing member to the group/project's success. | Provided leadership to project success. | |
| Total Score: | | | | | |

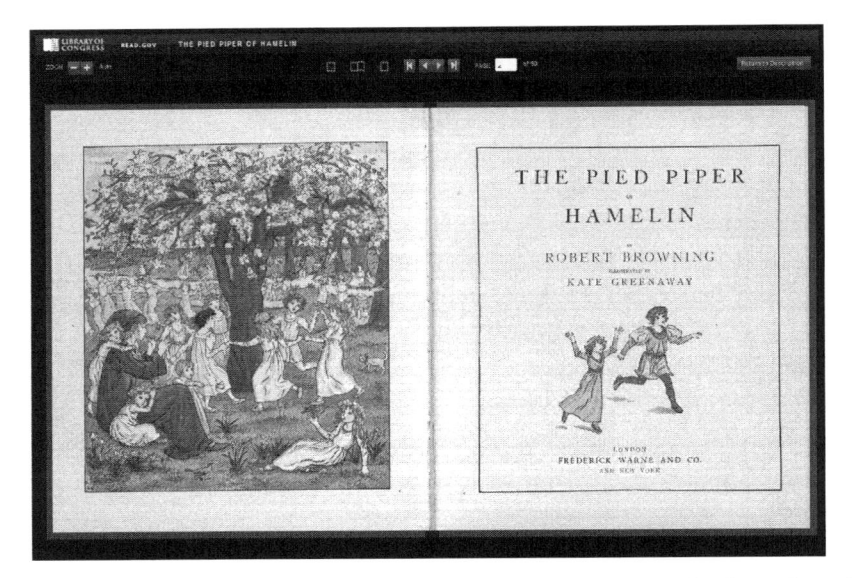

**FIGURE 7.2** An online reading version of *The Pied Piper of Hamelin* is available from the Library of Congress' Read.gov website

## ONLINE RESOURCES

**Amazon Uncle Wow stories illustrated by students:**

http://goo.gl/nenzZ

**Google Documents (presentation tool)**

http://docs.google.com

**"Our Stories" by students at the St. Elizabeth Catholic School in Ottawa**

www.daemonworks.ca/projects/LiteracyAlive/heart/table_contents.htm

**Storybook Castle**

www.storybookcastle.com/tales/

**Digital Media Repository http://libx.bsu.edu/cdm4/browse.php?CISOROOT=/HistChldBks**

Rare Books & Special Collections Reading Room www.loc.gov/rr/rarebook/digitalcoll/digitalcoll-children.html

**Library of Congress Read.gov's Classic Books**

www.read.gov/books/

**Children's Books Online: the Rosetta Project**

www.childrensbooksonline.org

# Chapter 8

# Online Tools for Creating Picture eBooks

Students and educators can use a variety of online websites to create eBooks and share them with others. These sites not only provide additional collections of online picture books for students to read, they also provide students with the tools to create their own stories.

Depending on the services offered by the websites, the student-created stories can be added to online collections or printed out to keep. The books can be illustrated by the students themselves or by using a library of professional artwork. Some websites even give students the option of adding their own narration to their stories.

Students using these sites do not have to be alone when writing their stories—the sites provide collaborative elements, including allowing students to rate and comment on the stories that they have read, and classes can have online discussions through chats or discussion boards.

Instructors might begin using one of these websites by first having students read, rate, and comment on stories they like. When students are ready, they can progress from reading to using the sites to write their own stories. Picture books are often written with careful and sparse word choices, making them excellent models for writing.

At the website My StoryMaker (www.carnegielibrary.org/kids/storymaker/), students create a picture book from existing options, and then print it out on their own printer. On other sites—Storybird (http://storybird.com), Mixbook (www.mixbook.com/edu), TikaTok (www.tikatok.com), and Storyjumper (http://storyjumper.com)—the stories that students create can be professionally bound and shipped as a printed book (for a fee), as well as being published online.

Little Bird Tales (littlebirdtales.com) is similar to the others, with students uploading their artwork and adding text. But Little Bird Tales also gives students the opportunity to express themselves in an additional medium, by recording their own voices into their digital books, which can then be emailed to others.

Teachers can have students create wordless picture books. This strategy serves as an excellent writing foundation because the illustrations contain opportunities for students to make inferences and critically analyze the story while providing the words. The lesson plan "Creative Writing through Wordless Picture Books" incorporates Wietzmann & Glasser's (2000) *You Can't Take a Balloon into the National Gallery*. It is available from Read-Write-Think (www.readwritethink.org/classroom-resources/lesson-plans/creative-writing-through-wordless-130.html).

Using online technology can provide students with 21st-century skills. It also encourages students to improve their writing. Research findings on the effects of computer technologies on reading and writing have found that students' written communications improved when going beyond the classroom (Kamil 2003). Technology makes it possible for students to write not only within the confines of their classrooms, but also to publish to the world at large.

# STORYBIRD

Each of the resources listed above uses a similar process for creating eBooks. Here, I highlight Storybird to show how students can create their own online stories.

The Storybird website allows students to create short, art-inspired stories by providing themed art collections to choose from. The story writing is actually a form of digital storytelling. With each step, instructional illustrations help in the creation of the book. The themed artwork serves as writing prompts as students develop their stories. Because the students are choosing which pictures they want to use, using Storybird would also be considered a differentiated instruction lesson. Students also select which images they want to use as their backdrop in presenting their online picture books.

Storybird has two kinds of user accounts, both of which are free. A student can have an individual account, but I recommend that teachers create a class account (although you can create your own personal account, too). With a class account, you can manage your students' accounts without requiring student email addresses, and have the ability to reset passwords (useful when students forget passwords). The class account is secure and has no student chat or personal profiles.

Under a class account, you can create an unlimited number of separate classes. For each one, you can determine privacy settings and moderate comments and discussions. You can also create assignments with due dates that appear every time a student logs in, and you can turn off the spell check feature if desired.

To create a class account:

1. Go to the Storybird site (http://storybird.com).
2. Click on the link to Sign up.
3. Select the account type option for Teacher/Class.
4. Fill in the boxes with your information, including username, password, email (no student emails will be required), and class name.
5. Once you have filled out the boxes, click on the button labeled "Create your account."

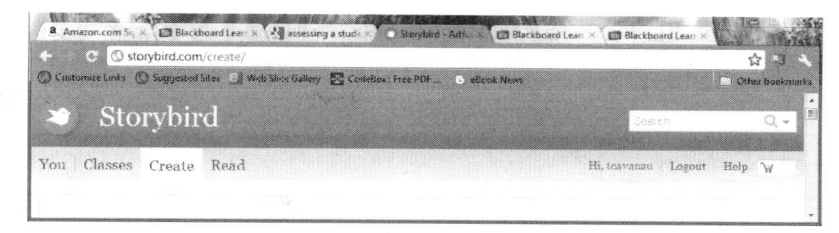

**FIGURE 8.1** Storybird header to create a new eBook

To create a Storybird book after logging in:

1. Click on the Create button (see Figure 8.1).
2. Select an art theme to work from (see Figure 8.2). Students can select from the image sets listed, or browse for other image collections, or use the word tag cloud at the bottom of the page for text themes. Click on the image or word in the cloud to see more associated pictures.
3. If you are satisfied with the image, click on the button labeled "Start a Storybird" with this art.
4. The page will now change to the editing section (see Figure 8.3). Here you can add pages to your story, pick the images you want to use from the collection, and then add text.
   a. To add a page to the story, click the plus button (+) on the storyboard at the bottom of the page. You can click on the pages to navigate through your story.
   b. To add or change the picture on the page, drag the image you want to use onto the page in the center of the screen. If you don't like the picture on that page, you can drag it off the center image to remove it.
   c. Each page has an add text section. Click inside the section and start typing in your story. The layout of the page's image with text can also be changed. Drag the picture to different

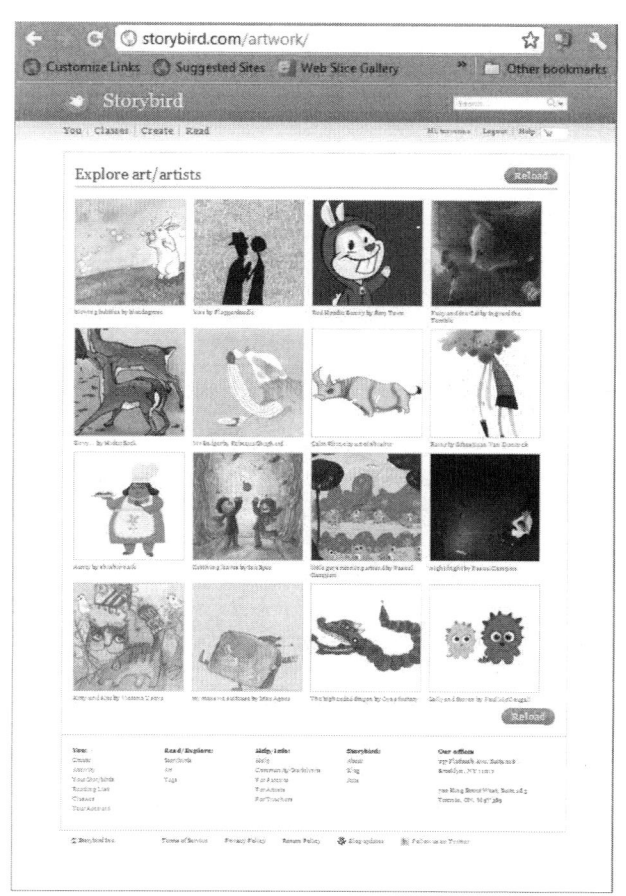

**FIGURE 8.2** Sample artwork selection for use in Storybird

**FIGURE 8.3** The Storybird editing window

parts of the page to see different layout possibilities.

d. Repeat steps a-c, adding pages, images, and text until your story is finished.
e. Click on the cover page to add the title of your Storybird book and your pen name.
f. When the story is complete, click on the Menu button and then choose the option to Publish this Storybird....

5. Now the page will change to the Storybird story information page (see Figure 8.4). The story isn't published yet. On this page you can make changes to the title or cover image, create a brief description of your story, add tags to help people find your story, set the story to public or private, and give an approximate age for the story's audience.
6. When everything is ready, click on the Publish button to publish your story to the Storybird library so that others can read it.

If your students create a really good story, you can have a hard copy printed for the classroom collection or the school library, in either paperback or hardback. The cost is reasonable. For example, to have a 20-page Storybird book printed costs approximately $20 plus shipping.

To have a book printed:

1. Log in to the site and browse to the Storybird story you want to have printed.
2. Click the Buy link in the top-right corner of your Storybird page.
3. Choose what type of format you'd like: softcover, hardcover, or premium hardcover.
4. Confirm the author(s) and, if you want, you can add a note.
5. Verify the page layout is the structure you want.
6. Add the Storybird to your cart and proceed through checkout.

**FIGURE 8.4** Storybird book information page

Online Tools for Creating Picture eBooks    97

# CAST UDL BOOK BUILDER

A different type of online tool is the Center for Applied Special Technology's (CAST) UDL Book Builder (http://bookbuilder.cast.org). The CAST UDL Book Builder allows users to create interactive Flash online books of text and images, which can then be read online or downloaded. Book components can include text, pictures, recorded sound, and reading coaches, which I explain below.

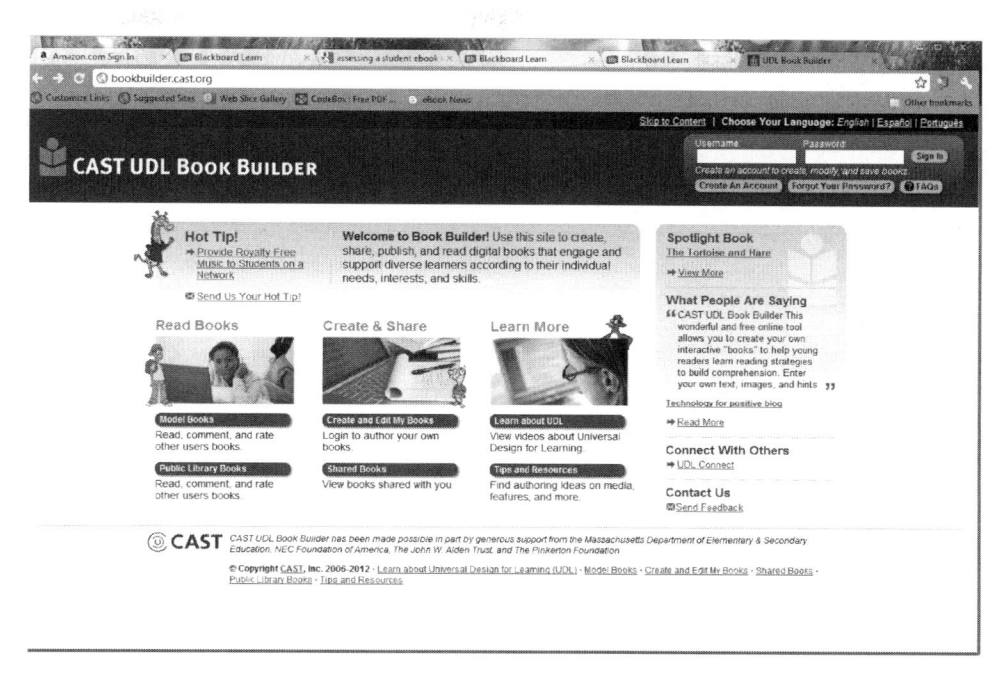

**FIGURE 8.5**  CAST UDL Book Builder log in

What makes the CAST Book Builder different from other online eBook creation tools is its Universal Design for Learning (UDL) format and how hints and reading strategies can be embedded within the eBook. UDL concepts embedded within the book-creation tool focus on three principles: representation, expression, and engagement.

Book Builder is also unique in its use of coaches that provide supports to help the reader. Supports can include reading strategies, questions, or additional content information. The coaches help keep the reader engaged with their reading and learning. The preset coaches for a new book appear as cartoon characters. My suggestion is to add the teacher or the librarian as one of the coaches.

Because you can have up to three coaches for each book, it is a good idea to create consistent roles for each coach, such as one for reading strategies or another to provide additional information. The preset coaches will read aloud whatever you type

**FIGURE 8.6**  The top section of Book Information defines the book and its intended audience

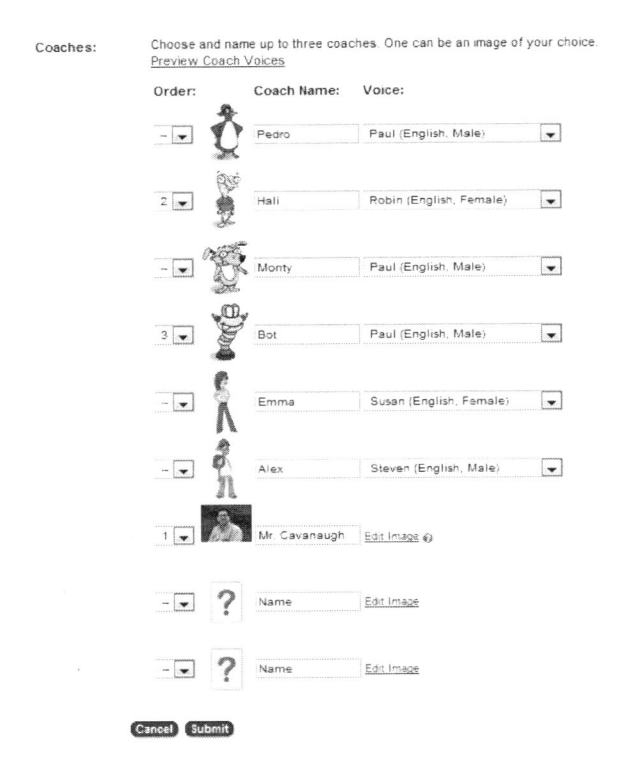

**FIGURE 8.7** Lower section of book information page where authors can select or add their own reading coaches

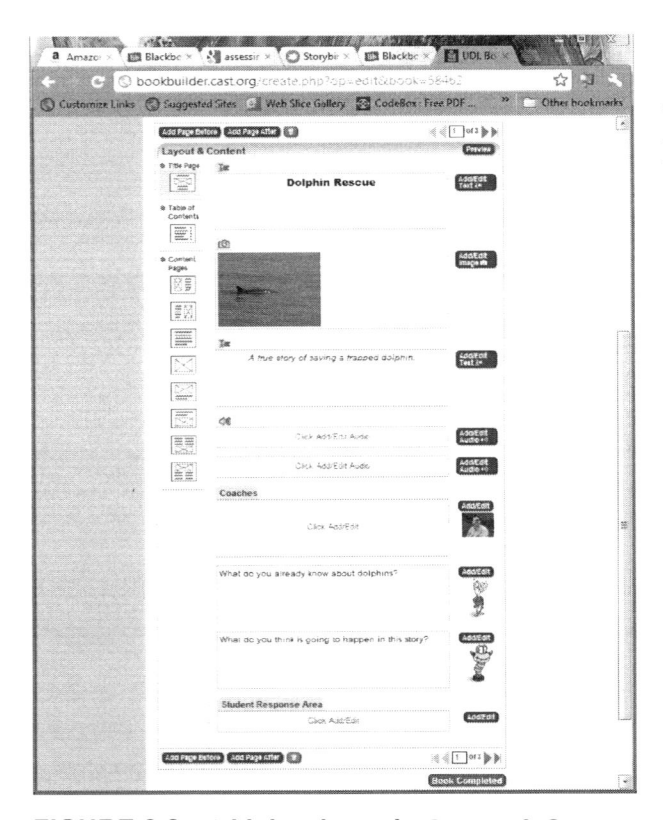

**FIGURE 8.8** Add details on the Layout & Content page

in their speech boxes. If you create your own coach, you will need to record your own audio and upload it.

Teachers will need to create their own account, but multiple students can access that account to create their own books individually or in cooperative groups. To create a class account:

1. Go to the CAST UDL Book Builder site (http://bookbuilder.cast.org).
2. Click on the link to Create An Account in the upper right-hand corner (see Figure 8.5).
3. Fill in the account information form with your information (username, first name, last name, email, and password).
4. Click on the button labeled "Create your account."
5. You will need to check your email for a verification email. When you receive the email, click on the link provided to complete the account registration process.

To create a Book Builder storybook after logging in:

1. Click on the Create and Edit My Books button.
2. Select the button titled Start a New Book.
3. You or the student can fill in information concerning the eBook that will be created. This includes some required and optional information, such as the book's title, author, school, content area, genre, grade level, language, and orientation (see Figure 8.6).
4. Also on this page, you can select up to three reading coaches (see Figure 8.7). My suggestion would be to add the teacher or the librarian as one of the coaches. Use the dropdown menus to

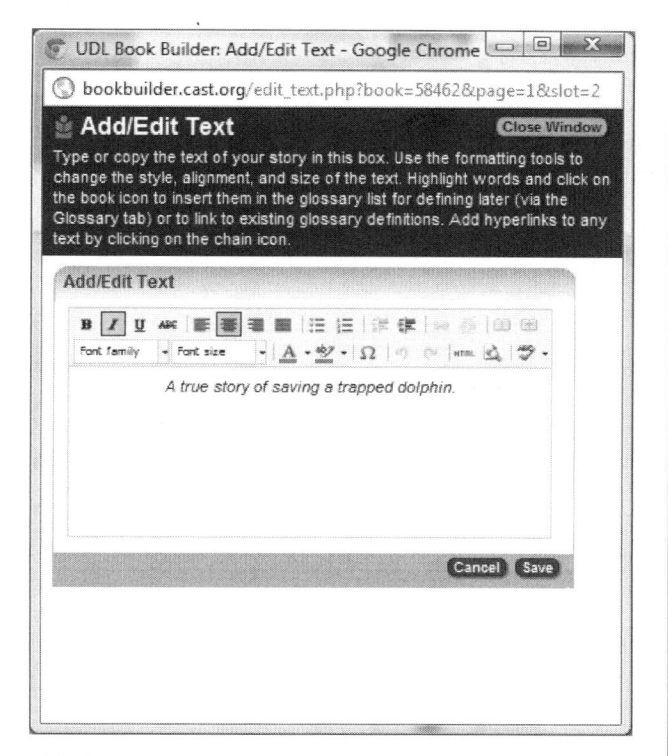

**FIGURE 8.9** Edit pages with the Add/Edit Text window

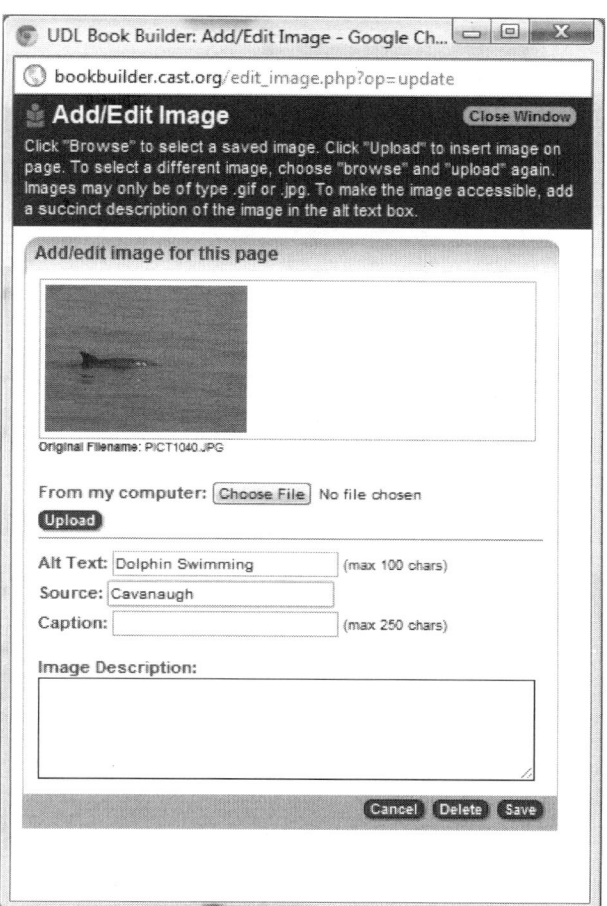

**FIGURE 8.10** Add images with the Add/Edit Image window

set the order of your coaches. To upload your own image, click Edit Image for one of the blank coaches, browse to your image on your computer, and select it.

5. When all the information is correct and the coaches have been selected, click on the Submit button.
6. You should now be in the book editing section at a blank page.
7. On the left edge are the available page layout templates (see Figure 8.8). Pick a layout, such as Title Page, and then edit the elements of the page.
8. To add text content, click on the Add/Edit Text button. This will open a pop-up window to add and format the text (see Figure 8.9).
9. To add an image to the page, click on the Add/Edit Image button. This will open a pop-up window so that you can upload either a GIF or JPG image (see Figure 8.10). Browse on your computer using the Choose File button to where your image is located, then open the file. Next, click on the Upload button to move the image into Book Builder. You should also now add a short description to the Alt Text box for your image, where the image came from for the Source, a Caption if you want, and a longer description of the image if appropriate.
10. If you wish to add your own audio narration for the page, you will need to record an audio file as an MP3 outside of Book Builder, such as with Audacity or with an MP3 recorder, and then upload the audio file. When you have your audio ready, click on the Add/Edit Audio button to open the audio window (see Figure 8.11). Next, click on the Choose

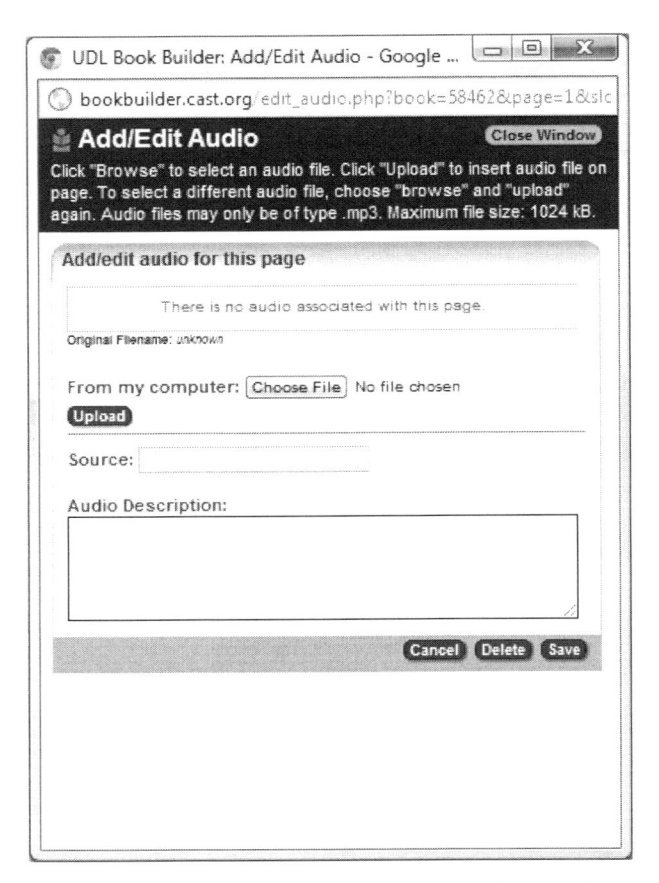

**FIGURE 8.11** Create MP3 files outside of Book Builder, then upload them using the Add/Edit Audio window

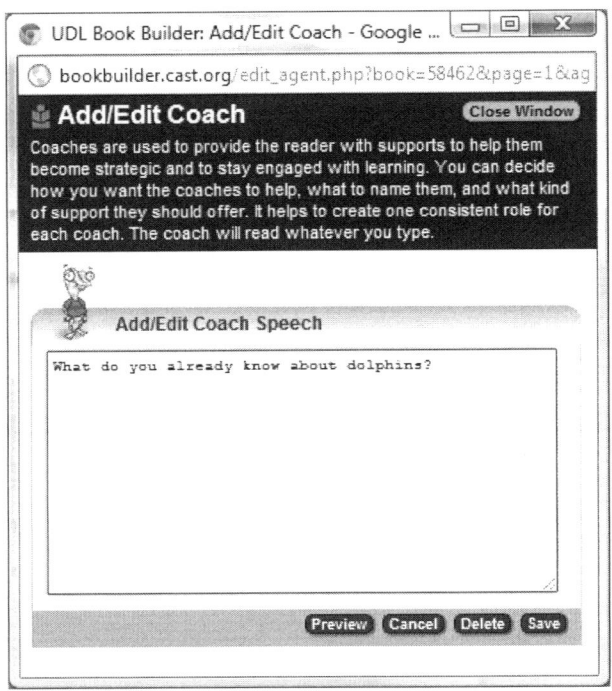

**FIGURE 8.12** Edit what coaches say to readers in the Book Builder Add/Edit Coach window

File button and browse to where you have saved the MP3 file (up to 1024 KB in size), and click Open. Then, click on the Upload button to move the audio into Book Builder. Use the Audio Description box to add a transcript of the narration. A second audio section is available for additional audio, such as narration of the text in another language or at a different speaking rate.

11. To add coach information, click on the Add/Edit button above the selected coach's image. This will open the Add/Edit Coach pop-up window (see Figure 8.12). Type in what you want the coach to say (the text will also be displayed) in the Add/Edit Coach speech box, and then click on the Save button. Do this for each of your selected coaches.
12. To add another page to your book, click on the Add Page Before or Add Page After button. To delete a page, use the arrows to go to that page and click the Trash Can button next to the Add Page After button.
13. With each page, choose a layout for the page and then click on the elements that you wish to add to that page: text, images, audio clips, and scripts for coaches. You can preview how your book will look by clicking on the Preview button. Continue adding pages, images, text, audio, and coaching until your story is finished.
14. You can also add a Glossary for your eBook. Click on the Edit Glossary link at the top of the page to go to the Glossary window. To add a new word to the Glossary, click on the Add New Glossary Term button. The window will change to a box where you can type in the term you wish to add. Then click on the Save button (see Figure 8.13). The page will now change to the Glossary Term Definition window. Add elements such as the definition, an image, and an audio recording, if you like. To finish adding the term to

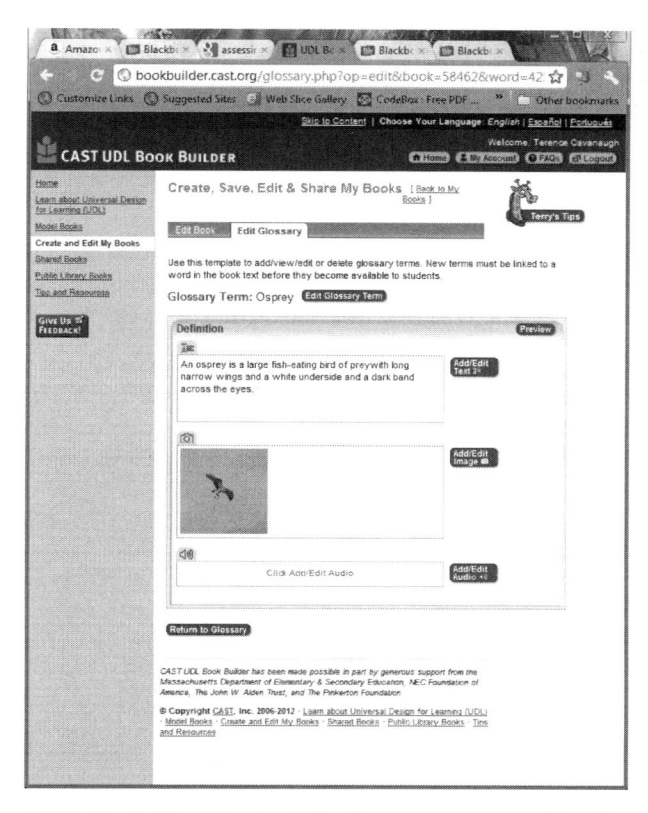

**FIGURE 8.13** Use the Edit Glossary page to add, edit, and delete glossary terms associated with the book

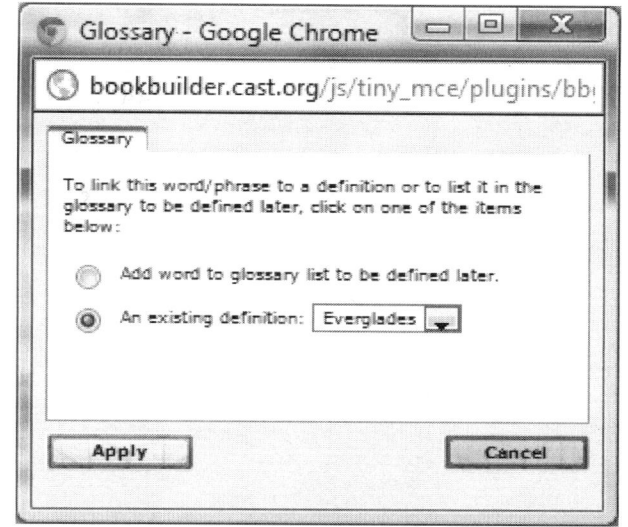

**FIGURE 8.14** Use this window to link words in the books to glossary definitions

the glossary, click on the Return to Glossary button. To return to editing the book, click on the Edit Book link at the top of the page.

15. To link a word in the story to the definition in the glossary, use the book page's text box. Edit the text and select the word you wish to link, and then click on the Glossary button (it looks like a small book). This will open a new pop-up window. Either select the option to add the word to the glossary list to be defined later, or select an existing definition and use the dropdown menu to select the glossary word (see Figure 8.14). Click on the Apply button to return to the Add/Edit Text window.
16. When your book is finished, click on the Book Completed button. This allows users to share the book with others, or publish the book to the Public Library eBook collection for others to read.

## CREATING COMICS

Don't forget other formats beyond picture books and text. Comics are a popular format for students, with many online resources for teachers. For example, more than 100,000 teachers have accounts at Bitstrips for Schools (www.bitstripsforschools.com), which offers educators a secure site for classroom use. So far, students have created more than six million original comic strips.

A complete lesson plan is available from Read-Write-Think on using comic strips for book reports (www.readwritethink.org/lessons/lesson_view.asp?id=195). The lesson plan includes planning sheets and a comic-strip rubric.

**FIGURE 8.15** Comic strips can be created with Strip Generator

For more information on using comics in the classroom, visit the Center for Cartoon Studies (www.teachingcomics.org), sponsored by the National Association of Comics Art Educators (NACAE). Resources at NACAE include guides, suggested books, syllabi, and resource links.

# ONLINE RESOURCES

## eBook Creation Sites

### CAST UDL Book Builder

http://bookbuilder.cast.org
CAST UDL Book Builder is an online eBook-creation tool for text and images

### Kerpoof

www.kerpoof.com
Owned and operated by the Walt Disney Company, Kerpoof lets you tell a story by creating artwork and turning it into an animated movie

### Little Bird Tales

http://littlebirdtales.com/
Little Bird Tales is an online eBook-creation tool that allows you to upload your own images and add your own voice

### Mixbook

www.mixbook.com/edu
Mixbook is an online eBook creation tool for text and images, which also allows you to have your eBook professionally bound

### My StoryMaker

www.carnegielibrary.org/kids/storymaker/
This online eBook-creation tool from the Carnegie Library of Pittsburgh allows you to print your eBook with your own printer

### Storybird

http://storybird.com
Storybird allows students to make, read, and share visual stories. The stories are organized in 19 topic categories from adventure to sci-fi/fantasy and in five age ranges, from 1–4 to adult

### Storyjumper

http://storyjumper.com
The StoryStarter section helps students write a story in seven steps. Students can then publish their text and images online, and for a fee they can have their eBook professionally bound

### TikaTok

www.tikatok.com
TikaTok from Pearson is an online eBook-creation tool that allows you to write, illustrate, and publish your eBook

## Cartoon Creation Sites

### Bitstrips for Schools

www.bitstripsforschools.com
Bitstrips for Schools allows you to create comics

### Bubblr

www.pimpampum.net/bubblr/
Bubblr allows you to create comic strips using photos from the Flickr.com website

### Comeeko.com

www.comeeko.com
Commeko.com lets you choose the comic layout, upload your own photos, and add thought, talking, or other bubble elements

### ComicsSketch

www.mainada.net/comics/
With ComicsSketch, you can create comic strips one panel at a time using online drawing tools

### Gnomz

http://en.gnomz.com/
Gnomz allows you to create your own characters or choose from characters available, select the background, and add dialogue to make your own comic strips

### MakeBeliefsComix.com

www.makebeliefscomix.com
Users can create two-, three-, or four-panel comic strips by using existing collections of characters and objects and adding dialogue

### *PikiStrips.com*

www.pikistrips.com
With PikiStrips.com, use tools to select story and character elements, and add dialogue to create a comic strip or comic book

### Pixton

http://pixton.com
Pixton lets you use existing collections of characters and objects and add dialogue to create comic strips

### ReadWriteThink's Comic Creator

www.readwritethink.org/student_mat/student_material.asp?id=21
Create comic strips by using tools that focus on the key elements, allowing students to choose backgrounds, characters, and props, as well as to compose related dialogue

### Scholastic's Captain Underpants Comic creator

www.scholastic.ca/captainunderpants/comic.htm
Use Scholastic's Captain Underpants Comic creator to make your own four-panel comic based on the famous character by grading images onto the frames

### Strip Generator

http://stripgenerator.com/
Use existing collections of characters and objects and add dialogue to create comic strips (see Figure 8.15)

### Toondoo

www.toondo.com
Toondoo claims to be the world's fastest way to create cartoons and comic strips with just a few clicks. It allows you to use tools to select story and character elements and add dialogue to create a comic strip or comic book

## Additional Resources

### Center for Cartoon Studies

www.teachingcomics.org
The National Association of Comics Art Educators (NACAE) includes resources such as guides, suggested books, syllabi, and resource links for using comics

## ReadWriteThink's Comic Lesson Plan

www.readwritethink.org/lessons/lesson_view.asp?id=195
ReadWriteThink's Comic Lesson Plan is a lesson plan for using comics as alternatives to traditional book reports

## ReadWriteThink's Creative Writing Through Wordless Picture Books

www.readwritethink.org/classroom-resources/lesson-plans/creative-writing-through-wordless-130.html <http://goo.gl/eJQnd>
ReadWriteThink's Creative Writing Through Wordless Picture Books is a lesson plan for creating wordless picture eBooks

# Chapter 9

# Creating eBooks with Productivity and Other Software

Many common applications and free software programs can be used to create or convert existing electronic text material into ebooks. Using standard productivity software, such as word processing or presentation programs, students can create their own ebooks. You can also use plug-ins or online tools with word processors to convert Microsoft Word documents into eBooks. Because presentation software is the most versatile program of this type, I explain in detail how to create PowerPoint eBooks with multimedia capabilities.

## CREATING TEXT (TXT) EBOOKS

The simplest form of eBook is the pure text eBook. Text-based eBooks are usually either text (TXT) or Rich Text Format (RTF), but they can also be other document formats. The common tool for creating these text eBooks is any word processor. With the book's text open in the word processor window, save the file as either plain text or rich text format. Saving the eBook as a plain text file means that the eBook will contain only unformatted text, without any pictures, special fonts, or formatting. To include images and other features in the eBook, save the file in rich text format (RTF).

Pure text eBooks can be read with word processors, web browsers, and other special eBook readers, such as Tom's eTextReader (http://www.fellnersoft.at/eTR.htm), which can also perform as a pure text eBook editor (see Figure 9.1).

# CREATING ADOBE READER (PDF) EBOOKS

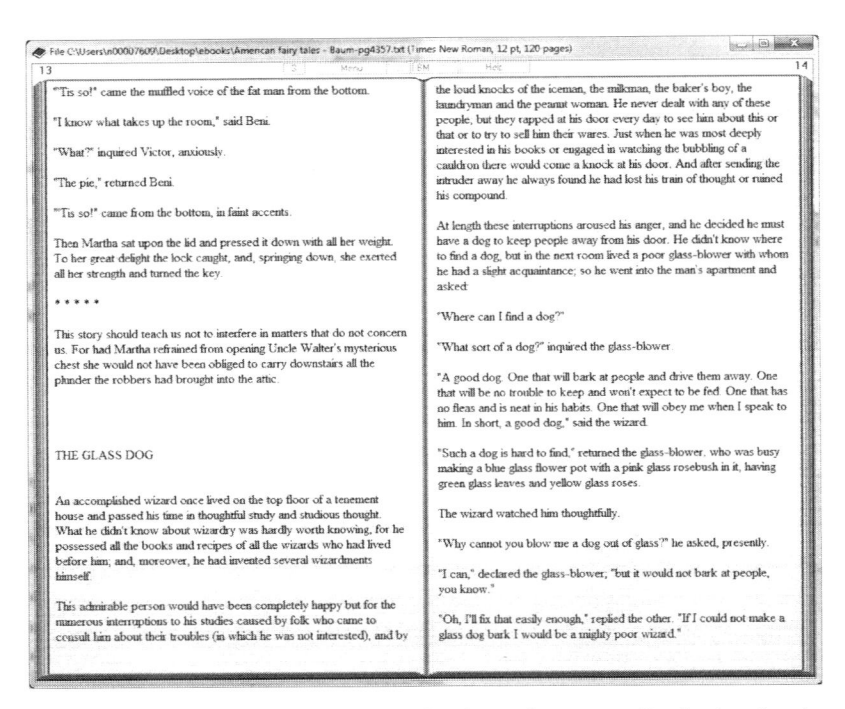

**FIGURE 9.1** Tom's eTextReader displays plain text eBooks in a book-like manner—in this case, Baum's *American Fairy Tales*. © Thomas Fellner

To create PDF eBooks, unless you have a specialized program like Adobe Acrobat, first you need to create the book in one format, and then convert or save it as PDF. Many word processors, such as Microsoft Office, OpenOffice, and Google Docs, have the ability to export or save their documents as PDF files.

If your word processor can't create PDF files directly, you can use an online converter. Online conversion programs convert text files and word-processed documents into PDF files. BCL Technologies hosts a free document-conversion service, PDFOnline (www.gobcl.com/convert_pdf.asp). With PDFOnline, users can upload and convert a variety of document formats, with a file size limit of five megabytes. The website program converts the files, zip compresses the created files, and emails them to the email address provided.

# CREATING EBOOKS FOR KINDLE OR NOOK READERS

There are a few relatively simple ways to create eBooks for dedicated eBook readers (such as Kindle, NOOK, Sony, and Kobo). The easiest method is to use a word processor and the Calibre program (see chapter 5). Other methods include using Microsoft Word with a special add-on program from Aspose (www.aspose.com) or using an online conversion service such as ePubConverter (www.epubconverter.org).

Creating eBooks to the EPUB format is a straight-forward process. Depending on your situation, you may first need to download and run the Aspose.Words Express program, available at www.aspose.com (Products > Free Utilities and Components). This program will convert a Word document into the EPUB format for eBook readers such as the Sony and NOOK.

To create an EPUB-formatted eBook with Aspose.Words Express, follow these steps.

1. Create the text using your word processor.
2. Save the eBook in the Microsoft Word document format (DOC or DOCX).
3. Start the Aspose.Words Express program (see Figure 9.2).
4. Browse to the desired Word document, select it, and then click on the Open button.
5. Use the other Browse button to place where you want the created document to be stored on the computer.
6. Click on the Convert button to create the EPUB eBook file.

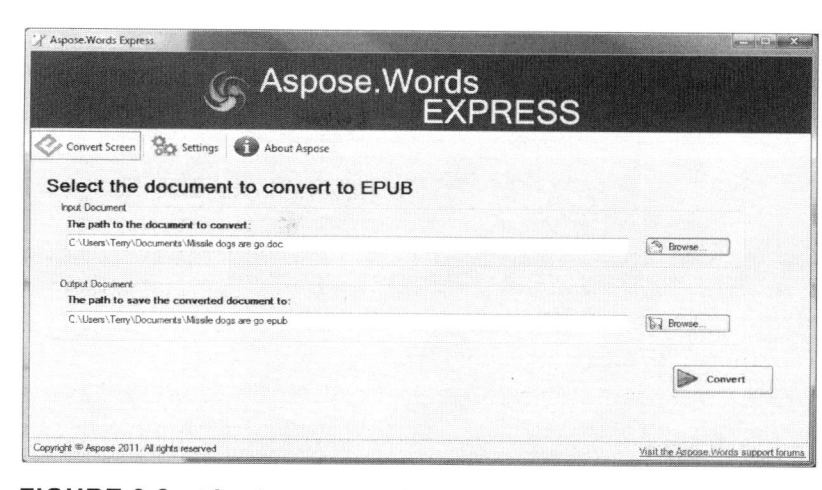

**FIGURE 9.2** The Aspose.Words Express program converts word processing documents to EPUBs

The file is now ready to be added to your eBook collection or transferred to a portable device.

You can also use Calibre to create eBooks with a standard word processor, such as Word, OpenOffice, or LibreOffice. Microsoft Word is a commonly available program, but if you don't already have a word processor, OpenOffice and LibreOffice are free programs that can be installed on PCs. Online alternatives such as Google Docs will also work. Calibre will create eBooks in more than fifteen formats for the most common eBook readers and programs.

To create an eBook with a word processor and Calibre:

1. Create the text using your word processor.
2. Using the Save As option, save the document in RTF or DOCX. Or, in Google Docs, click on the File menu, then Download As, and choose the Rich Text (RTF) or Microsoft Word (DOCX) option.
3. Start the Calibre program.
4. Add the RTF or DOCX file to the files section. Either click on the Add Books button and browse to the book file, or using drag and drop.

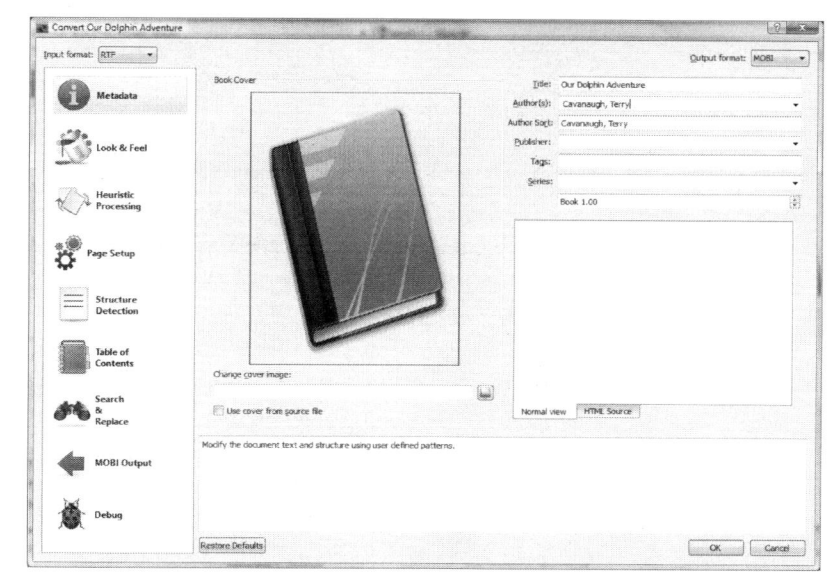

**FIGURE 9.3** The Calibre program can create and convert eBooks.
© 2012, Kovid Goyal

5. Select the book from the Calibre window and click on the Convert Books button.
6. In the Convert Books window, fill in the book information such as title, author, date, and description, and add a cover image.
7. Next, set the Output Format to the file type you prefer (MOBI for Kindle; EPUB for other readers such as the Nook), then click on the OK button (see Figure 9.3). This will start the conversion process and will save the eBook in the new format.

If you are creating a chapter book or longer document, you may prefer to have new chapters start on new pages. To do this, you will need to add information concerning the header of the document. First, go through the text and set the section titles to have a heading level of "1." Add a page break between each section. On the Insert tab, in the Pages group, click Page Break (go to Insert > Break > Page Break on a Mac). Or, press Control + Enter. Then use the Calibre program as described above.

## MORE WORD PROCESSING TOOLS

These are by no means all the ways to use a word processor to create an eBook. For example, Scrivener (www.literatureandlatte.com/scrivener.php) is a specialized writing program available for purchase across computer platforms that allows users to first write and then export a finished manuscript as a Word, RTF, PDF, HTM, EPUB, or AZW file.

Many more tools can be integrated to create books for other formats. For example, Microsoft makes an accessibility add-in for Microsoft Word that allows you to export your document as a DAISY eBook. Once the add-in is installed, Word documents can be saved in an accessible eBook format for people with visual disabilities. The add-in is available for download from Microsoft's Accessibility website (www.microsoft.com/enable/products/office2010/), and will allow Word to save documents in the DAISY eBook format, which can then be converted into a DAISY Digital Talking Book (DTB). A quick search online for word-processing eBook tools should allow you to find even more options.

## POWERPOINT AND OTHER PRESENTATION TOOLS

Another common productivity tool that you can use to create eBooks is presentation software, such as Microsoft's PowerPoint, which can be used to create your own talking electronic picture books. These books can be "played" on a computer or handheld device, or printed and bound. Another classroom application of the PowerPoint eBook is to use technology to create digital "big books" for class reading and other activities. By using a video projector or large-screen television connected to an online computer, a teacher can display the book to the whole class for an instructional reading activity or as example of writing, culture, or art. These digital big books would not by themselves cost anything extra, and they have the added advantage of being able to be placed onto a disc and made available for outside reading at students' homes.

To create a presentation eBook, make a folder in which to store all your files, such as pictures, and then create a template to use for your eBook. A PowerPoint eBook template is available at my Drs. Cavanaugh eBook website (www.drscavanaugh.org/ebooks/) that can get you started. Using a template saves time, because students don't have to repeatedly add items such as page turners. If PowerPoint is not available, try downloading and using OpenOffice or LibriOffice and their presentation tools. OpenOffice (www.openoffice.org) and LibreOffice (http://www.libreoffice.org/) are free productivity suites that include word-processing, spreadsheet, database, and presentation programs.

## Design Elements

Children's picture books contain just a picture and a few lines of text per page. This makes them an excellent project base for student writing. The average picture book is between 20 and 30 pages, with less than 500 words of text. It is important that the illustrations and text are balanced, because both are equally important to the storytelling. The words and the picture used on each page support and enhance each other.

A good eBook should follow a few standard presentation design principles:

- Limit the amount of text on the slide. A good rule is that there should never be more than 50 words on a slide.
- Use the standard mix of capitals and lowercase. Don't write in all capitals, unless it is to emphasize a single word or two, or as part of the title.
- Be consistent in use of font size and style. A good standard is a 24-point sans-serif font like Arial or Verdana.
- Keep the font and background colors the same through the book. Make sure that the colors contrast enough so the text can be seen easily.
- Use only one type of transition between slide pages for the entire story.

## The Template

Whether you are creating your own eBook template or downloading one, it should have some common elements of layout and control. You will most likely need at least two page-layout templates, one for the start of the eBook and another for the inside pages (see Figure 9.4). You will need page-turn buttons, too. If you are creating talking eBooks, you will need a speech button that will act as a placeholder. The page-turn buttons should have an Action Setting of going to the next or previous slide. You should also set your background color. Choose either white or a light pastel. Some pastel colors such as light yellow have actually been found to improve readability for many people.

Set the page transitions now. If you are going to have an action page change, one that moves the text to the left has a better reading design. Select Slide Show > Slide Transition. Choose a transition that changes the pages in a pleasing way and doesn't interfere with reading or become distracting—in other words, not too fast or too loud. Once you have selected which transition you want to use, click on the Apply to all Slides button.

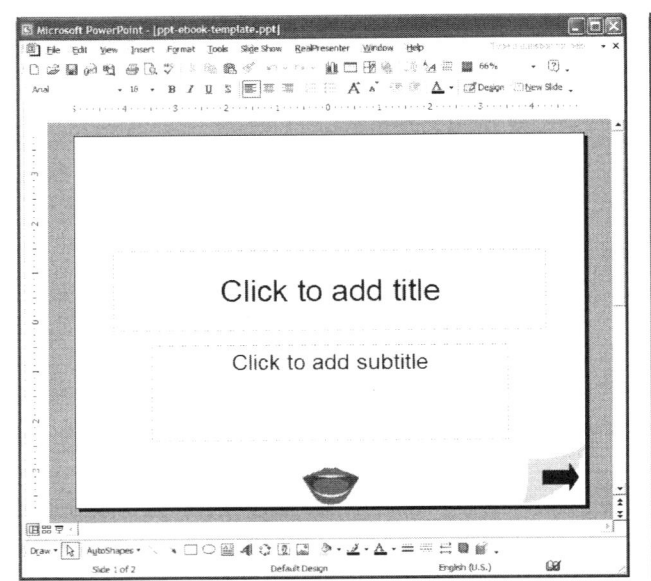

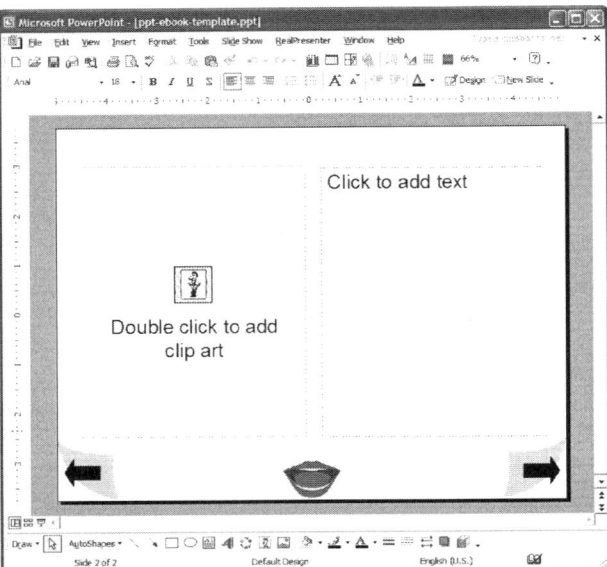

**FIGURE 9.4** Setting up a variety of PowerPoint eBook templates enables you to select the best design for each book project

Now that you have your template the way you want it, save it as a Design Template (.pot) with the name of your choice in the Templates folder. This way, the next time you want to create a PowerPoint eBook or have your students create one, the base template will be available.

## Creating the EBook

To start your new eBook in PowerPoint, select File > New. From the New Presentation menu, choose the General Templates button, and then from the General tab choose your eBook design. You are now ready to start writing your book.

To start your book, you will need a number of blank pages. You will also need to create a storyboard for your book. One easy way is to change to the Slide Sorter display from the View menu. Then copy the blank page and paste in as many pages as you need. To copy the blank page click on it once, then choose Edit > Copy. Select Edit > Paste repeatedly to add the pages you think you will need. If you are unsure, create about 25 pages. A quick way to add the blank pages is to press the Control + V keys to paste, or Control + D to duplicate.

## Storyboard

A good idea now is to print out a "Notes" version of your blank book to use in developing your storyboard. As you write your story, make rough sketches of what you want on each page. You can find or create the final pictures later.

Select Print from the File menu. In the pop-up window, change Print What to Handouts (3 slides per page). This gives you blank lines for making notes or writing the story. Now press the OK button, print out your storyboard pages, and start writing your story (see Figure 9.5).

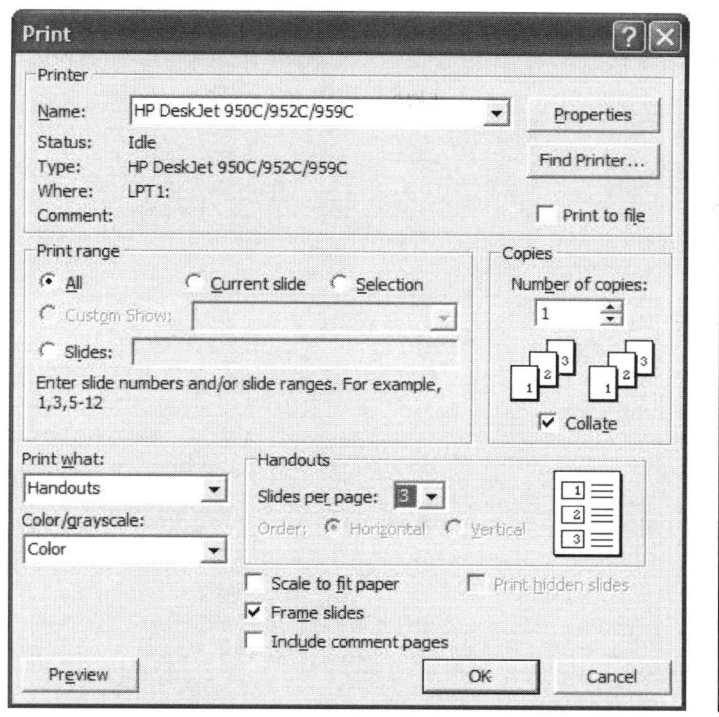

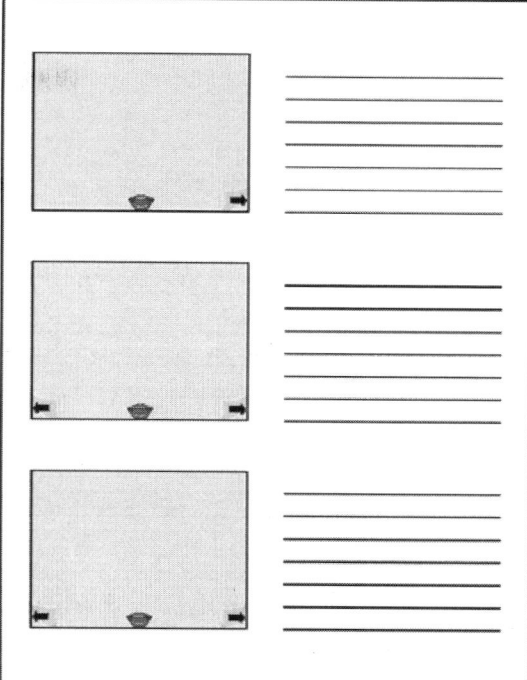

**FIGURE 9.5** Print out a storyboard to write your story

# Writing

Adding text to your eBook is not much different from using a regular word processor. On each page, you will find a text box labeled "Click to add text." Simply click in the box and write your story. You can reposition the text boxes or add a new text box from the Insert menu or with the drawing tools.

When you add text, the program may automatically resize the words to fit within the text box. You can leave it this size or resize it using either the font tools on the toolbar or the Format menu (Format > Font). Depending on your audience, you will have to judge how much text to have on a page.

# Images

Now it's time to add pictures to your PowerPoint eBook. Pictures can come from a wide variety of sources, such as digital cameras, scanned drawings, computer drawing programs, and even online sources of clip art and photographs. You can download copyright-free images from the Internet and manipulate them with software such as Photoshop, deleting or changing elements to turn them into different pictures.

Scanning is a great way to source pictures for an eBook. Have students create images for different pages using paint, colored pencils, or crayons, and then scan them. This can also be an effective strategy for a classroom with only a few computers. Connect the scanner to your computer, place the picture you want onto the scanner, and then scan and save the picture. All scanner programs should have both Scan and Preview options. Click the Preview option to make sure that the picture is correct, right side up, and lined up straight. You might want to change the resolution if the book is only for online use. Often the default is at 300 dpi (dots per inch), which is good for print. On computer screens, images look fine at only 75 dpi, so decrease the resolution to reduce the file size if you don't intend to print the book. Click the Scan button—your image will be scanned and saved on your computer for placement into your eBook later.

Because just about every cell phone has a digital camera, this is an easy option to take your own photographs to be placed in your eBook. You or your students can take pictures of artwork, live situations, or anything else you want to include in your eBook. Most digital cameras connect to the computer through a USB port. The computer doesn't see the cell phone as a camera, but as a storage drive. To insert the pictures in your PowerPoint eBook, select Insert > Picture, browse to the digital camera files, choose the picture that you want to use, and select Insert.

You can also get pictures from a variety of locations on the Internet. For example, using the Google search engine you can search for images on any subject, and then save them to your hard drive to be inserted into your book. Sites that provide copyright-free clip art and photographs include MorgueFile (www.morguefile.com) and Free Photo Gallery (www.freephoto galaries.com). Make sure that the copyright allows you to use pictures you find on the Internet.

If you like to draw with a computer, make your pictures with an art program like Microsoft Paint, and then save your pictures to the book folder. You can use the drawing tools in PowerPoint to create pictures, but the feature is limited in its tools and options.

Once you have saved an image to your hard drive, go to Insert > Picture > From File.... Browse to the picture and click Insert. Once you've placed the picture on the page, you can resize it by clicking once on the picture and then clicking and dragging on the corner marks. You can also use the picture toolbar to adjust a picture's color, contrast, and brightness, or crop and rotate it.

## Audio

With a microphone plugged into your computer, you and your students can add narration to your PowerPoint eBook. Make sure that your PowerPoint is set correctly so that it will embed the sound files and save them with the book file. Go to the PowerPoint Options menu (either under the Tools menu or by clicking on the Microsoft icon in the upper left-hand corner). Now choose the General tab (earlier versions of PowerPoint) or look under Advanced. Find the option for "Link sounds with files size greater than" and change the amount to 50,000 KB, which is the highest it will go, and then click the OK button.

To add speech to a page of your eBook, go to that page, and then choose Insert > Movies and Sounds > Record Sound (see Figure 9.6). A pop-up window will appear that you can use to record your voice reading your book. Click on the red circle to start recording and click on the square to stop. Click on the triangle button to play back your recording. Change the name of

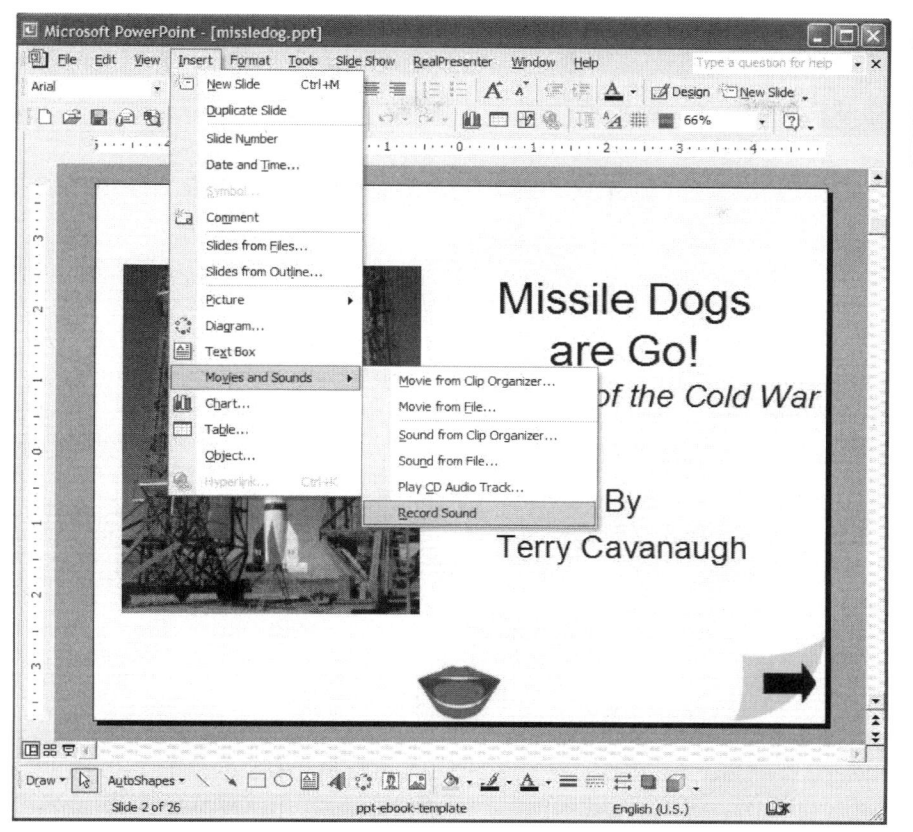

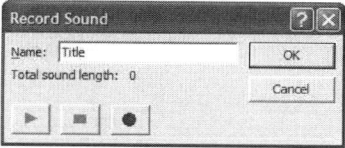

**FIGURE 9.6** PowerPoint's audio tools allow you to record speech for each page

the Record Sound file to the page number in the book, and then click OK. A speaker symbol will now appear on the eBook page.

To associate the sound with the mouth symbol, you will need to change the mouth's action settings. Click once on the mouth to select it. Then from the Slide Show menu, choose Action Settings. In the Action Settings pop-up window, put a check by Play Sound box, and then select the sound you created from the dropdown list. Now you can delete the speaker symbol from the page, and instead play the sound file by clicking on the mouth.

Once students have completed their eBook projects, they can be assessed as with any other classroom project. Table 9.1 is a sample rubric that can be used to assess a student-created eBook developed with presentation software.

# CREATING AUDIOBOOKS

You can create adapted audio versions of books that are already part of your classroom collection. For example, you can use the Franklin AnyBook Reader device (www.franklin.com) to create audio for picture books. Using the associated set of recording stickers, place one on each of the book's pages. Then press the Anybook Reader over the sticker and start recording

**TABLE 9.1** Presentation Software EBook Assessment Rubric

| Presentation Software Story Rubric | Excellent | Satisfactory | Not Satisfactory |
|---|---|---|---|
| **Design Elements** | All elements listed in design principles are followed. | All but one element listed is followed. | More than one element of the design principles is not followed. |
| **Image/Text Content** | All pages have both an image and text that support each other. | Up to two pages have only either text or images. | More than two pages do not have text or an image. |
| **Image Appropriateness** | All images relate to the content of the story. | One image doesn't relate to or support the story. | More than one image is inappropriate or does not support the story. |
| **Image Sequencing** | Pictures are sequenced so that they fit the story in a logical pattern. | Most pictures show appropriate sequencing, with only one or two out of appropriate sequence. | Pictures are not appropriately sequenced. |
| **Story content** | The story is well developed and has an engaging beginning, middle, and end. | The story has a good beginning, middle, and end, but lacks details to make it interesting. | The story is hard to follow; it does not have a good / clear beginning, middle, or end. |
| **Mechanics** | No mistakes in spelling and grammar. | Only a few mistakes in spelling and grammar. | Many mistakes in spelling and grammar. |

as you read the page. Repeat the process on each of the pages. The recordings can be done by a teacher, librarian, parent volunteer, or even students. The device comes in 15- or 60-hour recording time versions, and additional stickers can be purchased.

For more advanced audio recording, instructors or classes can use programs such as the Audacity (http://audacity.sourceforge.net) audio recording and editing program. Classes or instructors can participate with organizations like LibriVox (http://librivox.org), a public domain audiobook library, to record books in the public domain and share them with the rest of the world. If you plan to share your created audiobooks, make sure to only use public domain books or to get permission from the author and publisher.

## CREATING EBOOKS WITH IPADS

If your class or some of your students have an iPad, consider using eBook publishing apps for that device. One such tool is the Book Creator for iPad (www.redjumper.net/bookcreator) from Red Jumper Studio, available through the iTunes store ($6.99). Once installed, Book Creator for iPad can be used to create eBooks that will run in iBooks. Other similar products include Story Patch ($2.99), Strip Designer ($2.99), and My Story ($1.99), all available from the iTunes application store. With these apps, users can create various types of books—full-color picture books, student manuals, textbooks, and more. Using the iPad touchscreen, users arrange the text and pictures on each page. Images can be digital photographs or scanned images, and a wide variety of layouts is possible for each page. Once the book is completed, it can be read on an iPad using the iBooks app, sent though email or file sharing, and even submitted for possible publication though the iBook Store.

A more advanced app is iBooks Author (free), which allows educators to create their own multi-touch textbooks for use with the iBooks application. Another option is Toontastic (free) to make story videos. Using the Toontastic app, students follow the story elements to create their own animated story with music and their own voices (see Figure 9.7).

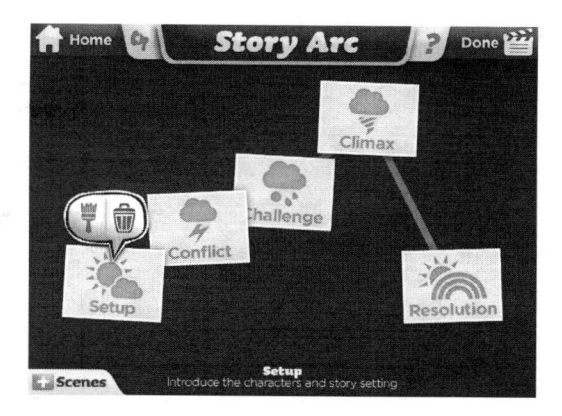

**FIGURE 9.7** Toontastic's "Story Arc" helps guide students in their story creation on the iPad. © 2011 Launchpad Toys

## PUBLISHING YOUR EBOOK

Once you or your class has created a great book, think about sharing it. You can easily share the eBook file with others in your school or the student's home. Students can actually become published authors by selling the eBook through bookstores such as Amazon, Barnes & Noble, and the iTunes Store. Make sure that you have permission on any copyrighted material first.

Amazon Kindle Direct Publishing (https://kdp.amazon.com/) allows registered users to self-publish and sell their eBooks through the Amazon's Kindle store. Authors receive royalties (35–70 percent) from their eBook sales. Kindle Direct Publishing accepts eBooks in various formats, including Word (DOC/DOCX), EPUB, TXT, MOBI, PDF, and RTF. Barnes & Noble has its own internal publishing service called PubIt! (http://pubit.barnesandnoble.com), where users can self-publish their books for distribution via the Barnes & Noble eBook store. PubIt! converts an author's uploaded eBook file to the EPUB format and makes it ready for sale. Again, royalties are paid for sales (40–65 percent). With either store, the sale price can be set at $0.00 to distribute the book for free. Another option is to distribute self-published eBooks through the iBook store via iTunes Connect (https://itunesconnect.apple.com/). The iTunes Connect system has an approval process, so eBooks in EPUB format will have to be approved before distribution is allowed.

## ONLINE RESOURCES

### Adobe's "How to Create Adobe PDF EBooks"

http://www.scribd.com/doc/122994668/How-to-Create-Adobe-PDF-eBooks <http://goo.gl/Bcgruy>
EBook on how to create Adobe PDF eBooks

### Amazon Kindle Direct Publishing

https://kdp.amazon.com/
Site to publish eBooks through Amazon's Kindle store

### Apose.Words Express

www.aspose.com
Tools for converting ePub eBooks from MS Word

### Audacity

http://audacity.sourceforge.net
Audio recording and mixing software that is free, open-source, and cross-platform

### Barnes & Noble PubIt!

http://pubit.barnesandnoble.com
Site to publish eBooks through Barnes & Noble for the NOOK

### Book Creator

http://www.redjumper.net/bookcreator
EBook-creation app for iPad from Red Jumper Studio

### Calibre

http://calibre-ebook.com/
EBook management and conversion software

### DrsCavanaugh PowerPoint EBook Template

www.drscavanaugh.org/Ebooks
Template for use with PowerPoint to create eBook slides

### Microsoft's Accessibility Tools for Office 2010

http://www.microsoft.com/enable/products/office2010/
MS accessibility tools for Office, such as an adaptor for creating DAISY eBooks

### ePubConverter

http://www.epubconverter.org
A program that converts a Word document into EPUB format for eBook readers such as the Sony and NOOK

### Franklin AnyBook Reader

http://www.franklin.com/
Audio recorder system that uses a stylus device to record your voice reading the text, and coded stickers that work much the way barcodes do

### Free Photo Gallery

www.freephotogaleries.com
Collection of more than 650 free, stock photos arranged in nine albums in categories ranging from Abstract/Stock to Travel

### goBCL.com

www.gobcl.com/convert_pdf.asp
Document conversion to HTML and Adobe PDF format

### Google Docs

http://docs.google.com
Online office suite of productivity tools, including word-processing, spreadsheet, database, and presentation tools

### iBooks Author

http://www.apple.com/ibooks-author/
Mac tool for creating interactive eBooks for the iPad and iPhone

### iPod EBook Creator

www.ambience.sk/ipod-Ebook-creator/ipod-book-notes-text-conversion.php
Converts text files into iPod notes

### iTunes Connect

https://itunesconnect.apple.com/
Site to publish eBooks through iTunes store

### iTunes Store

http://itunes.apple.com/
Online store for purchasing applications and eBooks

### Launchpad Toys

http://launchpadtoys.com/
EBook publishing app that can be used to create stories for the iPad

### LibreOffice

http://www.libreoffice.org/
Productivity tool suite; includes word processing, spreadsheet, database, and presentation tools

### LibriVox

http://librivox.org
Public domain audiobook library

### Microsoft's Accessibility Tools for Office 2010

http://www.microsoft.com/enable/products/office2010/
MS accessibility tools for Office, such as an adaptor for creating DAISY eBooks

### MS Word RMR Plug-in

www.microsoft.com/reader/developers/downloads/rmr.asp
Converts Word documents into MS Reader eBooks

### Morgue File

www.morguefile.com
Free photo archive of high-resolution stock photos

### OpenOffice

www.openoffice.org
Open-source productivity tool suite, which includes word processing (creating PDF, TXT, and HTML documents), spreadsheet, database, and presentation tools

### PDFOnline

http://www.gobcl.com/convert_pdf.asp
Online conversion tool to convert documents into PDF format

### Scrivener

http://www.literatureandlatte.com/scrivener.php
Specialized writing program for creating eBooks

### Tom's eTextReader

http://www.fellnersoft.at/eTR.htm
EBook reader program that displays plain text files in a book-like manner

# Part IV

# INTEGRATING eBOOKS INTO THE CLASSROOM

"Literacy arouses hopes, not only in society as a whole but also in the individual who is striving for fulfillment, happiness and personal benefit by learning how to read and write. Literacy... means far more than learning how to read and write... The aim is to transmit knowledge and promote social participation."
—UNESCO Institute for Education, Hamburg, Germany

The question of using variously formatted books in schools has been discussed before. From the 1930s "paperback revolution" to the 1960s young adult (YA) novels, people were concerned about whether or not paperbacks or YA book content would change the reading attitudes of students (Lowery & Grafft, 1968; Fraustino, 2004). Today, new technology formats are providing an efficient way of publishing books. In the 1930s, it was high-speed presses; today, it is Internet book delivery and inexpensive, high-capacity eBook readers.

The U.S. *Digital Textbook Playbook* helps schools make the transition to digital learning

A 2012 conference devoted to identifying persistent technologies highlighted the following as an important trend.

> The Internet is constantly challenging us to rethink learning and education, while refining our notion of literacy. Institutions must consider the unique value that each adds to a world in which information is everywhere. (New Media Consortium Summer Conference, Boston, 2012)

Today's students were born into and grew up in an information age where tools and technologies such as personal computers and cell phones always existed. Furthermore, we now have a push from the U.S. president and some state governors to have schools move to digital texts, especially for textbooks (Toppo, 2012; Florida Senate Bill § 2120, 2011). For more information about the United States' change to digital texts, see the Digital Textbook Playbook (www.fcc.gov/encyclopedia/digital-textbook-playbook). This guide helps K–12 educators and administrators begin the move to learning with digital texts.

In the long run, the switch to digital texts and technology integration may have one big advantage. It could end up costing less than would be spent on traditional paper books. Many school systems, state organizations, and private foundations are creating open-source public domain textbooks and sharing material freely, and this can result in real cost savings. It may well prove less costly to add a single technology device for each student to access a multitude of books across all learning areas and situations than to continue to purchase traditional paper products.

The first chapter in Part IV, chapter 10, introduces the modern student and discusses integrating technology into the classroom through collaboration with library media specialists. Management strategies cover classroom configurations, scheduling, and ideas for guiding students to digital books. Finally, we take a look at assessment tools.

Chapter 11 discusses picture eBooks and content area reading in mathematics, science, social studies, visual art and music, and foreign languages. Chapters 12, 13, 14, and 15 discuss working with struggling readers, gifted readers, ESL/ELL students, and students with special needs.

# Chapter 10

# eBooks in the Classroom and School

Today's generation of students, sometimes called millenials, represent the largest and most diverse group in our educational history (Patrick, 2004). Millenials have lived their whole lives with cell phones, personal computers, the Internet, and a myriad of other technology tools. They have never experienced a time without such technologies enabling them to express themselves, communicate at any time or any place, and be entertained (N.A. 2007). They are usually also technology savvy; by the age of five, 75 percent of children in the United States are already regularly using computers, with 22 percent of 5- to 8-year-olds using a computer at least once a day and another 46 percent using computers at least once a week (Blackstone, Karr, Camp, & Johnson, 2008; AVG, 2011; Common Sense Media, 2011).

Today's high school students spend their time in different ways from previous generations. Today's student's spend as a monthly average about 11 1/2 hours on the internet, 7 hours 13 minutes of mobile video a month, sent an average of 3,364 mobile texts, watch about 31% less TV than the average American, and are the smallest group of phone talkers outside the 65+ age group (Nielsen, 2009). Of course technology has always been there for them as a substantial portion of their time, just consider that today's 0-8 year old spends 104 minutes watching TV, 29 minutes listening to music, and 31 minutes using a computer or other video game device (they only get about 29 minutes reading books or being read to) (Common Sense Media 2011). Therefore, using a technology-integrated approach to reading should help teachers motivate their technology-integrated students. Children have stated that they want to read eBooks, and that they would read more if they had access to eBook reading devices (Scholastic, 2010).

# EBOOKS, LITERACY, AND READING

Technology has caused the concept of literacy to change. The Internet and other forms of information and communication technology (ICT)— word processors, web editors, presentation software, and email—are constantly redefining the nature of literacy. For a student to become fully literate in today's world, he or she must become proficient in the new literacies. Educators should integrate these technologies into today's literacy curriculum to prepare students for the literacy future. The International Reading Association (IRA) believes much can be done to support students in developing the new literacies that will be required in the future. The IRA (2002) states that students have the right to:

- have teachers who are skilled and effective at using new literacies for teaching and learning;
- a literacy curriculum that integrates these new literacies into the instructional program;
- instruction that develops these literacies for effective use;
- assessment practices in literacy that include electronic reading and writing;
- opportunities to learn safe and responsible use of information and communication technologies; and
- equal access to information and communication technology.

Historically, literacy meant the ability to read words on paper, including reading books, newspapers, and job applications. In the National Literacy Act of 1991, the U.S. Congress redefined literacy as "an individual's ability to read, write, and speak in English, and compute and solve problems at levels of proficiency necessary to function on the job and in society, to achieve one's goals, and develop one's knowledge and potential" (National Institute for Literacy, 1991). Today, literacy goes beyond paper to include reading from computers and personal devices, along with new aspects of literacy such as media literacy, technology literacy, and information literacy (Semali, 2001).

# INTEGRATING TECHNOLOGY

Using eBooks in the classroom is often no different from using paper-based materials, but they are substantially easier to share. Electronic texts can come in many forms—including books, documents, articles, reading lists, and reference works. Teachers can provide links to electronic versions of texts on classroom devices or classroom or school websites, or even email files directly to students and parents. Within the classroom or school environment, it will still be necessary for students to have access to the hardware—computers, tablets, or eBook readers—on which to read the eBooks.

With millions of eBooks freely available on the Internet (see chapter 4), eBook technology opens up new collaborative opportunities, both within the school and beyond, to the students' homes.

# Collaboration with Library Media Specialists

eBook technologies can provide an excellent opportunity for collaboration between teachers and school librarians, who are often referred to as media specialists. Here are examples of cooperative partnership opportunities.

**Standards.** Working with the classroom teacher, a library media specialist can provide assistance in the instruction and integration of technology and literacy to meet the National Education Technology Standards (NETS) and Common Core State Standards (CCSS) for students as they access and read electronic books.

**Research.** Today's students need to know how to effectively research with the new technology tools. Library media specialists can teach students and teachers to use technology resources to physically locate materials in the library, as well as use databases and conduct online research. The library media specialist can work with individual teachers to find available texts in print and digital formats for students to choose from as reading material.

**Computer Lab.** Library media specialists can educate both teachers and students on new technology skills. These professionals can also help schedule the school computer lab or portable computer collection, if such resources are available, so that students can have whole-class lab access for one-to-one computing opportunities. If whole-class scheduling is not possible, these professionals may be able to set up schedules so that single students or groups of students can use library computers as part of their class.

**eBook Access.** The school librarian can adapt the school library to be more accommodating to student-technology access. For instance, he or she can organize space within the physical library, creating centers for eBook access.

**School Website.** Because library media specialists are often responsible for the school web presence, they can also set up school websites with links to electronic book locations. In one school's library that I worked with, we took the list of books for that year's "Book of the Month," searched for electronic versions, and also searched for associated eBooks. For the month of October, the book of the month was *Stellaluna* by Janell Cannon. The librarian had planned to set up a collection of the physical books to be available in the school library along with a display. In searching we found out that the book was also available from SAG's Storyline Online (www.storylineonline.net/), in streaming video format, with the entire book being read by Pamela Reed, along with displaying all the text and images from the book. The link to the free online version of *Stellaluna* was sent to all the teachers, along with information about related activities available from the site. To match up with *Stellaluna*, we identified another free digital story about bats, *The Story of Echo the Bat* from NASA (http://science.hq.nasa.gov/kids/imagers/intro/) (see Figure 10.1), and links to that story were also sent to teachers. The links to both *Stellaluna* and *The Story of Echo the Bat* were distributed to parents in the monthly newsletter and placed on the library's website for the month, to encourage eBook reading at home.

# Classroom Technology Configurations

School libraries and classrooms have a variety of computer situations that mix desktop computers, laptops, and handheld devices. The computer configurations found in schools vary greatly but usually include some version of the following:

- a networked single computer
- two or several computers or devices clustered in an area of the classroom
- a digital reading center with several computers or devices
- the computer lab in a separate room
- a portable computer lab that can be brought to the classroom

**FIGURE 10.1** NASA's *The Story of Echo the Bat* is a great companion to *Stellaluna*

Regardless of the technology situation in your classroom or school, eBooks are affordable, immediately available, and relatively easy to integrate into a classroom's reading curriculum. I have successfully integrated technology literacy and eBook activities with my students in a variety of classroom configurations, from a one-computer classroom to a full computer lab. In addition to computers, other devices that your students can use to access eBooks include CD or MP3 players, eBook reading devices such as Kindle or NOOK, or tablet devices such as the iPad and Kindle Fire.

Each configuration provides different opportunities and has its own limitations. For example, fewer computers in class means less time for individual students to use the technology, but having computers there rather than in a lab increases convenience. Many teachers may feel that the one-computer classroom is not conducive for a class of students to use technology in activities, but every student doesn't have to be engaged in the same type of activity at the same time. A teacher can use the single classroom computer as a demonstration tool, or a small group can use it to read cooperatively. To increase technology access in the classroom, check to see if your school has a set of computers on a cart that can be used for whole-class projects and eBook reading activities.

Various strategies and methods can be used to integrate eBook technologies within the classroom, depending on the availability of technology (see Table 10.1). Integrating eBooks can be done with a single student, a small group (such as a reading group or reading center), or the whole class. For example, a teacher or school library media specialist can use a projector to display an eBook to a entire class. For small groups, you can schedule reading center activities that allow students to make use of technology-delivered reading material.

eBooks in the Classroom and School  127

**TABLE 10.1** eBook Activities in Various Classroom Configurations

| Class Design | Possible Activities |
| --- | --- |
| One-computer or device class | **Audiobook listening station:** Students listen to audiobooks individually or as class.<br>**Digital big books presentation:** Project an eBook onto a large display screen (see Figure 10.2).<br>**Download station:** Download eBook files onto students' personal storage media such as flash drives or DVDs.<br>**Print station:** Print either partial or complete documents.<br>**Reader's workshop:** Have a computer or device read a book with synchronized highlighting of text-to-speech.<br>**Reading assessment:** Copy sections of books and using tools such as Okapi to create individualized readability assessments.<br>**Reading station:** Students use the computer or device like a classroom bookshelf for open reading time.<br>**Research station:** Students use the computer or device for research individually or in small groups.<br>**Resource station:** Students use the computer or device as a reading support tool (such as with enlarged text or text-to-speech capabilities using headphones). |
| Centers or two-to-several computers or devices | In addition to activities above:<br>**Literature circles:** Group members read from an eBook, or technology-based groups take part in technology-related roles.<br>**Reader's theater:** Students read online scripts, or teachers record the reading. |
| One-to-one computing or full eBook access | In addition to activities in the two sections above:<br>**Whole-class reading.** All students follow along as an eBook is read aloud.<br>**Sustained silent reading.** Each student selects an eBook to read on her or his own.<br>**Class textbook reading.** Student use textbooks for assignments. |

It is possible, if somewhat challenging, to have students use eBooks in the classroom with only one computer or eBook device. One way to use the single computer is to add a projection device—a video projector, an LCD overhead panel, or even a large-screen television connected to a computer—and display the eBook to the whole class as a digital big book (see Figure 10.2). This is especially effective with picture books, for group reading, and for using eBooks during discussions to provide examples of writing, culture, and art. This form of big book can save you the cost of purchasing a large, printed big book version. An added benefit is that any eBook can be shown this way, not just the ones that publishers had decided to print as big books.

A classroom or library with several computers or devices can serve as a digital reading center. Instructors often find that having the

**FIGURE 10.2** A teacher uses a digital projector to display an eBook to the whole class

computers in the classroom is much more flexible than using a computer lab, because students can use them when time allows. Computer and device use can be rotated among individuals or groups. The number of computers determines the number of rotations and how long students have access. With multiple computers or devices, teachers or library media specialists may decide to dedicate each one to specific roles, such as an MP3 player for listening to audiobooks, a computer with Kindle software for reading from the classroom collection, and a tablet to play video eBooks.

A computer lab—whether part of the school media center, a separate room, or a portable set of laptops (sometimes known as COWs, Computers On Wheels)—allows more students simultaneous access, but scheduling issues and time restraints may limit access. For instance, you may only be able to schedule the lab for a single day of the week. When the lab is available, make sure that students are aware of the time restrictions and goals before beginning.

## Technology Management

For students to be effective in using eBooks, their instructors need to model effective and appropriate use of the technology as often as possible. Many factors contribute to the successful management of classroom technology. Being successful with technology means not only responding when problems occur, but also having a plan for how the technology will be integrated into instruction. For integration to be successful, the technology should primarily be used for an educational goal or activity, rather than solely as a reward.

Teachers and library media specialists should establish procedures to manage the technology so that technology-integrated activities will transition smoothly and every student is given access. The teacher should also make sure that all of the necessary equipment, such as batteries and software, are working. Before starting any technology-integrated activity, always have a backup plan in case there are problems, such as the network going offline or the computer crashing. Be prepared to do some troubleshooting of hardware and software—practice using it yourself.

Depending on their abilities and experiences, your students may need instruction on the computer basics, including how to use removable media, storing files on the network, using software, navigating on the Internet, and playing videos. To help them, consider having your more technology-savvy students serve as tech coaches. Teachers can also prepare information reference sheets or posters of common usage steps to place near computer stations.

---

### *Headphones for All*

If your class is using audiobooks or eBooks with audio support—such as text-to-speech, music, or sound effects—make sure that every student has a set of headphones, to avoid creating distractions and interruptions. Even cheap headsets from a dollar store can solve a lot of problems. You might also purchase a few audio splitters to enable a pair of students to read together on the same computer or device.

Before having students access an eBook website or use eBook software by themselves, consider demonstrating it to the whole class with a projection device. Students will make more efficient use of the machines once they are familiar with the tools. It is always a good idea to prepare students for what they will be learning, how to use the available tools, and what will be expected of them.

To avoid time off-task, make sure that the computer screens are visible to the teacher at all times. This could mean rearranging the room or adjusting the teacher's location, but when students know that you can see what they are doing, they are more likely to stay on task. If room design prohibits rearrangement and students' computer screens are not always visible to the teacher, there are solutions. Use a scan converter to display the screens on a television mounted for viewing by the instructor. Or use a computer monitoring software program to view and control the computers in the classroom. For a low-technology option, place mirrors on the walls so that you can see the monitors from elsewhere in the room.

**FIGURE 10.3** OK/HELP cards in green and red indicate which students need assistance

Another issue with computers in classrooms is making sure students know what to do when at a computer station or with an eBook device. To help them, educators should post guidelines near computers in the classroom. The guidelines should explain expected behavior and how to get help. Having a strategy for how students get help can keep them from interrupting you and the other students you may be teaching. Many teachers use some form of "Ask she/he before me," where students must first ask another student before asking the teacher for assistance. To get a teacher's attention and not have the students leave their computer stations, consider using some form of flag method to attract attention for assistance. One effective variation of the flag method is red and green plastic cups. The cups are placed on top of the monitor or on a dowel taped to the side of the monitor. When the green cup is showing, that means everything is OK. When a student needs help, the red cup is placed over the green. Another method is using self-standing triangle cards with the words OK and HELP showing on opposite sides (see Figure 10.3).

## Scheduling Ideas

There are a variety of strategies to assist in allocating students' time when using the classroom computers. To make the best use of scarce resources, you should schedule computer times efficiently for individuals or groups. For example, you can set up a class roster schedule set out in 15-minute blocks and posted next to the computer with a timer. Students set the timer for 15 minutes and then pass it to the next student waiting a turn.

A string-and-label method is another strategy for turn-taking. Hang a string horizontally with a "been there" label on one end and a "not yet" label on the other end. Then write student or group names on clothespins and attach them to the string. Place the labeled clothespins on the string near the appropriate label to indicate whether the student or group has used the computer. Once a student or group finishes using the computer, they move their clothespin to the "been there" label. A new "not yet" student or group gets to use the computer next.

Using one computer with a pair of students can also be an effective cooperative reading activity. Here are a few more tips on scheduling computer time.

- Use 3 × 5 index cards with computer names to identify computer users for each day or period.
- Leave a class roster by the computers so that students can check off their names after they have been at the stations.
- Use sign-up sheets for students who are ready.
- On a pocket chart, enter the student's or group's name and his or her computer time.
- Write each student's name on a craft stick, and place all the sticks in a blue plastic drinking cup. Place a red plastic drinking cup at each computer in the room. Randomly draw names from the blue cup for computer use and use a timer to limit the access time to, say, 10 or 20 minutes. If students have problems during their computer time, have them place the cup on top of their monitor to alert the instructor. This will avoid classroom disruptions.
- Start with students in the front of the class (or any random location in the room) and have them go to the computer stations either alone or in groups. As each student or group finishes, the next in line takes their place. Depending on the size of the class, this process may take more than one day to complete, so make sure to record for the next day where the pattern stopped.
- Use some form of printed technology "passport" that tracks student computer use. You can use stamps or stickers to indicate turns and usage.
- Post a schedule, and have students or groups rotate in 15-minute shifts.
- Create and post a weekly schedule and assign open blocks of time to students or groups.
- Use 3 × 5 cards or color-coded sticky note sheets (one for each week day) with student names to identify computer users for each day. Attach them to the wall next to the computer station. Students take turns rotating through the cards to complete their project.

Whatever the technology situation in your classroom, you can start integrating eBooks as part of the curriculum and managing the technology resources available to provide opportunities for student access. Just a bit of planning, practice, and arrangement can help develop technology-integrated activities that flow smoothly and ensure that all students have access to, and positive experiences with, the technology.

## BOOK CARDS

One problem that I have had with eBooks in the classroom or library has been student book browsing. Students are used to selecting books by looking at covers and briefly skimming the content. Choosing books in this way is difficult with eBook readers, especially when you consider that one device may have a good number of eBooks stored on it. So when students look at an eBook reader or MP3 player, they may not understand that there can be more than one book in it, because they may not be able to see the other titles as they would printed books on a shelf.

**FIGURE 10.4** Display book cards with each device to indicate the eBooks available

One solution that works for me is making book cards that are displayed on the shelf beside physical books (see Figure 10.4). I create these book cards using a word processor and my printer. Each card is about the size of a paperback book, or half a sheet of paper, and has the book's cover image and a short description. For chapter books, I include a sample of the text. I place the book cards on a shelf so students can browse the books available on the eBook reader or MP3 player. When I have multiple devices in a room, I laminate the book cards, punch a hole in the corner, and place them on a ring, which I place next to the device. For upper-level classes that use longer chapter books, I usually remove the cards associated with a device from the display until the device is returned.

## How to Make Your Own Book Cards

Word processors such as Microsoft Word or OpenOffice offer numerous layout and color options. Using a computer and standard printer, you can create card representations of book covers. You may wish to do this as an activity with your students. The standard 8 1/2 × 11-inch sheet of paper, when printed in landscape format and folded in half, will produce a printout that is about the size of paperback book, with just a little trimming.

### Page Setup

To begin creating book covers with your word processor, you will need to change the default page setup. In Word, go to File, and then select Page Setup or Page Layout (depending on your version of Word). In the Orientation section, select Landscape. In the Page Setup window (or Page Layout tab) change the margins so that the numbers match the following: Top = 0.82"; Bottom = 0.5"; Left = 0.75"; and Right = 0.75" (see Figure 10.5). Then click the OK.

On a blank page, insert a table of one row and three columns (three cells in all). These three cells will become the book's cover. The first cell is the back of the book, the middle cell is the fold of the book's spine, and the right cell is the front cover. Right click in the first cell and select the option for Table

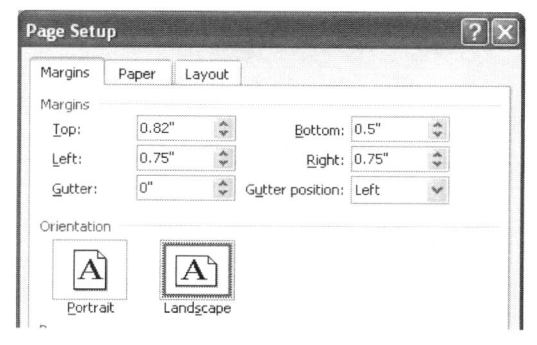

**FIGURE 10.5** Use this page setup in Word to make book cards

Properties. In the Table Properties window, choose the tab for the Row. In the Size section, select the option for a Specific Height, and set the size to 6.88". Select the tab for Cell, and set the Preferred Width to 4.25". Click OK. For the next cell, set the width to 1", and for the front-cover cell, set its width to 4.25". A ready-made template for Word with the correct margin and cell settings is available from the DrsCavanaugh eBook website (http://goo.gl/NAKr8).

Once you have your basic card template, it is time to make some book cards.

### *The Front Cover*

The right-hand cell is the front cover. Copy a large, good-quality cover of the book from a website and paste the image into the front-cover cell. One fun option is for students to make their own book-cover cards for books they like, using their own drawings or photographs in the cover design.

Next, adjust the size of the image so that it fits within the front cover space. Do this by clicking on the image and then moving the corners or sides by clicking and holding to adjust the size. Place your image in front of the text—right-click on the image, select Order, and click on In Front of Text. Alternatively, use the Picture Tools tab to adjust the text wrapping to In Front of Text. You can also adjust your image by lightening, cropping, or adjusting the contrast. Do this by using the Picture toolbar (if your picture toolbar is not showing, right-click on the image and turn the toolbar on) or right-clicking and choosing Format Picture.

### *Back Cover*

The back cover of a book is usually designed to entice the reader. Back covers often have information about the story, the author, other books the author has written, or short reviews. A great place to find blubs, reviews, or quick author studies is to go to the book's Amazon.com page.

I provide additional information, too, including the type of eBook, its location in the classroom, what device it is on, its reading level and length, and any associated tests.

### *Finishing a Book Card*

When you have finished making the book card, print it onto card stock or heavy paper, then trim and fold it. Use a glue stick or double-sided tape to stick the two sides together. To protect the card, seal it with the school laminator or spray film.

For a chapter book, rather than gluing front to back, I make a folded card. I copy a selection of the book's text and paste it to the inside of the card. Use the same template, but paste the text into the front and back cover boxes. Remember this time to start in the front box.

## ASSESSING WITH EBOOKS

You can use eBooks to create assessments, such as for Content Based Assessment (CBA) of fluency and comprehension. Using public-domain digital libraries, you can copy a selection of text, from 75 to a few hundred words, and then paste it into a tool that will adapt the text for assessment. With such a tool, you can use various texts to create a range of reading assessments covering numerous topics and genres.

Intervention Central (www.interventioncentral.org) offers two assessment tools that work well with eBooks: The Oral Reading Fluency Probe and the Maze Passage Generator. These tools allow you to create reading assessments in comprehension and fluency based on text topics that interest students.

The Oral Reading Fluency Probe can be used to evaluate students' proficiency in reading chosen text. The Maze Passage Generator creates multiple-choice cloze passages that can be used to track student reading comprehension. With the Maze assessment, the first sentence is left intact; after that, every seventh word from the passage becomes a multiple-choice response item (original word plus two foils).

## Creating a Fluency Probe

Select a passage from an eBook that is a few hundred words long (the maximum is 900 words). To find the word count, copy and paste the passages into Microsoft Word and use the Word Count option from the Tools menu. Then go to the Oral Reading Fluency Passage Generator from Intervention Central (http://www.interventioncentral.org/teacher-resources/oral-reading-fluency-passages-generator) <http://goo.gl/8ooiiG>. Give the passage a title and author, and copy and paste the eBook passage into the appropriate spot on the passage generator site.

**FIGURE 10.6** The Maze Passage Generator creates multiple-choice cloze passages to assess reading comprehension

Select the option to run a readability analysis on the passage to check for appropriateness. If you have more than 75 words in your passage, click on the Compute button to run 10 different readability formulas. Next, choose how you want to receive your probe. The created PDF will be sent to you by email or you can download it directly. This will cause the system to create your fluency assessment. The created probe will contain the student's reading page and the teacher/examiner page. This type of assessment is administered to individual students.

## Creating a Maze Passage Generator

Select a passage from an eBook that is a few hundred words long (the maximum is 900 words). To find the word count, you can copy and paste the passages into Microsoft Word and use the Word Count option from the Tools menu; the Maze Passage Generator also displays a word count under the passage section. Then go to the Maze Passage Generator from Intervention Central (http://www.interventioncentral.org/teacher-resources/test-of-reading-comprehension) <http://goo.gl/Mvq1al>. Give the passage a title and author, then copy and paste the eBook passage into the appropriate spot on the passage generator site.

Select the option to run a readability analysis on the passage to check for appropriateness. If you have more than 75 words in your passage, click on the Compute button to run 10 different readability formulas. Next, choose where you want the foil or distractor options to come from. You can choose from a basic list of common English words or words from elsewhere in the passage, or you can create your own word list. Then click Next.

You will now see your passage with the seventh words in bold and the foils in parenthesis in red. You can click on the foils to change them to different words or click on the "Edit Distractors by Hand" button to write in your own words. Once the words appear the way you want, click Next.

In the final steps, you tell the system how you want to receive your examiner page and student probe. You can either have the resulting PDFs sent to you by email, or you can download them directly (see Figure 10.6). Your examiner page can have the readability calculated from any of the options and will have the passage with the correct words in bold. The student's page contains the text with all three word choices in bold, so that they can select the appropriate words while silently reading the passage. This type of assessment can be administered individually or to the whole class.

# ONLINE RESOURCES

### Amazon.com

www.amazon.com
The Amazon website is an excellent source of information about books, authors, and other information that can be used for book-cover blurbs

### Book Card Template

www.drscavanaugh.org/ebooks/bookcards/BookCardTemplate.doc
http://goo.gl/NAKr8
The Drscavanaugh eBook website has many tools to help you develop your class eBook projects such as this Word template that include all margin and cell settings

## Intervention Central's Fluency Assessments

www.interventioncentral.org
Intervention Central provides teachers, schools, and districts with free resources to help struggling learners and implement Response to Intervention and attain the Common Core State Standards

## NASA's *The Story of Echo the Bat*

http://science.hq.nasa.gov/kids/imagers/intro/ <http://goo.gl/k1OeMv>
The National Aeronautics & Space Administration (NASA) Foundation presents the entertaining, informative story of Echo the Bat as an extension or background on bats to go with the book, *Stellaluna*, the popular tale of a fictional fruit bat

## SAG's Storyline Online

www.storylineonline.net
The Screen Actors Guild (SAG) Foundation website offers online streaming videos of well-known SAG actors reading children's books aloud

# Chapter 11

# Picture eBooks and Content Area Reading

Co-written by Gigi David and Katrina W. Hall

Children's book collections are a staple in the elementary classroom. They can be used in a number of ways: from reading instruction and practice, to understanding diverse cultures, and even for learning about STEM topics—science, technology, engineering, and math.

For teacher Sylvia Koontz, children's literature promises a way to increase her third-grade students' experiences with STEM. While she already has a number of non-fiction books that focus on STEM areas, she has decided to expand the children's literature available in the classroom with open-source (free) books that support STEM concepts. Also, she will be using some of the children's literature she found online in her lessons, integrating STEM concepts with reading.

For instance, in one lesson Sylvia is using the International Children's Digital Library (www.childrenslibrary.org) to access B. Cory Kilvert's *The Kite Book*—the story of a boy lifted away on his kite by strong winds and an excellent resource for working on onsets and rimes. She uses the problems that occur to characters in *The Kite Book* to make problem-solving experiences more authentic for her students. In tandem with the reading, students learn about physics (the forces of tension, lift, and drag), math concepts (modeling and measuring), and engineering (following plans and construction). They create their own kites as part of the project. After learning about forces and flying, students build, decorate, and fly their own kites made out of grocery bags. A PDF of the kite plan is available at http://www.drscavanaugh.org/sci/kite.pdf.

# EBOOKS IN CONTENT AREAS

Teachers aren't limited to textbooks—they can also use trade books in their classes. eBooks provide an easy way for teachers and students to access trade books for content area reading. According to McGovan and Guzzetti (1991), using trade books within a subject provides students with

- **variety** with a wide range of books and interest levels
- **interest** with engaging formats and writing styles
- **relevance** through connections to life experiences
- **comprehensibility** through the development of concepts.

Electronic books and libraries provide reading material for both literary and technical reading. Most modern standardized reading assessments include elements from both. Educators can find eBooks from bookstores, public library collections, and specialized online libraries devoted to subject-area books that can be used within content areas for resource, research, and reading materials.

# PICTURE EBOOKS

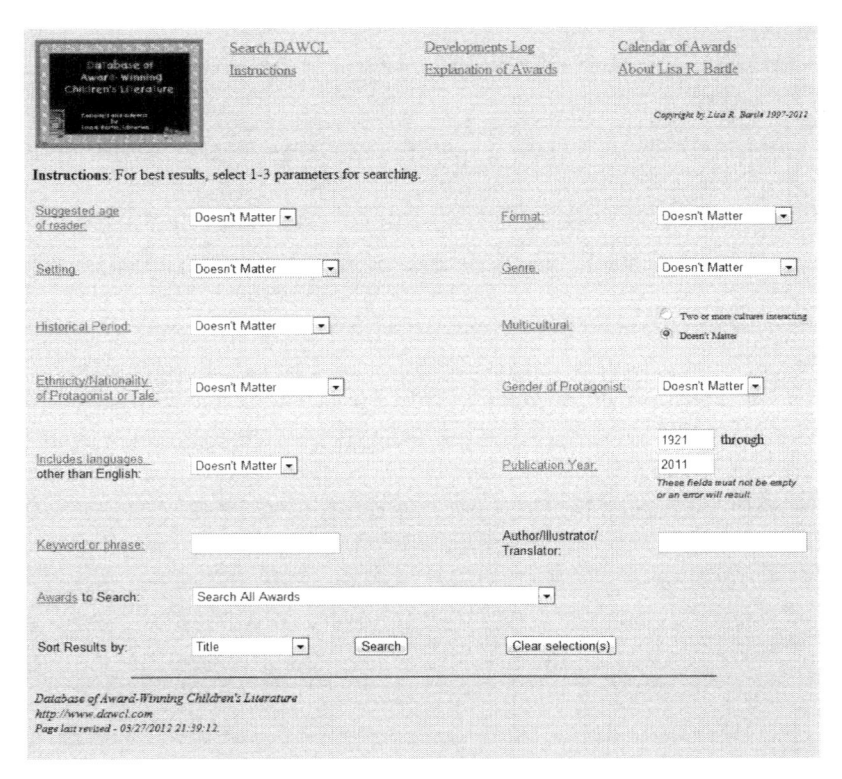

**FIGURE 11.1** Database of Award Winning Children's Literature is a flexible, searchable resource. © Lisa R. Bartle, California State University, San Bernardino

In our visually oriented society, classroom teachers strive to make learning concrete and to help students visualize and comprehend many different concepts throughout the year. To access prior knowledge, address misconceptions, and get students on the same page, many teachers choose to introduce and reinforce new concepts using picture books.

Picture books are books usually intended for children that contain text and illustrations integral to the storyline (Nodelman & Reimer, 2003). Picture books may contain sophisticated vocabulary, yet the language demands are often low because of the integral nature of the illustrations and text. The illustrations provide a visual scaffolding to support the text. Together, two elements forge a bridge to facilitate understanding, making them accessible to all students. Students of all ages and reading levels, as well as English language learners, respond to the focused nature of picture books. Students also increase cultural competence as they see themselves and their classmates in the books, or meet realistic characters from a variety of cultures that live in faraway lands.

Choosing the best picture books for particular topics can be time-consuming, although resources are available online to support teachers. Once the teacher is clear about her learning objectives for a particular lesson, she is ready to search for a picture book that supports her learning goals for the students.

Sylvan Dell Publishing (www.sylvandellpublishing.com) releases a number of its eBooks for free from its paid subscription library. The books may integrate science, math, or geography and have audible text and additional language support. Another useful resource is *Book Links!* magazine, published by the American Library Association. Each issue features books focused on a targeted content area. Other excellent online resources include the Database of Award Winning Literature (www.dawcl.com) (see Figure 11.1) and the Children's Picture Book Database (www.lib.muohio.edu/pictbks/).

Once you have identified books you want to include in your collection, find out whether a digital version is available for purchase or borrowing.

# MATHEMATICS

The National Council of Teachers of Mathematics standards (NCTM, 2000) includes process standards that emphasize the role of written and oral communication in supporting mathematical content development. Through the use of picture books, print or digital, students learn about practical applications of mathematical concepts in a meaningful context. Mathematical vocabulary is introduced and reinforced in fiction picture books as characters solve the problems they face.

A range of math eBooks are available, from math theory to math romance. For instance, *Happy Maths: Measurement* is just one of a series of thirteen such books from Read India available from the International Children's Digital Library (www.childrenslibrary.org). It contains stories on applying math measurement concepts. *All About Geometry with George*, from the CAST UDL Bookbuilder library (http://bookbuilder.cast.org/library.php), presents information on the geometric concepts of points, lines, and surfaces.

For a more textbook-like experience, try eBooks such as *Place Value* from K12 Handhelds (http://k12opened.com/ebooks/). This math eBook, available either for online reading or download, is very textbook-like, and includes simple explanations and problems on place value and decimal concepts. School Sparks (www.schoolsparks.com) offers a collection of free eBooks. One, *Fun Math for Young Learners*, covers early math concepts and is structured like a workbook. It is available for download in PDF format. (Other titles offered by School Sparks include *All Children Can Be Great Listeners*, *Early Writing*, and *Early Reading*.)

Teachers can also access high-quality, standards-based mathematics lesson plans for PK–12 from sites such as Illuminations (http://illuminations.nctm.org/) sponsored by NCTM. These lessons are organized according to math standards; many incorporate the use of picture books and are linked to interactive sites for children. Websites such as CoolMath4Kids (www.coolmath4kids.com) and Mathwire (www.mathwire.com) provide opportunities for children to practice skills as they engage in problem-solving activities that provide immediate feedback and can challenge the user at an appropriate level.

# SCIENCE

Inquiry-based instruction is embedded in the National Science Education Standards (NSES, 1996). Children are encouraged to take ownership of their learning by asking relevant questions, designing procedures to answer these questions, and then collecting the data to analyze and answer their questions. This process can be teacher-directed, such as in the case of a structured inquiry, or student-directed, such as in the case of guided inquiry or open inquiry (Colburn, 2004). In either case, the teacher sets the stage for the students to engage in hands-on inquiry.

Both fiction and nonfiction picture books targeting science concepts capture students' attention through engaging text and illustrations that help make abstract concepts more concrete (Mayer, 1995).

The National Science Teachers Association, in conjunction with the Children's Book Council, publishes an annual list called Outstanding Science Trade Books for Students K–12 (www.nsta.org/ostbc), many which are available for purchase from bookstores such as Barnes & Noble.

Freely available eBooks in different formats can also be used to teach science. Non-fiction examples include the

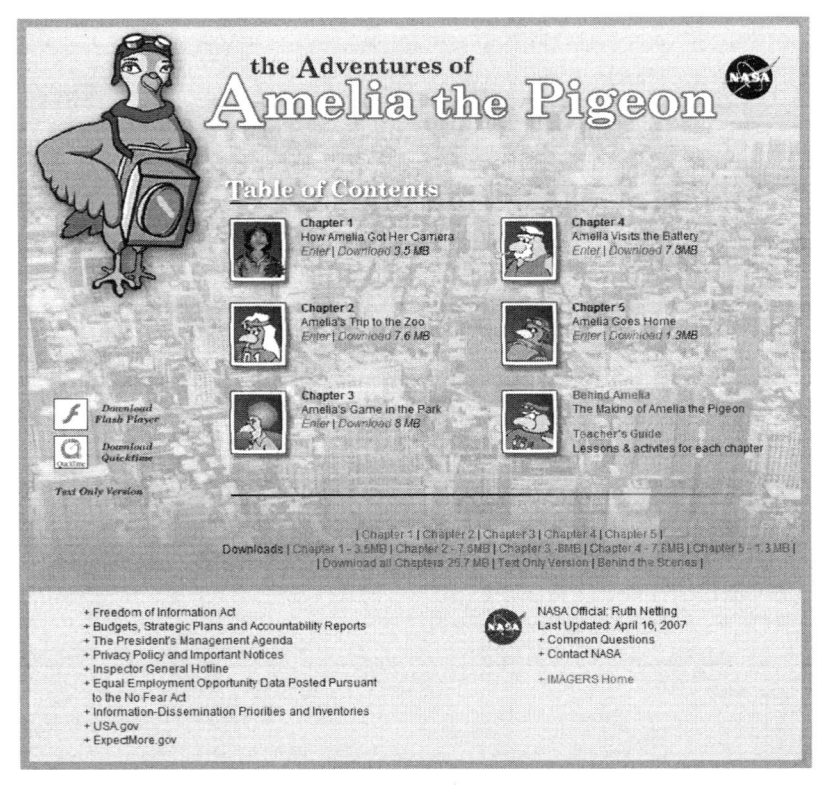

**FIGURE 11.2** NASA's Imagers page offers *The Adventures of Amelia the Pigeon*

emagazine *Science News for Kids* (www.sciencenewsforkids.org) and the K12 Handhelds eBook *The Water Cycle* (http://k12opened.com/ebooks/). Fiction can also be used to teach science; for example NASA's *The Adventures of Amelia the Pigeon* (http://science.hq.nasa.gov/kids/imagers/) makes a great introduction to the real science of remote sensing, along with providing related history information (see Figure 11.2). Storyline Online (www.storyline online.net) has a video eBook edition of *Somebody Loves You, Mr. Hatch* that makes a great introduction to cooking science (chemistry and physics), and the Rare Book & Special Collections of the Library of Congress (www.loc.gov/rr/rarebook/digitalcoll/digitalcoll-children.html) offers Peter Newell's classic *The Slant Book*, which can be used as a great introduction to inclined planes, gravity forces, speed, and acceleration.

# SOCIAL STUDIES

Each year, the National Council for Social Studies (www.ncss.org) publishes annotated book lists that include picture books for students in Grades K–8. Notable Tradebooks for Young People highlights books that are culturally diverse and encompass a range of topics; these bibliographies can be found at www.socialstudies.org/notable. Other sites useful to social studies instruction include the U.S. Central Intelligence Agency (CIA) and the International Children's Digital Library. The CIA, an organization whose job is to be expert on other countries, produces the *World Factbook* (https://www.cia.gov/library/publications/the-world-factbook/index.html), <http://goo.gl/nqZw>, an up-to-date encyclopedia of the current nations of the world, and provides information on each country's history, people, government, geography, and international issues (see Figure 11.3). The International Children's Digital Library (www.childrenslibrary.org) has more than 4,500 books in 60 languages. Here students can read books from all over the world (many books are translated), giving them first-hand experience with what children in other countries are reading.

Years ago, many teachers packed up Flat Stanley and sent him across the world, marking his travels with pins in a map (www.flatstanley.com). Digital technology now makes it possible to do much more, allowing teachers to integrate GIS (geographic

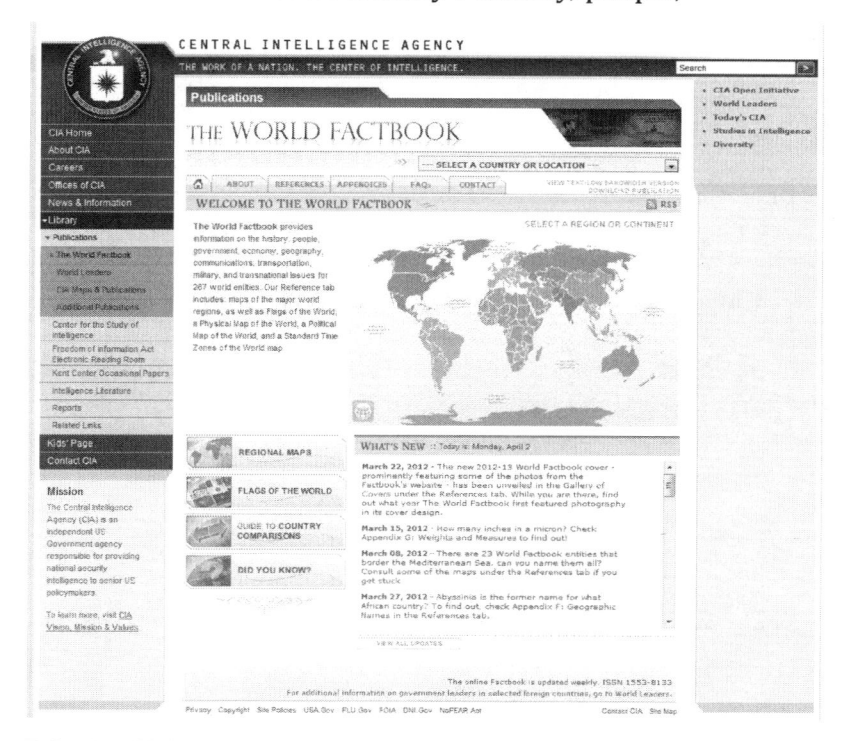

**FIGURE 11.3** The CIA's *The World Factbook* is an encyclopedia of all nations

information systems) in a myriad of ways. A helpful PDF guide to getting started is available from the Google Lit Trips site (www.googlelittrips.com).

One multimedia way to experience a book is through a Google Lit Trip (see Figure 11.4). This award-winning site created by educator Jerome Burg allows readers to create or to follow the journeys taken by characters in books. Each interactive, multimedia "trip" is stored as a KMZ file that can be "played" with programs such as Google Earth or Google Maps. As of this writing, more than 20 elementary lit trips are available, including trips for works such as Robert McCloskey's *Make Way for Ducklings* and Mem Fox's *Possum Magic*. Google Lit Trips also provides background information on Google Earth and Google Maps for teachers.

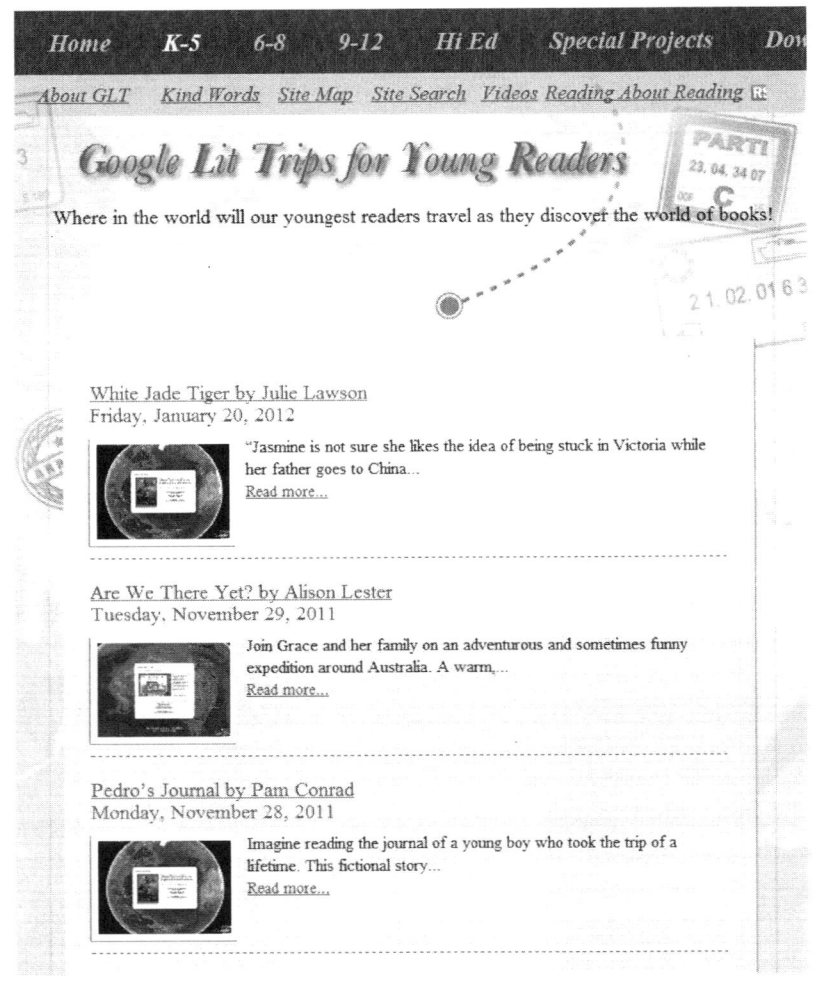

**FIGURE 11.4** Jerome Burg's Google Lit Trips site explores books with Google Earth

In addition to tracking individual books, Google Lit Trips can be created by teachers and students for units such as the Civil Rights Movement or African American History. Award-winning author Elizabeth Partridge's *Marching for Freedom: Walk Together, Children, and Don't You Grow Weary* (2009) contains video clips and background information detailing the 1965 Selma March. On Partridge's website (www.elizabethpartridge.com), teachers can download curriculum guides and other information. Her lessons can be paired with information from other sites, such as the U.S. National Park Service's standards-based lesson plan on the Selma March (http://goo.gl/2RiF6).

## VISUAL ART AND MUSIC

Picture books can introduce children to artists and musicians and to people from distant lands, giving them the opportunity to think about the similarities and differences of cultures. As children read and learn more, they come to realize that all cultures express themselves through the arts. Historic styles and periods of art and music come alive in the words and illustrations in picture books, which help us visualize and appreciate the contributions and experiences of our ancestors. They also serve to increase our aesthetic awareness and appreciation for diversity in terms of perspective and styles of personal expression.

The Kennedy Center for the Performing Arts (http://artsedge.kennedy-center.org/educators.aspx) has an interactive educational website with standards-based integrated lesson plans in visual arts, music, theater, and dance for K–12. One example is a visual art, math, and language arts integrated lesson using the picture book *Go Away, Big Green Monster!* by Ed Emberley (1992). This cleverly assembled book isolates each adjective describing the face of a monster. The Adjective Monster (K–4) lesson introduces the techniques of paper sculpture and reinforces knowledge of basic shapes and adjectives. Children create their own paper-sculpture monster faces with geometric and organic shapes and choose adjectives to describe each feature.

With the assistance of picture books and museum sites, children can visit an art museum virtually before ever stepping foot into one. Many museum sites have interactive children sections that include cultural and historical information as well as games and activities that help students learn about topics such as symbolism in artwork or the techniques used by famous artists. One museum site that is user-friendly and engaging for kids is the National Gallery of Arts' NGA Kids (www.nga.gov/kids/kids.htm). This site provides opportunities for children to create landscapes, portraits, collages, still life, and more. Links within the NGA site lead to Family Guides and Inside Scoop (see Figure 11.5), which provide access to more than 60 digital booklets targeting specific artists and artwork. All of the material is age-appropriate and provides a meaningful context for students along with online interactive lesson units (www.nga.gov/education/classroom/).

Each year, the American Library Association (ALA) recognizes the author and the book providing the most

**FIGURE 11.5** The National Gallery of Arts offers for download sample online books on artists and styles

**FIGURE 11.6** Booktrack provides soundtracks of music and ambient sound (© 2012, Booktrack)

distinguished contribution to American literature for children with the Newbery Medal and Honor (often two separate distinctions). The foremost book illustrator is also recognized each year and awarded the Caldecott Medal. Many Newbery and Caldecott winning books are available in eBook form from electronic bookstores, electronic collections at public libraries, and specialized free libraries. The digital library at the University of Pennsylvania has a free collection of Newbery Honor Books and Medal Winners written by women and published between 1922 and 1964 (http://digital.library.upenn.edu/women/_collections/newbery/newbery.html). The Celebration of Women Writers collection of Newbery books includes works such as Cornelia Meigs's *The Windy Hill* (1921) and Emily Cheney Neville's *It's Like This, Cat* (1992). The 2009 Newberry Medal-awarded book *The Graveyard Book* by Neil Gaiman is available as a series of streaming videos in which the author reads the entire book (http://goo.gl/3EnOM).

The Caldecott Medal has been awarded since 1938. Books illustrated by the medal winners display a wide range of techniques and artistic styles. Sites such as Barnes & Noble's Storytime (www.barnesandnoble.com/storytime/), SAG's Storyline Online (www.storylineonline.net), and PBS's New Hampshire Public Television Caldecott Literature Series (http://video.nhptv.org/program/caldecott-literature-series/) also make available free online streaming video versions of Caldecott-winning books. These include titles such as Chris Van Allsburg's *The Polar Express*, Tomie dePaola's *Strega Nona*, and Marcia Brown's *Stone Soup*.

Teachers can guide students to have a deeper understanding of the choices an artist must make to illustrate a text. Denise Matulka (www.picturingbooks.com), author of *A Picture Book Primer: Understanding and Using Picture Books* (2008), has created a website where teachers and students can learn more about the artistic process of illustrating picture books. She discusses issues such as media and basic elements and principles of art, and has links to websites of artists who have illustrated children's books.

In addition to visual arts, music is an important part of children's educational development. Exposing children to different styles of music can begin with a picture-based eBook.

Booktrack (www.booktrack.com) is an eBook application and library that offers children's books with their own soundtracks (see Figure 11.6). It is available for all standard platforms (iPad, PC, Android) and matches music and sounds to the student's reading speed based on page-turn speed. The eBook application for iPad, *The Fantastic Flying Books of Mr. Morris Lessmore* (http://morrislessmore.com) becomes a piano keyboard during part of the story, allowing the reader to play music. The eBook version of *Chicka Chicka Boom Boom* not only presents all of the book, but also provides the book's text performed in song form by Ray Charles.

Music has a role in children's literacy skills, and many children's songs have been made into picture books, such as the *Itsy Bitsy Spider*, available from RIF's Book Zone (http://www.rif.org/kids/readingplanet/bookzone.htm). This is just one of a number of story songs for reading and listening in which the text is synchronized with the audio, much like karaoke. Other websites that offer music to accompany familiar songs. The Kididdles website (www.kididdles.com) includes activity worksheets, song sheets, and music sheets to accompany each song.

## FOREIGN LANGUAGE

eBooks are a natural fit for virtually any foreign language study. Most eBook retailers such as Amazon and Barnes & Noble offer eBooks in many languages as well as audiobooks spoken in other languages. There are sites that specialize in foreign-language public-domain texts. One, Multilingual Books (http://multilingualbooks.com/ebooks.html) offers a range of titles in Chinese, Dutch, French, German, Italian, Portuguese, Russian, Spanish, and Swedish. The International Children's Digital Library has picture books in over 30 languages.

## A LITTLE RESEARCH GOES A LONG WAY

The Internet provides a near-infinite number of resources to complement your book use across the curriculum. Think about how you can create effective interdisciplinary experiences for your students as you choose books to read. With online research to see what is available, you can provide your students with an effective multimedia experience that melds reading and content information.

## ONLINE RESOURCES

### American Library Association's Book Links!
www.ala.org/offices/publishing/booklist/booklinks
A quarterly supplement to *Booklist*, *Book Links* magazine is designed for teachers, youth librarians, school library media specialists, reading specialists, curriculum coordinators, and others interested in connecting children with high-quality literature-based resources.

### Barnes & Noble's Storytime

www.barnesandnoble.com/storytime/
Streaming video stories

### Booktrack

www.booktrack.com
eBooks that include music and sound effects matched to the students' reading speed

### CAST UDL Bookbuilder Library

http://bookbuilder.cast.org/library.php
An online book-creation and book-sharing resource

### Children's Picture Book Database

www.lib.muohio.edu/pictbks/
Database of quality children's picture books, searchable by keyword such as areas of study

### CIA *World Factbook*

https://www.cia.gov/library/publications/the-world-factbook/index.html
Encyclopedic eBook from the CIA with information about every country in the world

### CoolMath4Kids

www.coolmath4kids.com
Online resource site for math, including games, puzzles, flash cards, and lesson plans

### Database of Award-Winning Literature

www.dawcl.com
A database of quality children's literature that identifies award-winning books

### Picturing Books

www.picturingbooks.com
A celebration of picture books by author Denise Matulka

### Elizabeth Partridge

www.elizabethpartridge.com
This website by an award-winning author includes curriculum guides and other information for teachers

### *The Fantastic Flying Books of Mr. Morris Lessmore*

http://morrislessmore.com
A website about the story of Morris Lessmore

## FlatStanley

www.flatstanley.com
Teachers and student everywhere packed up the fictional character Flat Stanley and sent him around the world, marking his travels with pins on a map

## Google Lit Trips

www.googlelittrips.com
An online resource that uses Google Earth to show book locations
Google Lit Trips guide (PDF)
www.googlelittrips.com/GoogleLit/Lit_Trip_Tips_files/GoogleEarthResources.pdf
http://goo.gl/kPsDw

## Grocery Bag Kite

http://www.drscavanaugh.org/sci/kite.pdf
A PDF by Dr. Cavanaugh that provides plans for constructing kites out of paper grocery bags

## *Graveyard Book* by Neil Gaiman

www.neilgaiman.com/p/Cool_Stuff/Video_Clips/The_Graveyard_Book_Tour
http://goo.gl/3En0M
Collection of videos of author Neil Gaiman reading *The Graveyard Book*

## Illuminations Lesson Plans

http://illuminations.nctm.org/
Standards-based lesson plans and activities for teaching math, as well as links to other resources

## International Children's Digital Library

www.childrenslibrary.org
Online library of children's eBooks from all over the world

## K12 Handhelds eBooks

http://k12opened.com/ebooks/
Library for early reading though upper elementary and middle school, with fiction and non-fiction eBooks and textbooks for English language arts, math, social studies, and science

## Kennedy Center for the Performing Arts

http://artsedge.kennedy-center.org/educators.aspx
Standards-based lesson plans for art

## Kididdles

www.kididdles.com
Online database of children's songs with lyrics

## Mathwire

www.mathwire.com
Math education resource site with activities and worksheets

## Multilingual Books

http://multilingualbooks.com/ebooks.html
Online library of foreign-language public-domain texts

## NASA Imagers

http://science.hq.nasa.gov/kids/imagers/
Online eBooks on science topics by NASA

## National Council for the Social Studies (NCSS)

www.socialstudies.org
Professional association for social studies

## NCSS Notable Tradebooks for Young People

www.socialstudies.org/notable
Annual lists of social studies trade books compiled by the National Council for the Social Studies

## National Gallery of Arts's NGA Kids

www.gov/kids/kids.htm
Art resource for children, also includes editions of the emagazine *NGA Kids Inside Scoop*

## National Gallery of Arts's NGA Classroom for Teachers

www.nga.gov/education/classroom
Interactive lessons and resources for teaching about art

## National Park Service—Selma March

www.nps.gov/history/nr/twhp/wwwlps/lessons/133SEMO/133selma.htm
http://goo.gl/2RiF6
Lesson plan on the Selma March

## Outstanding Science Trade Books for Students K–12

www.nsta.org/publications/ostb/
Lists of science books from the National Science Teachers Association, with links to purchase eBooks

## PBS New Hampshire Public Television Caldecott Literature Series

http://video.nhptv.org/program/caldecott-literature-series/
Streaming video stories of Caldecott-awarded books

## Rare Book & Special Collections of the Library of Congress

www.loc.gov/rr/rarebook/digitalcoll/digitalcoll-children.html
Online library of classic children's books

## RIF Book Zone

www.rif.org/kids/readingplanet/bookzone.htm
Reading Is Fundamental's online library of animated stories and songs, with text synchronized to audio

## SAG's Storyline Online

www.storylineonline.net
Streaming video stories read by famous actors who are members of the Screen Actors Guild

## School Sparks

www.schoolsparks.com
Site dedicated to assisting parents to better prepare students for success in the classroom. Free eBooks in PDF format include:

*All Children Can Be Great Listeners*
http://www.schoolsparks.com/assets/ebooks/all-children-can-be-great-listeners.pdf
<http://goo.gl/ziC9c>
*Early Reading*
http://www.schoolsparks.com/assets/ebooks/stepping-stones-for-early-readers.pdf
<http://goo.gl/AGVcp>
*Early Writing*
http://www.schoolsparks.com/assets/ebooks/early-writing-for-little-hands.pdf
<http://goo.gl/PlqoB>
*Fun Math for Young Learners*
www.schoolsparks.com/blog/new-e-book-fun-math-for-young-learners
<http://goo.gl/gk56c>

## *Science News for Kids*

www.sciencenewsforkids.org
Science News for Kids is the youth edition and companion to Science News, the magazine of the Society for Science & the Public

## Sylvan Dell Publishing

www.sylvandellpublishing.com
Publishing house of picture eBooks that integrate science, math, and geography

## University of Pennsylvania's Newbery Honor Books and Medal Winners

http://digital.library.upenn.edu/women/_collections/newbery/newbery.html
Collection of seventeen Newbery-noted eBooks written by women and published 1922–64

# Chapter 12

# eBooks and Struggling Readers

## Co-written by Lunetta Williams and Andrea Thoermer

The students in Esperanza Williams's second-grade class have a variety of ability levels. In evaluating her students, she found that eight of her twenty-five students were struggling with reading, and she wanted to provide them with more assistance. However, class time is limited, and she also needed to provide reading resources for the rest of the class.

To help these students, Esperanza created a read-aloud station students could use during literacy time. At the station, students follow along in a book while listening to stories being read out loud by the teacher or professional readers.

Now when you enter her Grade 2 class, you find students actively engaged in different literacy activities using various technological devices. They move enthusiastically around the classroom without realizing the literacy growth they are gaining. In a corner closest to the teacher's desk is the read-aloud station. Three children listen excitedly to the remaining pages of *Romeow and Drooliet* at Storyline Online (www.storylineonline.net), read aloud by popular actress and singer Haylie Duff. After the reading is over, students create a small circle to take turns discussing their favorite parts of the story—making predictions and connections and asking questions for clarification. After completing the related activities, they cannot decide whether to read *Thank You, Mr. Falker* or *My Rotten Redheaded Older Brother*, both written by Patricia Polacco.

In another corner of the classroom, children clap their hands to the beat of the nursery rhyme *The Grand Old Duke of York*, printed out from the nursery rhymes section of the Famous Quotes website (www.famousquotes.me.uk). Then they close their eyes and visualize the picture they would draw to go along with the nursery rhyme. Once they've drawn their picture, they share them with each other, giving them an even more expansive view of the nursery rhyme.

# STRUGGLING READERS

Struggling readers are students who perform below grade level in reading. Students struggle for a variety of reasons. Some have difficulty with decoding, while others might have trouble with vocabulary and comprehension.

Struggling readers continue to concern educators. In 2011, the National Assessment of Educational Progress (NAEP) reading tests revealed that 33% of Grade 4 students in public schools were at or below the "basic" level (NCES, 2011). Further improvement is needed, particularly when considering the reading achievement gap that exists among mainstream and minority students (NCES, 2011).

Students who struggle with reading are more likely to become alliterate (able to read but not interested in doing so) than students who are successful readers (Brinda, 2008). Struggling readers are usually affected by what is known as the "fourth-grade slump," the notion that some students fall further behind when content reading increases in Grade 4 (Hirsch, 2003). Students having to cope with increasingly difficult textbooks become frustrated and discouraged, and, as a result, they read less and less. Some develop negative attitudes toward reading and learning in general.

Strategies to assist struggling readers include providing small-group instruction, increasing vocabulary lessons, building background knowledge, tailoring reading to student interests, integrating multimedia and different forms of text, offering independent leveled reading materials during silent reading time, and reading aloud. Providing access to eBooks can help motivate struggling readers to become more successful. This chapter provides the following suggestions for using eBooks with struggling readers.

- adapting text
- reading aloud
- building background knowledge
- using songs, poetry, and nursery rhymes
- setting up a readers theater
- providing wide access to books.

# ADAPTING TEXT

Text can be adapted for struggling readers in numerous ways. For example, the font size can be increased, the text can be simplified, and pictures can be added for selected words.

## Increase Font Size

A simple way to help struggling readers is to increase the font size of the text (Redford, 2012). A larger font results in fewer words on a page, which makes the text less intimidating for students, and allows students to read more easily and quickly.

In the past, teachers would need to search for large-print books from the library. With today's eBook readers, you can easily adjust the font to a larger size, such as 14 points. In many cases, you can also adjust the style to a sans serif font, such as Arial, which is generally easier to read for beginning readers (Benard, Mills, Frank, & McKown, 2001).

## Simplify the Text

Another way to assist struggling readings is to rewrite the text to make it easier to understand. If you can get an editable version of a book that the class is reading, you can simplify the text by using shorter words and more contemporary language (make sure that the content is not lost). Echevarria and Graves (1998) suggest four methods of economizing texts to make them more comprehensible:

1. Use graphic organizers.
2. Outline the text.
3. Rewrite the text.
4. Use audio recordings. (See below for more on reading aloud.)

Some books are already available in a simplified format. For example, in 1910 Mary Godolphin adapted classic texts by rewriting them in words of one syllable. When she could not find a one-syllable word for a specific word, she broke it into syllables with hyphens to help decode the pronunciation (see "tor-toise", Figure 12.1).

## Add Pictures for Selected Words

If you can get an editable version of a book that the class is reading, you can use software to add picture symbols for selected words in the text. Pictures matched with words strengthen the association of text with vocabulary, which helps develop vocabulary and makes text more meaningful and easier to remember. This helps struggling readers comprehend the written word.

Several commonly used picture symbol programs can be purchased: Picture It from Suncastle Technology (www.suncastletech.com), SymWriter from Mayer-Johnson Co. (www.mayer-johnson.com), and Clicker from Crick Software (www.cricksoft.com/us/home.aspx).

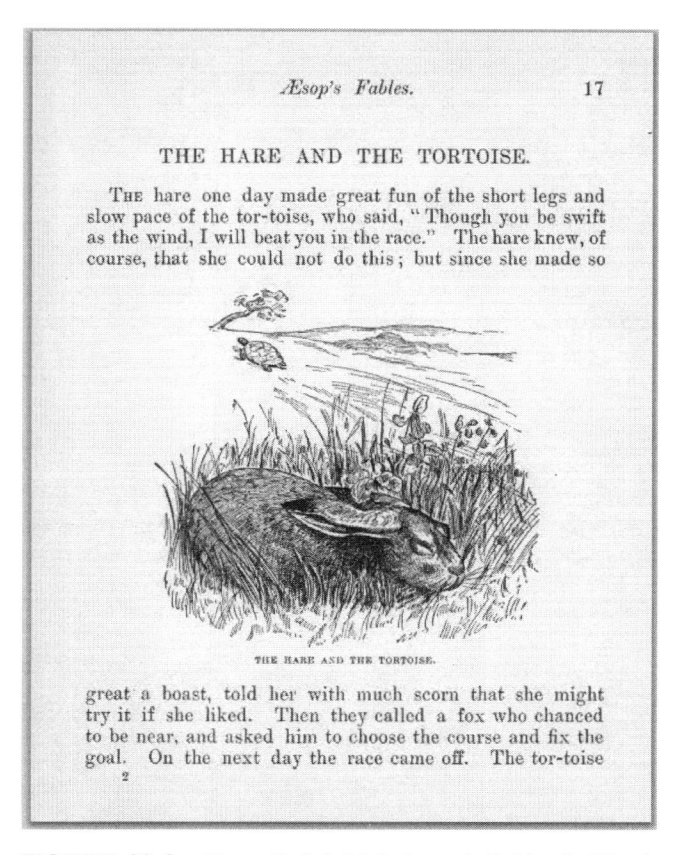

**FIGURE 12.1** *Mary Godolphin's Aesop's Fables in Words of One Syllable* is available from the Internet Archive

Over time, as students' reading improves, picture-symbol support can be faded out to encourage reading of connected text. Start-to-Finish from Don Johnston, Inc. (www.donjohnston.com/products/start_to_finish/) has a library of books on CD-ROM for students who want to read the classics or autobiographies but have delayed reading abilities.

# READING ALOUD

Reading aloud is a beneficial strategy for struggling readers because it serves as a model for reading fluently (Lynch-Brown & Tomlinson, 2008). It can also increase students' vocabulary, print concepts, and comprehension (van Kleeck & Stahl, 2003). "Reading aloud is one of the most important things I do," states Debbie Miller, teacher, staff developer, and consultant in the Denver Public Schools (2002).

Many websites feature read-aloud eBooks. With these sites, your classroom computer can be used to read aloud to struggling readers. Some of these sites deliver books in video format, while others provide synchronized highlighting of the words in the text as they are being read aloud, which can further assist struggling readers in word identification.

Storyline Online (www.storylineonline.net) from the Screen Actors Guild (SAG) Foundation is an online streaming video program that features actors reading children's books aloud. For example, James Earl Jones reads *To Be a Drum* (Coleman, 1998), Betty White reads *Harry the Dirty Dog* (Zion, 1956), and Tia and Tamera Mowry read *No Mirrors in My Nana's House* (Barnwell, 1998). As the book is read aloud, the illustrations and text from the book are displayed so that students can follow along.

At Read to Me (www.readtomelv.com/current-books/), streaming video eBooks are read by Las Vegas personalities. Books include Jackie Urbanovic's *Duck Soup* and Jane O'Connor's *Fancy Nancy* (see Figure 12.2).

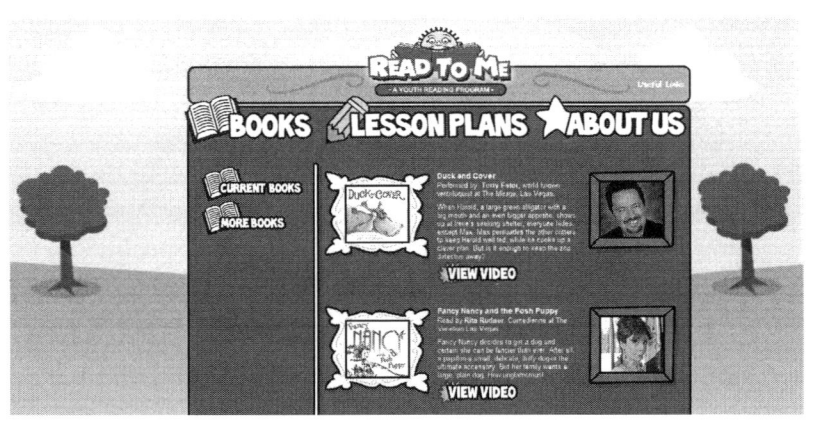

**FIGURE 12.2** The Read To Me site offers video streaming eBooks (© 2009, Clark County Education Association Community Foundation)

Online Storytime by Barnes & Noble (www.barnesandnoble.com) offers streaming videos of popular children's books read by authors or celebrities. The collection has more than 15 titles including Rachael Ray reading Dr. Seuss's *Green Eggs and Ham*, Laura Numeroff reading her own *If You Give a Mouse a Cookie*, and Maurice Sendak reading his award-winning *Where the Wild Things Are*.

eBooks and Struggling Readers   155

Reading is Fundamental (RIF) provides Reading Planet's Book Zone (http://www.rif.org/kids/readingplanet/bookzone/read_aloud_stories.htm), which has audio stories and songs that display the text as it is read aloud. Each word is highlighted as it is read aloud to further engage students in matching speech to print.

Starfall (www.starfall.com) offers many eBooks with simple text focused on a particular vowel sound. For example, the eBook *Zac the Rat* focuses on the short "a" sound. When a student clicks on a word in the text, each sound in the word is pronounced, while each letter representing the sound is highlighted. After all the sounds in a word are pronounced, the whole word is read aloud.

For children who enjoy the *Clifford* stories, Scholastic makes available several *Clifford* eBooks in English and Spanish (http://teacher.scholastic.com/clifford1/index.htm). Children can press a button next to each line of the story so that the text is read aloud. Also, the last line on each page has another interactive feature—children choose a word to complete the sentence, and the whole sentence is then read aloud to them.

Fairytales such as *Rapunzel* and *Cinderella*, as well as stories with a moral such as *The Persistent Rain Cloud* and *Windswept*, are located on the Light Up Your Brain website (http://lightupyourbrain.com/audio-stories-for-children.html). These audio stories can be quickly downloaded and played using iTunes or MP3 programs.

Inkless Tales (www.inklesstales.com/stories/) offers audio stories with illustrations that feature a character named Fanny Doodle. Another group of stories, *Dolch Stories*, includes many words from the Dolch word list in bold text along with color illustrations.

Older students might like watching Neil Gaiman read *The Graveyard Book* (http://goo.gl/3En0M), where the author was filmed reading different chapters of the entire book on the book's tour.

**FIGURE 12.3** An audiobook of *A Princess of Mars* by Edgar Rice Burroughs is available for download from LibriVox

## Audiobooks

Today, most schools, libraries, and bookstores have audiobooks, so nearly everyone is familiar with them. Audiobooks can be considered eBooks because they contain digital or electronic information that is "displayed" with an electronic device. Many audiobooks are available for free, either on discs (CD) or as MP3 files. The online library LibriVox (www.librivox.org) allows users to download thousands of free unabridged books (see Figure 12.3). Users at LibriVox select the audio format they want—from lower quality (64 KB/sec) to higher quality (128 KB/sec).

The C.S. Lewis literary estate granted special permission for one organization to provide free online streaming and MP3 download of all seven books of *The Chronicles of Narnia* series (http://goo.gl/KX1Xa).

Students' reading can improve when they are exposed to many styles of learning, and that includes listening. Often teachers and parents see a reluctant reader who is troubled when reading a passage, but that same student may display good comprehension from listening to the same passage. A report for the U.S. DOE's Commission on Reading stated, "The single most important activity for building the knowledge required for eventual success in reading is reading aloud to children." (Anderson, Hiebert, Scott, & Wilkinson, 1985, p. 23). This was reinforced when the Family Literacy Foundation (2002) found that one of the most important things to prepare children for success in school is to read aloud to them, because it helps build listening skills, vocabulary, and memory.

## BUILDING BACKGROUND KNOWLEDGE

Students enter the classroom with varying background experiences. Some are fortunate to be provided with rich literacy opportunities; others are not as lucky. It is during these "experiences" that students add to or change existing beliefs, ideas, and preconceptions that shape their schema. According to Merriam-Webster's 2010 Medical Dictionary online, schema is "the organization of experience in the mind or brain that includes a particular organized way of perceiving cognitively and responding to a complex situation or set of stimuli." Life experiences affect and build upon students' schema by altering their attitudes, thoughts, and feelings toward current and future experiences.

Struggling readers who lack background experiences may have a distorted or incoherent understanding of different people, places, and things (Karchmer, 2004) because of their preconceptions. This poor understanding lessens students' ability to construct meaning as well as formulate relevant questions when dealing with unfamiliar pieces of literature.

Teachers can alleviate this distortion by equipping struggling readers with the proper tools before reading a text, enabling them to make connections to new material through pre-reading activities. This scaffolding encourages students to learn, enabling them to gain self-confidence as a member of a literacy community (Cumming-Potvin, 2007). In turn, students read with more ease and enjoyment and make reading gains (Willett, 2007) because, according to Cumming-Potvin (2007), scaffolding draws on students' cultural and intellectual resources.

Using eBooks can strengthen and develop literacy familiarity and acquisition. With eBooks, teachers can provide positive literacy experiences for their struggling readers to use in constructing background knowledge. The following online eBook resources can help students make connections and predictions, acquire new vocabulary, and provide multiple and diverse exposures before they begin their reading.

Google Lit Trips (www.googlelittrips.com) gives students an opportunity to learn about a book through the use of a literature virtual road trip using Google Earth. Furthermore, Google Lit Trips can be used in conjunction with teaching social studies. Teachers, librarians, and students are encouraged to create their own lit trips.

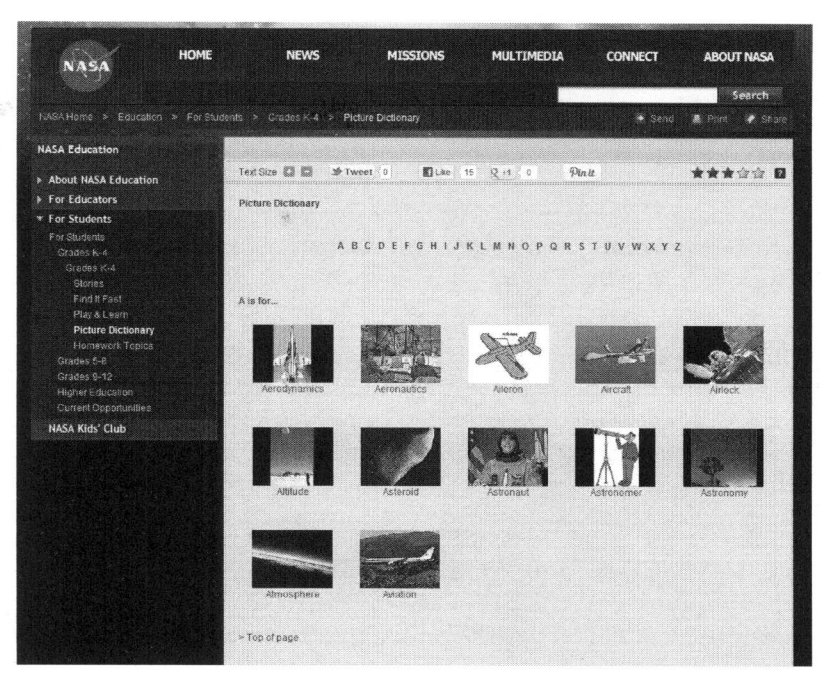

**FIGURE 12.4** NASA Education provides an online Picture Dictionary of science words for Grades K–4

Greene Bytes (www.greenek12.org/co/gbytes/index_files/Page504.htm) contains numerous virtual field trips in the categories of language arts, social studies, history, science, math, guidance, health and physical education, fine arts, and "just for teachers." Tramline (www.field-trips.org/trips.htm) offers additional virtual field trips in the areas of science, literature, social studies, and "other" categories. Similar to Google Lit Trips, opportunities are provided to create added virtual field trips. Kid's Zone (www.agclassroom.org/kids/tours.htm) provides agricultural virtual field trips to farms. offers a dictionary of science vocabulary NASA (www.nasa.gov/audience/forstudents/k-4/dictionary/index.html), which can be interwoven with reading (see Figure 12.4).

## USING SONGS

Songs can be considered a type of short story. Singing, through the use of electronic karaoke or songbooks, can motivate, challenge, engage, and improve the literacy skills of struggling readers. Singing can be an alternative form of reading—once students know the melody, they can focus on following along with the lyrics, whether they are highlighted on a screen or appear in a songbook.

Integrating music moves "beyond the linear world of printed text," providing additional support in the literacy development of a struggling reader (Biggs, Homan, Dedrick, Minick,

& Raskinki, 2008, p. 197). Scientists studying the effects of music on the brain have discovered that musical training enhances literacy skills. Therefore, music can be a valuable tool in providing support for struggling readers, especially during classroom instruction.

In addition, singing is an effective supplemental literacy tool to aid in vocabulary achievement (Korat, 2010) and improve fluency, reading prosody, and word automaticity (words the reader automatically knows and recognizes) through melodic and rhythmic beats (Biggs et al., 2008), while simultaneously increasing text comprehension (Korat, 2010). The rhyme, rhythm, and repetition in most popular songs all contribute to improved comprehension and memory. Linebarger, Piotrowski, and Greenwood (2009) found that reading tasks improved with at-risk students who were given the opportunity for "repeat exposure to on-screen print paired with visual and auditory inputs" (p. 162).

Finding musical resources to use in the classroom is not difficult—the lyrics and music of a large number of songs are available online. Electronic books in the form of songs provide extra support for the struggling reader and can be accessed through various websites. A free downloadable karaoke player, Karafun, can be downloaded from EFL Classroom 2.0 (http://community.eflclassroom.com/page/karafun-get-the-player-and), along with many popular songs, nursery rhymes, and even math songs. The site also has directions on how to take any song and make it karaoke-accessible using iTunes and lyrics found at www.azlyrics.com.

Krazykats Karaoke (www.krazykats-karaoke.co.uk/karaoke_kids.html) provides other links to relevant websites that contain singing and songs. Bus Songs (http://bussongs.com/) contains lyrics, video, and music for 2,108 children's songs and nursery rhymes.

As an added benefit, singing can build a student's confidence. Biggs et al. (2008) explain that struggling students are aware of their lower academic performance compared to their peers. Motivation initiates and shapes peer interaction, which affects a student's performance (Eisenkopf, 2010). Because peers induce higher motivation in the learning process, teachers can counteract low self-esteem by encouraging students to sing, which helps struggling students feel successful.

## USING POETRY AND NURSERY RHYMES

Poetry appeals to people of all ages and helps foster a love of reading. Struggling readers can be enticed by the alliteration, rhythm, and beat of poems (Rasinski & Padak, 2008), as well as the short format (Allor, Mathes, Jones, Champlin, & Cheatham, 2010). Struggling students may be intimidated by long, laborious passages of text. But these same students are often motivated to read poems repeatedly, aiding in fluency, an essential skill of proficient readers (Hudson, Lane, and Pullen, 2005).

The rhythmic patterns of poems and nursery rhymes can help struggling readers develop their phonemic awareness (separating the individual sound units of a word). Learning different phonemes, or word families, helps readers decode new words (Rasinski, Rupley, & Nichols, 2008).

The *Mother Goose* nursery rhymes have been captivating children since they first appeared in the eighteenth century, and young readers are still attracted to them today. Many websites are available for downloading *Mother Goose* nursery rhymes. For example, Project Gutenberg has a 1916 illustrated version of *The Real Mother Goose* (www.gutenberg.org) available in multiple formats (see Figure 12.5). Super Parents Talk (http://superparentstalk.com) has a free downloadable *Mother Goose* nursery rhyme eBook. Online Mum (www.onlinemum.com) has a free downloadable *A–Z of Popular Nursery Rhymes* eBook. Nicky's Nursery Rhymes (www.nurseryrhymes4u.com) contains nursery rhymes with midi music, wav songs, or voice accompaniment. Fanpop (www.fanpop.com/spots/nursery-rhymes) is another site with many nursery rhyme eBook options.

**FIGURE 12.5** *The Real Mother Goose* is available from Project Gutenberg in HTML, ePub, Kindle, and TXT

## SETTING UP A READERS THEATER

Readers theater is a "performance of a written script that demands repeated and assisted reading that is focused on delivering meaning to an audience" (Young & Rasinski, 2009). Basically, a readers theater performance is a live or recorded form of a radio play that uses little or no acting, props, or costumes. Giving students the responsibility of creating a recording or performing in front of peers can motivate struggling readers to practice reading. As these readers reread parts of a script before performing for others, their accuracy, automaticity, and prosody can increase (Young & Rasinski, 2009).

Using a story or text as a basis, teachers or a whole class can create their own scripts for a readers theater presentation. However, if developing scripts from scratch seems too much for your class, online resources provide complete electronic versions of readers theater scripts. About 50 scripts are available at www.readinglady.com (see Figure 12.6) based on books such as *The True Story of the Three Little Pigs* (Scieszka, 1996) and *Dog Breath: The Horrible Trouble with Hally Tosis* (Pilkey, 1994). Aaron Shepard (www.aaronshep.com/rt/) offers 40 readers theater scripts and, for each, indicates genre, age range, theme, approximate length of performance, and number of readers needed.

One way to help students read their scripts is to use a word processor to replace each character's name with that of the student. This can further personalize the script and draw readers' attention to their lines. Simply use the Find and Replace function on your word-processing program to replace the character names with student names.

The Reading Lady provides access to a readers theater script based on *The Three Little Pigs*, retold and illustrated by James Marshall (1989). Table 12.1 provides an excerpt of the original script and the same script with original character names replaced with students' names.

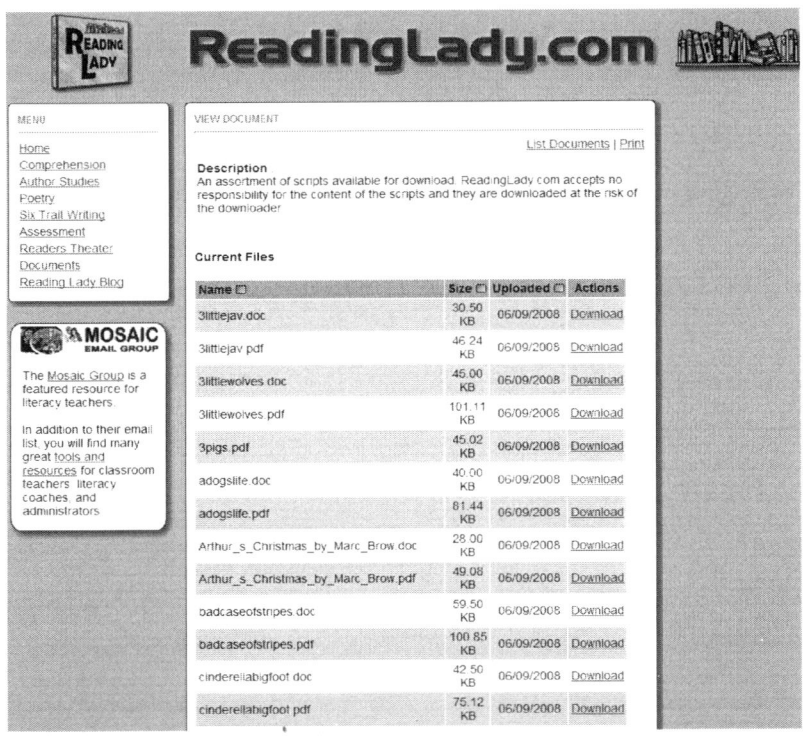

FIGURE 12.6 ReadingLady.com offers downloadable scripts for reader's theater performances

## PROVIDING WIDE ACCESS TO BOOKS

Hundreds of studies demonstrate that successful readers read more than unsuccessful ones (Donahue, Finnegan, Lutkus, Allen, & Campbell, 2001), so the amount of reading in which struggling readers engage is important. You can increase the likelihood that struggling readers will read more by providing increased access to a variety and number of books. With eBooks, you can radically increase the number of books available to your students. Some struggling readers might be embarrassed to let their peers see them reading a lower-level book. However, eBooks provide more privacy because students can read at a computer without others seeing what they are reading.

Of course, when we select books for students, we take into consideration their interests (such as football, dinosaurs, or famous people) as well as their reading levels (Lynch-Brown & Tomlinson, 2008). Fortunately, a wide variety of eBooks are available, covering most interest areas. The NASA Education website provides articles focused on various science concepts, such as the sun and climate, for K–4 students. Illustrations and videos are included within some of the articles to provide further information about a concept. Also, online libraries such as the International Children's Digital Library (http://en.childrenslibrary.org/) and the Pitara Kids Network (www.pitara.com/talespin/folktales.asp) feature books about many cultures. Books at the International Children's Digital Library are categorized in a variety of ways, such as by length, genre, and ethnicity.

**TABLE 12.1** Downloaded Reader's Theater Script with Character Names Replaced with Students' Names

| Original Script | Script with Name Replacement by Students |
|---|---|
| **Characters**:<br>Reader 1, 2, 3, 4, 5, 6<br>Pig 1, 2, 3<br>Wolf<br>Mama<br>Man 1, 2, 3 | **Characters**:<br>Reader 1 (Marcus)<br>Reader 2 (James)<br>Reader 3 (Lydia)<br>Reader 4 (Mykeisha)<br>Reader 5 (Julio)<br>Reader 6 (Meiko)<br>Pig 1 (Gloria)<br>Pig 2 (Fadia)<br>Pig 3 (John)<br>Wolf (Chris)<br>Mama (April)<br>Man 1 (Cody)<br>Man 2 (Nate)<br>Man 3 (Jarvis) |
| Reader 1: Once upon a time, an old sow sent her three little pigs out into the world to seek their fortune.<br>Mama: Now be sure to write. And remember that I love you.<br>Reader 2: The first little pig met a man with a load of straw.<br>Pig 1: I know! I'll buy your straw and build a house. | Marcus: Once upon a time, an old sow sent her three little pigs out into the world to seek their fortune.<br>April: Now be sure to write. And remember that I love you.<br>James: The first little pig met a man with a load of straw.<br>Gloria: I know! I'll buy your straw and build a house. |

# ONLINE RESOURCES

## Adapting Text

### Clicker from Crick Software
www.cricksoft.com/us/home.aspx
Award-winning literacy tool for special needs students

### Picture It from Suncastle Technology
www.suncastletech.com
Picture-symbol software program

### Start-to-Finish from Don Johnston, Inc.
www.donjohnston.com/products/start_to_finish/
Library of books on CD-ROM for students with delayed reading abilities

### Storyline Online (SAG)
www.storylineonline.net
Streaming video program that features actors (members of SAG) reading children's books aloud

**SymWriter from Mayer-Johnson Co.**

www.mayer-johnson.com
Picture-symbol software program selling specific solutions for specific needs

## Simplified eBooks

### Internet Archive

archive.org

>*Aesop's Fables in Words of One Syllable,* by Mary Godolphin
>http://archive.org/details/aesopsfablesinwo00aeso

### Project Gutenberg

www.gutenberg.org

>*Alice in Wonderland—Retold in Words of One Syllable*, by J. C. Gorham
>www.gutenberg.org/ebooks/19551
>*Black Beauty, Young Folks' Edition*, by Anna Swell
>www.gutenberg.org/ebooks/11860
>*The Pilgrim's Progress in Words of One Syllable*, by Mary Godolphin
>www.gutenberg.org/etext/7088
>*Robinson Crusoe in Words of One Syllable*, by Mary Godolphin
>www.gutenberg.org/etext/6936
>*Swiss Family Robinson in Words of One Syllable*, by Mary Godolphin
>www.gutenberg.org/etext/6692

## Reading Aloud

### Apple iTunes

www.apple.com/itunes/
Search for audiobooks, many of which are free

### Audiobooks.org

www.audiobooks.org
Online audiobook collection including some free, classic, public domain titles, as well as best sellers for sale, including *Red Badge of Courage*

### Audiobooks for Free

www.audiobooksforfree.com
Classic audiobooks including fiction, nonfiction, and children's books read by professionals

### Candlelight Stories

www.candlelightstories.com/Stories.asp
Audiobooks include *Pirate Jack* by Alessandro Cima and *Robinson Crusoe* by Daniel Defoe

### *The Chronicles of Narnia* by C.S. Lewis

www.ancientfaith.com/podcasts/series/the_chronicles_of_narnia
http://goo.gl/KX1Xa
Free online streaming and MP3 download of all seven books.

### Clifford Interactive Storybooks

http://teacher.scholastic.com/clifford1/index.htm
Clifford eBook stories in English and Spanish from Scholastic.

### *Graveyard Book*, by Neil Gaiman

www.neilgaiman.com/p/Cool_Stuff/Video_Clips/The_Graveyard_Book_Tour
http://goo.gl/3En0M
A video series where the author reads the entire eight chapters of his book

### Inkless Tales

www.inklesstales.com/stories/
Collection of audio stories with illustrations that feature a character named Fanny Doodle; the site also includes poems, games, activities, and *Dolch Stories*

### Kids Space—Hear a Story

http://kidsspace.torontopubliclibrary.ca/genStoryArchive_All_1.html
The Toronto Public Library provides a collection of 100 audio narrations from children's books in different languages

> Virtual edition of Barbara Reid's *The Party* http://media.torontopubliclibrary.ca/virtual-book/48/

### LibriVox

librivox.org
A free online library of audiobooks from the public domain

### Light Up Your Brain

http://lightupyourbrain.com/audio-stories-for-children.html
Collection of free short audio stories for downloading and playing in MP3 format

### Online Audio Stories

www.onlineaudiostories.com
Classic children's stories in audio format for online play or download, with associated text

### Online Storytime by Barnes & Noble

www.barnesandnoble.com/u/online-storytime-books-toys/379002381/
Streaming video of popular children's books read by authors or celebrities

### Open Culture

www.openculture.com/freeaudiobooks
This resource site offers hundreds of links to websites with audiobooks

### Read to Me

www.readtomelv.com/current-books/
Streaming video eBook site that has books read by Las Vegas personalities

### Reading Planet's Book Zone

www.rif.org/kids/readingplanet/bookzone/read_aloud_stories.htm
This Reading is Fundamental (RIF) site has audio stories and songs that display the text as it is read aloud

### Starfall

www.starfall.com
eBooks with simple books focused on particular vowel sounds.When a student clicks on a word, each sound is pronounced, while each letter representing the sound is highlighted. After all the sounds in a word are pronounced, the whole word is read aloud

### Story Cove

www.storycove.com
A collection with 22 leveled picture books with folktales from around the world and two read-along storybooks

## Background Knowledge

### Google Lit Trips

www.googlelittrips.com
Virtual field trips based on story locations

### Greene Bytes

http://greenetn.schooldesk.net/Departments/CurriculumandInstruction/TeacherResources/Newsletters/GreeneBytes/VirtualFieldTrips/tabid/12327/Default.aspx (http://goo.gl/5v1mX)
Virtual field trips for language arts, social studies, history, science, math, guidance, health and physical education, fine arts, and more

### Kid's Zone

www.agclassroom.org/kids/tours.htm
Agricultural virtual field trips to farms

### NASA's Dictionary Website

www.nasa.gov/audience/forstudents/k-4/dictionary/index.html
Dictionary of science vocabulary with images arranged alphabetically, terms defined and used in sentences for students K–4

### Tramline
www.field-trips.org/trips.htm
Free virtual field trips in the areas of science, math, literature, social studies, and other topics, and it includes teacher's resources

## Songs
### A–Z Lyrics Universe
www.azlyrics.com
Lyrics database featuring word to thousands of songs listed by title and artist

### Bus Songs
bussongs.com
Lyrics, video, and music for over 2000 children's songs and nursery rhymes

### EFL Classroom 2.0, Karafun
http://community.eflclassroom.com/page/karafun-get-the-player-and
A free downloadable karaoke player for download, along with hundreds of songs

### Krazykats Karaoke
www.krazykats-karaoke.co.uk/karaoke_kids.html
Links collection to sites that contain singing and songs to use karaoke as a learning tool to build self-confidence and improve reading skills

## Poetry and Nursery Rhymes
### Fanpop
www.fanpop.com/spots/nursery-rhymes
Nursery rhyme eBook collection with images, videos, articles, and links

### Nicky's Nursery Rhymes
www.nurseryrhymes4u.com
Nursery rhymes and songs with midi music, wav song, or voice accompaniment

### Online Mum
www.onlinemum.com/baby/activities/the-online-mum-free-download-of-popular-nursery-rhymes.html
Free downloadable *A–Z Popular Nursery Rhymes* eBook in PDF format

### *Real Mother Goose*
http://www.gutenberg.org/ebooks/10607
Project Gutenberg has the 1916 illustrated version of *The Real Mother Goose* available in multiple formats (see Figure 12.5)

**Super Parents Talk**

http://superparentstalk.com/articles/free-ebook-mother-goose-nursery-rhymes.html
Downloadable *Mother Goose* nursery rhyme eBook in PDF format

## Readers Theater

### Aaron Shepard

www.aaronshep.com/rt/
Collection of readers theater scripts and tips by Aaron Shepard

### The Reading Lady

www.readinglady.com
Collection of free readers theater scripts available for download

## Wide Access

### International Children's Digital Library

http://en.childrenslibrary.org/
Online library of children's stories from around the world, arranged by geographic area

### NASA Education for Students, Grades K–4

http://www.nasa.gov/audience/forstudents/k-4/index.html
Stories and games that define and explain science terms with visuals

### Pitara Kids Network

www.pitara.com/talespin/folktales.asp
Collection of folktales, myths, fairy tales, and legends from around the world

# Chapter 13

# Gifted Students and Advanced Readers

## Co-written by Christine Weber

At the beginning of her third year teaching fourth grade, Marsha Rodriguez has been told to expect a cluster group of gifted students in her mixed-ability classroom. Gifted students are those in the top 3–5% of ability, and they are often gathered together (clustered) in a single class of a particular grade level. Marsha's group will consist of three to six students identified as gifted.

Although she has had some training in teaching exceptionally capable students, Marsha realizes that having learners with different ability levels will require her to reconsider how to develop and teach differentiated lessons. Her district uses a basal reading program, and she believes several of her students could already pass the basal comprehension assessments before she even teaches them the material. Because Marsha does not want her students to spend time in school doing work they already know, she wants to be sure that she creates a learning environment in which all of her students will be stretched to learn. This means she needs to:

- provide opportunities for faster pacing of new material,
- incorporate students' enthusiastic interests into their independent studies,
- facilitate sophisticated research investigations,
- offer flexible grouping opportunities for the entire class.

Marsha thinks it is important that students at this age are encouraged to choose books themselves to maintain their interest in reading. But the school budget is limited, so purchasing more challenging reading material is out of the question. How can she help each student make academic gains without spending additional money on reading materials or resources?

With an emphasis on inclusionary classrooms, the chances you will encounter a gifted child are about one in 20. As a result, you need to be prepared to provide opportunities to differentiate reading for gifted and advanced readers in your classroom. Unfortunately, there is little research focused on identifying talented readers, teaching them, or using the pedagogy of gifted education to encourage and develop advanced and continuous reading progress in gifted readers (Jackson & Roller,1993; Renzulli & Reis, 1989). It can be a daunting task to try to meet the needs of a variety of learners in the same classroom and help all students, including the gifted, make academic gains.

In the article "Worthy texts: Who decides?" Gilmore (2011) suggests that students who read for pleasure tend to read a variety of texts, except in the classroom. The opportunity to read and enjoy a book of one's choosing is often overshadowed by what Gilmore calls a "mandate" to read it. We know that teachers and schools make many of the decisions about what children read. Gilmore (2011) states that ".... schools ... fail to motivate students through choice." By expanding this choice through digital texts, students can start to select what they read and begin the process of critically analyzing their choices and comparing them to the required classical readings in the field.

## CHARACTERISTICS OF GIFTED READERS

Because gifted readers have unique characteristics, they may require a differentiated approach to teaching reading that will match their abilities and needs. Gifted readers often read earlier and tend to read more independently. In fact, many gifted students come to school already knowing how to read, so they may grow bored and distracted if not challenged. It is important to note that primary gifted readers are those who, "upon entering first grade, are reading substantially above grade level or who possess the ability to make rapid progress in reading when given proper instruction" (Bonds & Bonds, 1983). They also tend to be better readers, requiring less drill for mastery of skills (Halsted, 1990).

Gifted readers can digest a large quantity of information about a topic in which they are interested. Many gifted readers are strongly motivated to read. Because of their ability to understand the nuances of language, make connections, and deal with the abstract, gifted readers enjoy provocative stories and solving plots with twists. Books with characters who are gifted, complex, or multidimensional are also appealing.

Abilock (1999) identified the following five facts about gifted readers:
- They are skilled, flexible readers who read often.
- They monitor their own reading.
- Linguistically rich texts are especially suited to them.
- They use other strengths in response to the particular demands of the text.
- They are passionate readers who find books to love.

Catron and Wingenbach's research identifies the following specific skills gifted readers possess (as cited in Vosslamber, 2002, p. 15):

- anticipation of meaning based on visual clues,
- use of prior knowledge and experience, personal identification, and reader purpose,
- awareness of cognitive processing of a text for information/concept gathering,
- making links between the present text and what was previously read, resulting in forming and developing concepts.

As educators, it is important for you to keep in mind that even gifted and advanced readers lose enthusiasm and interest in reading as they progress through their school years (Anderson, Tollefson, & Gilbert, 1985; Henderson, Jackson, & Makumal, 1993; Martin, 1984). Once students lose interest in reading, it is difficult to win them back.

## DIFFERENTIATING INSTRUCTION

Keeping these facts in mind, it is crucial that when you have students who enter school reading at a considerably higher and more sophisticated rate than their peers that you provide some type of accommodation to keep these advanced and gifted readers engaged and involved in reading.

How can you provide access to a variety of genres that may interest advanced readers? How can you extend the reading content above the current level? In what ways can students be engaged in complex texts? Digital texts may be part of your answer.

One way to differentiate instruction for gifted readers is to provide exposure to quality reading materials from a variety of genres and at different levels of difficulty. Reading instruction that emphasizes depth and complexity, is offered at an appropriate pace for the learner, and allows for self-selection is crucial to keeping gifted and advanced readers excited and motivated to read. Using eBooks to promote reading can provide the interaction, enrichment, and challenge for gifted readers that may be missing from the existing classroom reading instruction. eBooks provide a variety of ways to differentiate reading content to meet the cognitive needs that can set gifted and advanced readers apart from their peers. Access to a wide variety of books encourages exposure to the following:

- new and challenging information
- varied subjects
- areas of interest
- difficult vocabulary and concepts

eBooks provide an avenue for parents, teachers, and librarians to help gifted readers grow intellectually. By using eBooks, you can provide a greater variety of available, challenging reading materials—often at no cost.

# USING EBOOKS WITH GIFTED READERS

Reis, Gubbins, and Richards (2001) recommend that gifted readers have access to an array of classroom and library books. On the web, you and your students can find sites that offer free eBooks ranging from single books to special collections, along with entire online libraries. These sites expand the opportunities for students to have access to books. Through these websites, students can find favorite authors or books, related titles, other books in a series, or books by the same author that may not be available at either the school or local public library. For example, most school libraries have the classic children's favorite *The Wizard of Oz* by L. Frank Baum, but they may not have the other titles in the series. The online libraries Feedbooks (www.feedbooks.com) (see Figure 13.1) and Project Gutenberg (www.gutenberg.org) freely distribute all 14 books in the *Oz* series.

Some online libraries provide entire collections of special topics or authors. For example, Cornell University's Making of America collection (http://moa.library.cornell.edu/) provides 900,000 pages of primary source material on a variety of subjects. The U.S. Geological Service (USGS) General Interest Publications (http://pubs.er.usgs.gov/) has 100,000 reports issued by that agency in the past century, including excellent nonfiction materials for scientific research (see Figure 13.2). The Electronic Text Center at the University of Virginia Library (http://goo.gl/6Vt00), in its Modern English Collection, has electronic book sections on African American, Native American, and women writers. A student can use this electronic library to obtain such rarities as 13 works written by Booker T. Washington or 39 volumes by George Washington. An advantage of using these resources is the student's speed of access. If you or your student find an interesting book, it can be downloaded in seconds.

Although eBooks can be used to present text and images, just as a paper-based book can, eBooks also contain features that can be classified as accommodations or as assistive technology tools for reading. These accommodations can include alternative formats, scaffolds, and supports for reading activities to reach all students, including those who may be experiencing print or reading difficulties or disabilities. The latter

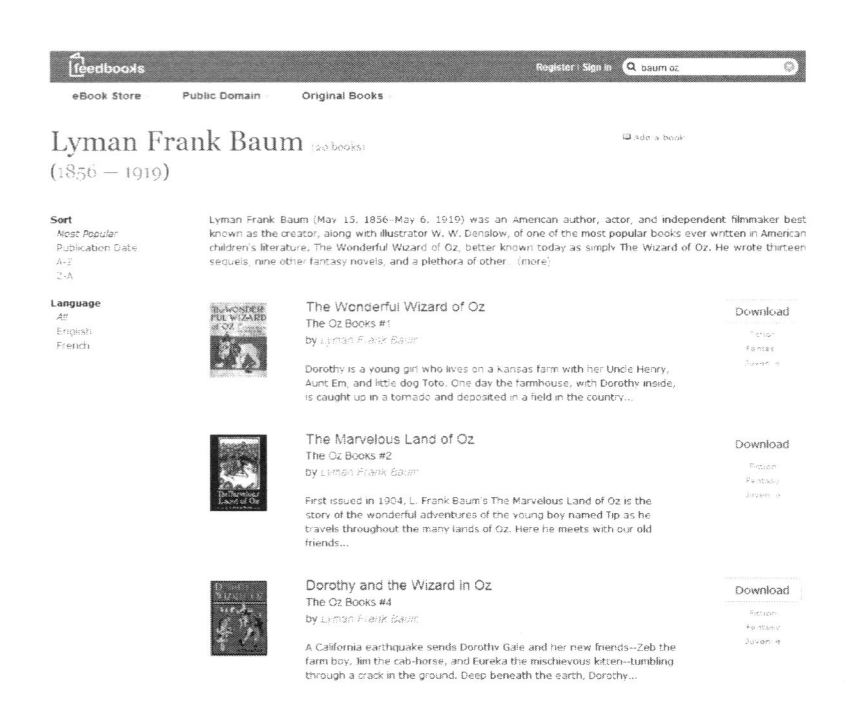

**FIGURE 13.1** Feedbooks' L. Frank Baum collection contains all 14 of his *Oz* books along with others in ePub, Kindle, and PDF formats (© Feedbooks 2006–12)

includes gifted and advanced readers, since the incidence of learning disabilities in the gifted population is 10–15% (Silverman, 2003). Some of the accommodating features that eBooks can provide include adjustable text size for large print, highlighting, bookmarking, note-taking, interactive dictionaries, and read-alouds through text-to-speech (see chapter 15).

## Suggested Books for Gifted Readers

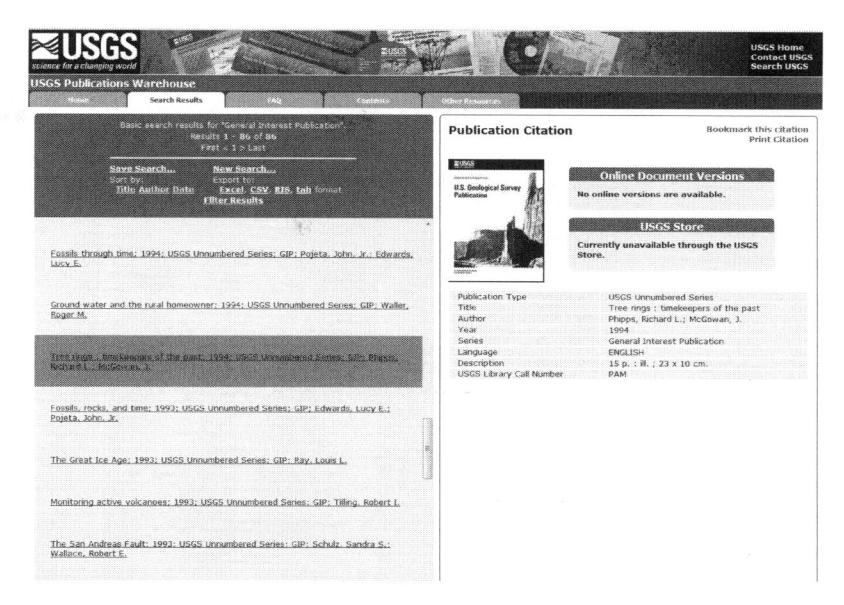

**FIGURE 13.2** The USGS Publication Warehouse contains more than 80 short books that cover a wide variety of science topics

Below is a brief selection of free eBooks that may be appropriate for gifted readers as suggested by some gifted instructors. All of these books are available from the online library Project Gutenberg (www.gutenberg.org) in a variety of formats, including TXT, Kindle's AZW, EPUB, HTML, and audiobooks. To find these books, simply use the search tool on the Project Gutenberg site. Each of these books is also available from other online libraries (see chapter 5), which may offer them in other formats.

Alcott, Louisa May. *Little Women*
Burnett, Frances H. *The Secret Garden*
Burroughs, Edgar Rice. *Tarzan of the Apes*
Dodge, Mary Mapes. *Hans Brinker*
Doyle, A. Conan. *The Adventures of Sherlock Holmes*
Dumas, Alexandre. *The Three Musketeers*
Grahame, Kenneth. *The Wind in the Willows*
Grimm, Jacob and Wilhelm. *Grimm's Fairy Tales* (includes *Rumpelstiltskin*, etc.)
Kipling, Rudyard. *Captains Courageous*
Lang, Andrew. *The Blue Fairy Book*
London, Jack. *The Call of the Wild*
London, Jack. *White Fang*
Stevenson, Robert Louis. *Kidnapped*
Stevenson, Robert Louis. *Treasure Island*
Verne, Jules. *A Journey to the Center of the Earth*
Wyss, Johann David. *The Swiss Family Robinson*

## Online Libraries with Challenging Materials

Gifted readers can use online libraries to access a wide variety of challenging books, information, materials, ideas, and issues that interest them, but that may not be available in their school library or teacher's classroom collection. Below is a list of general and secondary eBook libraries that provide challenging material for gifted readers. (For a larger list of general and secondary eBook libraries, see chapter 5.)

**Baen Free Library**

www.baen.com/library/
More than 120 relatively new science-fiction books in Kindle (AZW), EPUB, LIT, Rocket (RB), RTF, and Sony LRF format.

**Electronic Text Center at the University of Virginia Library**

http://etext.lib.virginia.edu/modeng/modeng0.browse.html
http://goo.gl/6Vt00
Modern English Collection contains fiction, nonfiction, poetry, drama, letters, newspapers, manuscripts, and illustrations for online reading.

**Making of America (MOA)**

http://cdl.library.cornell.edu/moa/
Digital library created by Cornell University Library containing primary sources in American social history (antebellum through reconstruction periods), with a full text/image journal site of 22 magazines from the 1830s to the 1900s.

**USGS General Interest Publications**

http://pubs.er.usgs.gov/#search:basic/query=General%20Interest%20Publication/page=1/page_size=100:0
http://goo.gl/qN9o3
Listings of online books, reports, and pamphlets published by the U.S. Geological Survey that cover a variety of science topics (mostly Earth science).

**Wired for Books**

www.wiredforbooks.org
Collections of audiobooks and interviews contain full versions of *The Wonderful Wizard of Oz, Alice in Wonderland*, and Beatrix Potter stories, along with short stories and excerpts from other books (Real Audio and MP3).

# NEXT STEPS

eBook libraries can increase the interaction between home and classroom and expand reading experiences for gifted readers by providing additional reading options. It is estimated that there are more than 5 million eBooks available on the Internet. The unique features and capabilities of eBook technologies provide the attraction, options, and accommodations that not only promote reading, but keep students interested in reading. Dr. Del Siegle at the University of Connecticut provides PDF resources at his website (www.gifted.uconn.edu/siegle/Conferences/Creating%20EBooks.pdf http://www.gifted.uconn.edu/siegle/Conferences/

Creating%20EBooks%2060%20min.pdf) <http://goo.gl/3Asauu> information concerning using eBook resources to motivate students.

For gifted students interested in writing, Siegle (2006) provides an excellent description on how to create and share eBooks. Quindland (2011) emphasizes the importance of authentic experiences to foster deep and lasting learning. Creating a real book that is then shared on the Internet is more authentic that creating a project for a class homework assignment. Levy (2008) indicates that when student work culminates in a genuine product for an authentic audience, it encourages students to put forth their best effort. Providing an opportunity for gifted students to create their own eBooks and share them with others encourages a connection with what is taught and what is learned. (For more information on creating eBooks, see chapter 7.)

# WHERE TO START?

Hoagies' Gifted Reading Lists (www.hoagiesgifted.org/reading_lists.htm) provides many ideas about books appropriate for gifted and advanced readers. Some can be found in eBook versions. The site provides an abundance of information for parents, educators, and gifted children themselves.

# ONLINE RESOURCES

### Australian Gifted Support Centre
http://nswagtc.org.au/
Resource site with lists of books appropriate for gifted students

### Baen Free Library
www.baen.com/library/
Collection of relatively new science-fiction resources from Baen Publishing in a variety of formats (Sony, Kindle, EPUB, LIT, Rocket, and RTF)

### Electronic Text Center at the University of Virginia Library
http://etext.lib.virginia.edu/modeng/modeng0.browse.html
<http://goo.gl/6Vt00>
General eBook collection with a wide variety of texts including fiction, nonfiction, poetry, drama, letters, newspapers, manuscripts, and illustrations for online reading

### Feedbooks
www.feedbooks.com
General eBook collection with a wide variety of texts (see Figure 13.1)

### GT World Reading Lists

http://gtworld.org/gtbook.htm
Lists in the Books section summarize the reading recommendations from Gifted and Talented Families

### Guiding the Gifted Reader

www.kidsource.com/kidsource/content/guiding_gifted_reader.html
Information about guiding your gifted reader

### Hoagies' Gifted Reading Lists

www.hoagiesgifted.org/reading_lists.htm
Reading lists for the gifted child

### Making of America (MOA)

http://cdl.library.cornell.edu/moa/
Digital library created by Cornell University Library containing primary sources in American social history (antebellum through reconstruction periods), with a full text/image journal site of 22 magazines from the 1830s to the 1900s

### PlanetEsme.com

www.planetesme.com
Author site for Esmé Raji Codell, author of *How to Get Your Child to Love Reading*

### Project Gutenberg

www.gutenberg.org/
General eBook collection with a wide variety of texts in a variety of formats. See list above for suggested books to download

### ReadWriteThink

www.readwritethink.org
Resource site for educators and parents to provide materials and instruction for reading and language arts

### Schoolwide Enrichment Model-Reading at the University of Connecticut

www.gifted.uconn.edu/semr/
SEM-R information on how teachers use student reading time to meet individually with students to provide individual instruction in strategy use as well as higher order questions to challenge and engage readers

## USGS General Interest Publications

http://pubs.er.usgs.gov/#search:basic/query=General%20Interest%20Publication/page=1/page_size=100:0

http://goo.gl/qN9o3

Lists of online books, reports, and pamphlets published by the U.S. Geological Survey that cover a variety of science topics (mostly Earth science)

## Wired for Books

www.wiredforbooks.org

Collections of audiobooks and interviews containing full versions of *The Wonderful Wizard of Oz*, *Alice in Wonderland*, and Beatrix Potter stories, along with short stories and excerpts from other books (Real Audio and MP3)

# PRINT RESOURCES

Codell, E. (2003). *How to get your child to love reading: For ravenous and reluctant readers alike.* Chapel Hill, NC: Algonquin Books.

Fredericks, A. D. (1987). *The gifted reader handbook.* Tucson, AZ: Goodyear Books.

Halsted, J. (1994). *Some of my best friends are books: Guiding gifted readers from pre-school to high school* (2nd ed.). Scottsdale, AZ: Great Potential Press.

Kingore, B. (2002). Reading instruction for the primary gifted learner. *Understanding Our Gifted*, 15, 12–15.

Polette, N. J. (2000). *Gifted books, gifted readers: Literature activities to excite young minds.* Littleton, CO: Libraries Unlimited.

# Chapter 14

# eBooks and ESL / ELL Students

Co-written by Jin-Suk Byun

Nando Sanchez is a Grade 3 mainstream classroom teacher with three English language learners (ELLs) in his class. One of the three ELLs, Uranchimeg, arrived in the United States from Mongolia only two months ago and does not yet talk in class. Nando does not know any other Mongolians, nor has he experienced Mongolian culture. As part of his job, however, not only must he teach Uranchimeg to read, write, and function in English, he also needs to support Uranchimeg's original language. In researching Mongolia, he finds the International Children's Digital Library (ICDL, www.icdlbooks.org). This online library has children's books in more than 50 languages, including more than 200 titles in Mongolian.

Because all the books in ICDL are in English as well as in other languages, Nando uses one of the bilingual eBooks to teach Uranchimeg. Nando also has the option of creating a bilingual text. That way, Uranchimeg can read the text in Mongolian, be exposed to English at the same time, and be able to compare the words in both languages. Moreover, Mr. Sanchez encourages Uranchimeg to read eBooks in the ICDL at home or in a public library.

---

### ELL, ESL, ESOL, EL

In this chapter, we use the term English language learner (ELL). However, other terms such as English as a second language learner (ESL learner), English to speakers of other languages learner (ESOL learner), and English learner (EL) are used interchangeably.

# THE ELL STUDENT

All teachers in the United States today must be prepared to support English language learners (ELLs) in their classrooms. According to survey results (NCELA, 2010), it is estimated that as of 2008 more than 5 million ELLs are enrolled in PK–12 in U.S. public schools, or 10.56% of the total public school population. In other words, one out of every 10 public school students is an English language learner (ELL), and that number is growing. It is estimated that the ELL population has grown by 53.25% since the school year of 1997–98. This is an enormous increase when you consider that the total public school enrollment rose just 8.45% for the same period. The rate of increase of ELLs' enrollment is more than six times greater than average.

The *number* of ELL students is not the only issue; so are the *types* of ELLs. There has been an enormous increase in the variety of languages in public schools. A recent biennial report to Congress (2004–06) shows that ELLs in public schools in the United States speak more than 400 different languages. So, it is not just a matter of having bilingual English–Spanish resources. Teachers must consider the other 399 languages as well. How can you help this fast-growing population of ELLs? One way is through eBooks.

Reading eBooks employs at least two important tools for English acquisition: technology and reading. The use of technology to teach content has been emphasized in education, and educators are encouraged to use it (Cavanaugh, 2006; Dexter, Doering, & Riedel, 2006). The use of eBooks is exactly in line with the new mandate of education. In general, the use of technology is becoming more popular in second-language acquisition (SLA) (English is the second language for these students), with technology developed for Computer-Assisted Language Learning (CALL) or Multimedia-Assisted Language Learning (MALL).

eBooks can also be used to help ELLs improve their English through extensive reading. Practice makes perfect may be an ancient cliché, but just as English language readers improve their reading skills the more they read, ELLs will improve their English language skills the more they read in English. The positive effect of extensive reading has been accepted in both English as a second language (ESL) and English as a foreign language (EFL) reading instruction programs. Moreover, because these programs have begun to include the Internet (Silva, 2009), eBooks are exactly in line with this trend of reading for ELLs. In other words, the large amount of free reading materials available online will help ELLs to improve their English skills without paying a large amount of money for traditional books.

# EDUCATIONAL APPLICATIONS

eBooks are a useful tool if you have English language learners in your classroom. Many eBook sites provide a variety of second-language supportive reading materials for students from linguistically and culturally diverse backgrounds. When ELLs go through their second-language (L2) acquisition process, the use of their native-language (L1) literacy becomes important, especially when they do not speak any English at all. It helps to provide ELLs with comprehensible input, activate their background knowledge, and scaffold the acquisition of English and content knowledge.

However, because more than 400 languages are spoken by ELLs, you probably won't be able to find books in all of these native languages in your local Barnes & Noble or Books-a-Million. Even if you could, the cost would be prohibitive. So, what can you do? A good place to start is the International Children's Digital Library (ICDL), where you will find many good materials for your English language learners (see Figure 14.1). As mentioned previously, the ICDL has books in more than 50 languages, as well as many bilingual books. The bilingual books help ELLs improve their English while simultaneously maintaining their native language. Even the books available only in the student's native language will help them improve their English indirectly, because there is a close relationship between L1 and L2 literacy development (Cummins, 1984; Kahn-Horwitz, Shimron, & Sparks, 2005; Sparks, Patton, Ganschow, & Humbach, 2009).

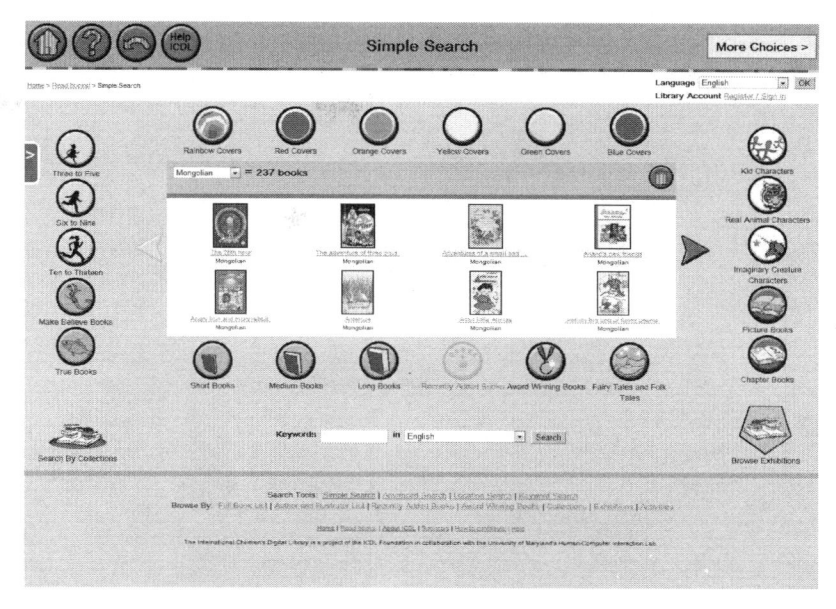

**FIGURE 14.1** The International Children's Digital Library offers eBooks in more than 50 languages, including Mongolian

According to Cummins (1979), low L1 proficiency leads to low L2 proficiency. In other words, learners who are not proficient readers in their native tongue will probably be weak in reading in their target language as well. This is why you should encourage English language learners to read books in their native language. This is especially true for ELLs at the beginning stage of their English acquisition. One way to do that is by using eBooks from numerous sites on the Internet.

# THE CONNECTION BETWEEN SPOKEN AND WRITTEN LANGUAGE

ELLs may miss many words when they are spoken because they mishear or confuse the sequence of sounds. Students' opportunities for learning increase when they hear the words as they read them. For example, an ELL student named Jinsuk had trouble understanding the word "ruin" when he started learning English because the letter "i" in the word formed an

FIGURE 14.2 *June the Prune* from the Amazing Adventure Series is an online eBook with audio support (© 1997, Thomas and Heidi Tosi)

unstressed syllable. Unstressed syllables in English tend to become weak and reduced vowels (such as the schwa sound, /∂/). One day, however, Jinsuk encountered a script for the audiotape he was using, and realized the word was "ruin." After that, he almost never missed the word when he heard it. As this example demonstrates, the connection between written and spoken language is helpful for second-language learners, and eBooks with audio support can effectively promote the connection.

Some eBooks provide audio and video formats and can be read on screen. For example, Amazing Adventure Series (www.tosiproductions.com/_amazing adventure/) (see Figure 14.2), Between the Lions (http://pbskids.org/lions/stories/), and CBeebies Story Circle (www.bbc.co.uk/cbeebies/stories/) all have eBooks that provide audio along with text. Most also provide synchronized highlighting of the text on screen as the words are read. This is especially helpful for ELLs because the connection between spoken and written language is effective in helping them to improve their English (Berninger, Vaughan, & Abbott, 2000; Bochner & Bochner, 2009). Of course, if for some reason you are not able to obtain eBooks with audio support, much the same effect can be achieved by using audiobooks in tandem with books that students are reading. Hearing the words spoken while following along on the pages or on screen is an effective mode of language acquisition. This process helps all students, not just ELLs, to learn pronunciation and make the letter-sound connection.

## TEXT-ENHANCING FUNCTIONS

Second-language acquisition (SLA) research has focused on the effect of many different types of language input in language learning. For example, one way of enhancing language input is to provide in a passage many tokens (occurrences of unique words) of target vocabulary or grammatical structures. This is called input flooding (Trahey, 1996; Trahey & White, 1993). In other words, you can expose ELLs to the target vocabulary and the target grammatical structure repeatedly without explaining them explicitly (see Figure 14.3).

Another way to enhance language input is to emphasize the target vocabulary and the target grammatical structure. This is called enhanced input or textual enhancement (Smith, 1991,

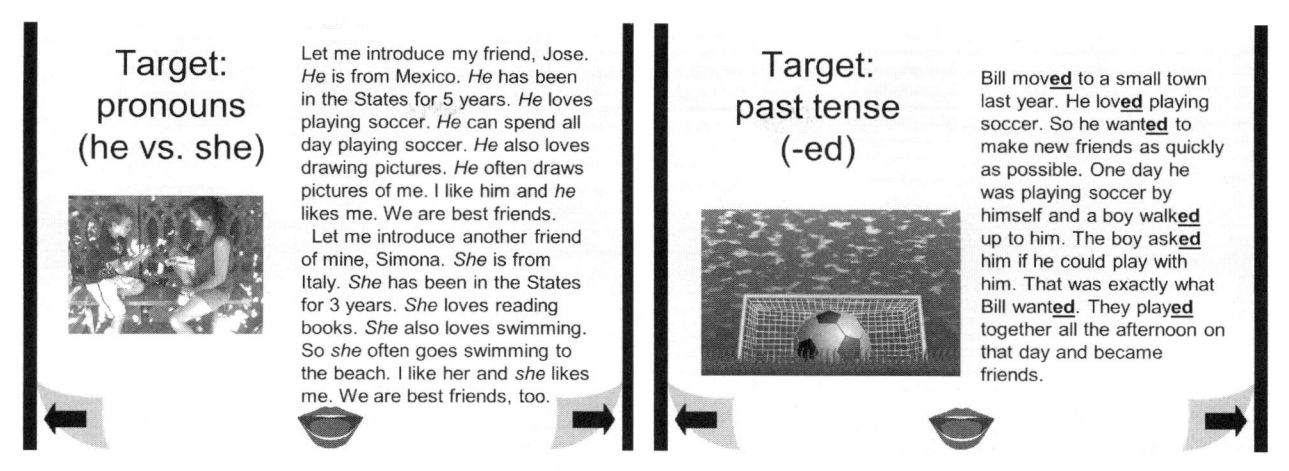

**FIGURE 14.3** These sample pages of eBooks created with PowerPoint display input flooding of the pronouns he and she (top) and textual enhancement of past tense (-ed)

1993). Through textual-enhancement techniques, ELLs pay attention to particular target vocabulary or grammatical structures and gradually acquire them.

With their text-enhancing functions, eBooks can be effective tools to help ELLs. Because you can easily add, delete, change, or copy and paste material on electronic files, eBooks can systematically provide your ELLs with language input appropriate for their developmental stage of English. To develop the texts, you can use Microsoft Word, PowerPoint, or a story-maker website such as Storybird (http://storybird.com).

With an eBook you can easily incorporate textual-enhancement techniques into ELLs' lessons. You can change the size and color of text, such as putting specific parts in different formats (italic, bold, or underline). This helps ELLs process what they need for their current developmental stage of English.

Remember, you can use free tools to create your own eBook stories that highlight important words and concepts, or even target grammatical structures (see chapters 7, 8, and 9 for information on creating your own eBooks).

## ON-DEMAND REFERENCING

Various reference functions of eBook programs can help ELLs. For example, most eBook programs and eBook readers have an interactive dictionary (see Figure 14.4), which can facilitate students' acquisition of second-language (L2) vocabulary. Whenever students come across a word they don't know, they can touch or click on it and be taken directly to the word's definition. The dictionary may also have examples of the words used in context, the correct pronunciations, and sometimes even translations into the students' native languages. This is especially helpful to ELLs for their content vocabulary acquisition, which is, in turn, important for their acquisition of subject matter (VanDeweghe, 2007).

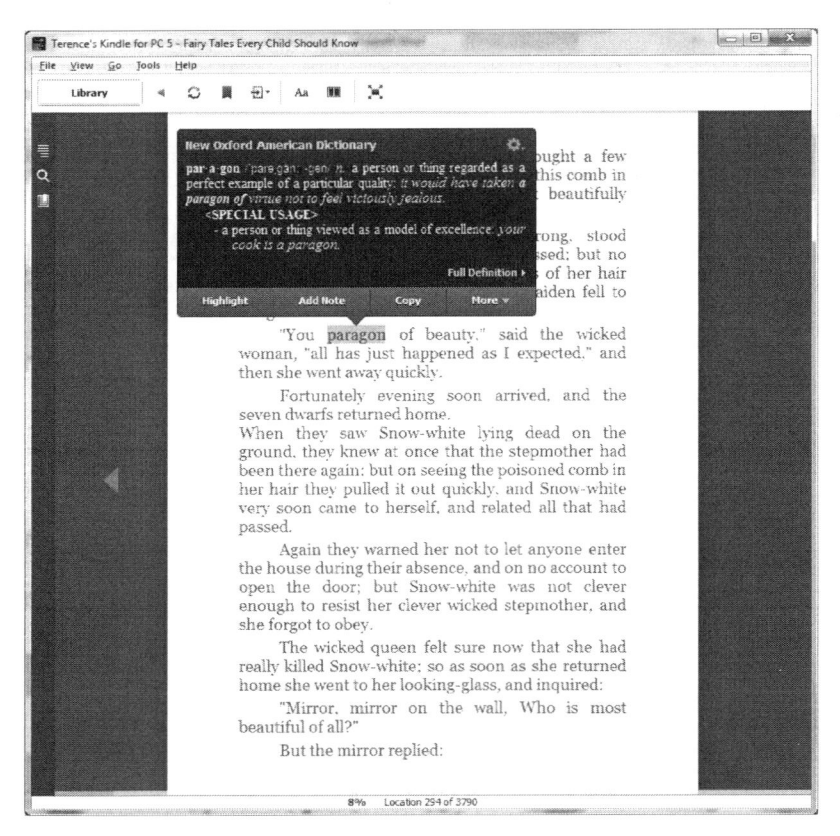

Some ELLs already have academic knowledge of certain subject matter. For these students, the acquisition of subject matter may require simply renaming in English the content words or concepts they already know. In this case, having an interactive digital dictionary available will quickly help with their reading comprehension.

**FIGURE 14.4** Interactive dictionary use in a Kindle program running on a desktop computer

# PROMOTE INTERACTION IN THE CLASSROOM

Interaction between you and your students and between students themselves is an important factor for second-language acquisition. Interaction plays an important role in second-language learning because languages are acquired through the negotiation of meaning in conversation (Long, 1996). This means that the more interaction you promote in your classroom, the more English acquisition will occur.

With eBooks, you can use technology to promote interaction in the target language. For example, you may pair an English language learner (ELL) with a non-ELL and ask them to read a bilingual book online together. The ELL can explain how her or his native language works using the words and concepts in the story, and the non-ELL can explain how English works. While they work in pairs, they will interact in English to accomplish assigned tasks, which will help the ELL improve his or her English.

# MORE SITES TO COME

With the ever-increasing number of English language learners (ELLs) and the rapid development of technology, educators in elementary schools are now more than ever expected to be prepared to use technology-related tools for their ELLs.

One of the tools to cover both English-to-speakers-of-other-languages (ESOL) accommodations and modern technology is an eBook. Since an eBook provides ELLs with many visuals, sounds, highlighting, L1 support, and fun, it motivates and helps ELLs to improve their English through extensive reading with ESOL accommodations. eBooks can quickly, easily, and cheaply expand the size of a classroom reading collection that will accommodate all levels and backgrounds of ELLs.

Also, because English learning is getting more and more popular all over the world, no doubt more useful eBook sites will be developed in the near future. Therefore, it is highly recommended that you include eBooks into your repertoire for lesson plans, especially for the rapidly growing number of ELLs in the United States.

# ONLINE RESOURCES

## Bilingual eBooks—in English and in ELL's Native Language

The following is a list of eBooks with content in multiple languages (for instance, English and Spanish). In this case, the ELL would be learning English, and his or her native language would be Spanish.

### International Children's Digital Library

http://en.childrenslibrary.org/
Links to eBooks in more than 30 languages

### Fairy Tales by Grimm Brothers

www.fln.vcu.edu/grimm/grimm_menu.html
eBooks in German and English

### Story Place

www.storyplace.org
eBooks in Spanish and English

### Children's Books Online: The Rosetta Project

www.childrensbooksonline.org
eBook translations into Armenian, Chinese, Italian, Japanese, Portuguese, Romanian, Spanish, and Turkish

## eBooks in English

The following is a list of English eBooks with content that is well known in English. These eBooks are useful for cultural understanding and idioms.

### *Aesop's Fables*
www.umass.edu/aesop/index.php

### Maya Culture—Traditional Storytellers' Tales
www.kstrom.net/isk/maya/mayastor.html

### Irish Storyteller's Website
www.irishstoryteller.com/

### Folklore and Mythology Electronic Texts
www.pitt.edu/~dash/folktexts.html#b

### Classic Bookshelf
www.classicbookshelf.com/library/

## eBooks with Audio/Video Files

The following eBooks provide audio or video as well as text.

### Amazing Adventure Series
www.tosiproductions.com/_amazingadventure/

### Between the Lions
http://pbskids.org/lions/stories/

### CBeebies Story Circle
www.bbc.co.uk/cbeebies/stories/

### Aborigine Tales
http://australianmuseum.net.au/Stories-of-the-Dreaming

### Storyline Online
www.storylineonline.net

### Lil' Fingers: Storybooks
www.lil-fingers.com/storybooks/index.php

### Story Place
www.storyplace.org

## eBooks in Other Languages

The following library resources support an ELL's native language.

### Antologia della Letteratura Italiana

www.crs4.it/HTML/Literature.html
Libre Libre http://www.liberliber.it/libri/index.php Free Italian eBook site that has book on architecture, plays, stories, poems and more

Italian novels, poetry, plays, and other texts, both classic and contemporary, available in HTML, for reading online

### Aozora Bunko

www.aozora.gr.jp
Site with more than 2,000 works of Japanese literature in HTML, ZIP, and Japanese eBooks (no English text at all)

### Athena Textes en Français

http://un2sg4.unige.ch/athena/
Ten thousand French eBooks by French and Swiss authors on French literature, philosophy, history, economics, science, and more

### Belarusian E-Library

http://knihi.com
Belarusian literature in Cyrillic script, with some English, German, and other translations

### Bibliothèque nationale de France

http://gallica.bnf.fr
More than 2 million digitized French documents from the National Library of France

### Biblioteca Virtual do Estudante Brasileiro

www.bibvirt.futuro.usp.br/index.html?principal.html&2
Several hundred Brazilian Portuguese eBooks

### Digital Library of India

www.dli.ernet.in/
More than 1 million eBooks predominantly in Indian languages

### Ebookgratis.it

http://www.ebookgratis.it/category/recensioni_ebook/ebookgratuiti/
<http://goo.gl/7mlsX>
Italian blog site that lists and links to free eBooks in Italian. Genres include novels, poetry, classics, plays, biographies, horror, and fantasy

### Libros Tauro (Argentina)

www.librostauro.com.ar/
Several thousand eBooks in Spanish

### New Threads Chinese Cultural Society

www.xys.org
Electronic library archive of classic Chinese texts

### ngiyaw eBooks (German)

http://ngiyaw-ebooks.org/
German works with some classic English and Hungarian books in PDF, PRC, LIT, and HTML formats for your web browser

### Online Books Page Links to Foreign Language Libraries

http://onlinebooks.library.upenn.edu/archives.html#foreign
A resource page with links to more than 70 foreign-language libraries. Resources include those in harder-to-find languages such as Afghan, Maori, and Yiddish

### Ozoz Cyberbooks

www.ozoz.it/cyberbooks.htm
Classic texts in English, Italian, and Latin, in HTML, RTF, and TXT formats

### Panjab Digital Library

www.panjabdigilib.org/webuser/searches/mainpage.jsp
This website preserves and makes accessible the Panjab heritage, with books, magazines, newspapers, and photos related to the Sikhs and the Indian region of Panjab

### Project Gutenberg Europe

http://pge.rastko.net/
More than 17,000 books in 58 languages

### Russian Science Fiction and Fantasy

www.rusf.rue
Books in both Russian and English in ZIP and HTML formats (all text on the website is in Cyrillic)

### Terra VirtualBooks for Children

http://virtualbooks.terra.com.br/v2/infantil/
<http://goo.gl/Ez8JC>
Free eBooks in Portuguese for children with stories by Brazilian authors and other world classics

# Chapter 15

# Students with Special Needs

Maria is a fifth-grade student with cerebral palsy (CP). She is motivated and on grade level. However, her CP restricts her to a motorized wheelchair. Her CP has made her weak and she tires easily, so much so that she cannot lift anything more than a pound. As a result, although Maria likes to read, many of the books in her classroom and the school library are too heavy for her to lift on her own and she requires assistance.

Because of these health issues, as part of her individualized educational program (IEP) all of her textbooks have been made available in a digital format. The textbooks are loaded onto a Kindle Fire, which sits on a stand on the desk that is built into her wheelchair. A switch control was considered for her eBook reader (see Figure 15.1), but her physical therapist thought using the touch screen would be good practice for her fine motor control.

To expand her personal reading materials, the school district subscribed to websites for students with disabilities, including Bookshare and Accessible Book Collection. Maria uses Read:OutLoud text-to-speech software to help her read books on her laptop. She and her teacher coordinate with the school librarian to help her access materials from the local public library's special-needs collection.

Educators in today's classroom need to be prepared to work with a diverse range of students, including those with special needs, such as disabilities or second-language issues (see chapter 14). Many students with special needs require accommodations in the school or classroom to help them learn and achieve their personal goals.

An accommodation is a change in how instruction is presented without changing the content of the instruction, the skill being learned, or the material being assessed. Text and textbooks provided in standard print format can create barriers for students with dyslexia, visual impairments, and other disabilities. eBook readers, in comparison, can serve as assistive technology tools that provide accommodations for reading with alternative formats, scaffolds, and supports to make information more accessible to all students. In this way, eBook devices and programs classify as a form of assistive technology, and assistive technologies must be considered for any student with an IEP (individualized education plan).

## ACCOMMODATIONS PROVIDED BY EBOOKS

According to the Center for Applied Technology (CAST, www.cast.org), educational materials need to be flexible and adaptable for all learning styles in order "to reach learners with disparate backgrounds, interests, styles, abilities, disabilities, and levels of expertise" (Rose & Meyer, 1998). One of the most common accommodations for students with special needs is providing the required text in electronic format. Once text is digital, it can be adapted for special-needs students in a number of ways.

Many eBook reader devices contain features that can be classified as accommodations or as assistive technology. Students with physical impairments benefit from the smaller reader devices and accessories such as switch controls (see sidebar, "Switch Control for Kindle"). eBooks can be more accommodating than printed text because of features such as adjustable text format, scanning assistance, highlighting, bookmarking, note-taking, multi-language interactive dictionaries, and text-to-speech capability.

Using the interactive features of modern eBooks, educators can create reading material for students that includes features such as advance organizers, concept maps, cooperative

---

### Switch Control for Kindle

PageBot is both a stand mount and a control for the Kindle. It can interface directly with a variety of adaptive switches, creating a simple interface for page control for people who cannot hold the Kindle or press its buttons.

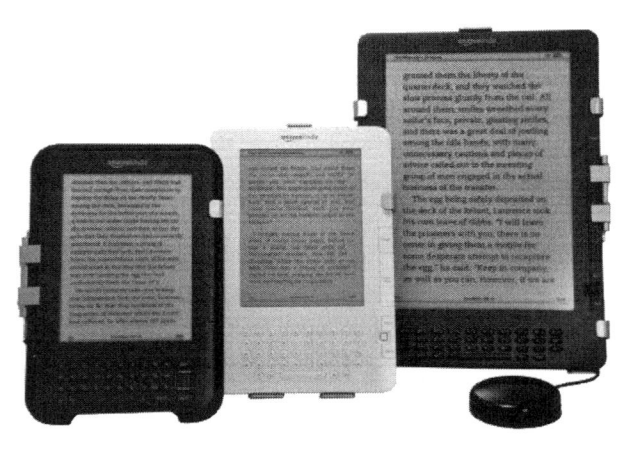

**FIGURE 15.1** The PageBot from Origin Instruments (http://estore.orin.com/) for Kindle allows for switch-operated control of Kindles with external page control

activities, and reading guides. Options such as text-to-speech and eBook interactions offer new ways for users to receive information as the material on screen is read aloud and students interact with the text. All these features can make using eBooks much more accessible to students with disabilities.

## Reduced Weight and Other Benefits

With their current size, battery life, memory, and display technology, handheld eBook devices add a degree of mobility and access to texts that was previously impossible. Compared to standard textbooks, eBook devices are very lightweight.

Many students who are physically impaired are unable to carry the average upper elementary 20-pound backpack (*Consumers Reports*, 2008) filled with books, workbooks, notes, and other resources. Compare that to popular eBook readers, which often weigh less than half a pound (the Nook Simple Touch weighs only 7.5 ounces). These devices can run for more than a month on a single charge and hold gigabytes of material. The amount of text in an eBook takes no additional space and adds no additional weight to the book, making eBook versions highly accessible to students with physical disabilities.

Not only are handheld reading devices accommodating with their size and weight, many also have a touch screen that allows the device to be controlled with a single finger. Other accommodations provided by eBooks include text-to-speech software and summary analysis programs, which analyze the text in a textbook or other book and extract material to make a summary. (These tools were built into many versions of Word and there are a number of applications available online; see "Online Resources".)

## Adjustable Text Display

Standard paper-based, printed text often presents barriers for dyslexic and visually impaired students. eBook text is adaptable, allowing students to select from a variety of sizes and font styles and to choose the one that is most appropriate or accommodating. Simple changes in the text display, such as enlarging the font, changing to boldface, or increasing the contrast between the text and background, can serve as accommodations.

Larger text sizes especially can assist students who have vision issues or have motor disabilities that affect eye movement. According to the Reluctant Reader Center (www.galeschools.com, 2004), many teachers, librarians, and media specialists already use large-print materials for their students who have the following:

- attention-deficit/hyperactivity disorder (ADHD)
- difficulty with encoding or decoding
- dyslexia
- large or small motor deficits
- amblyopia or "lazy eye"
- light sensitivity

- short-term memory deficits
- tracking issues
- visual impairments

While large-print text has usually been associated with visually impaired students, it also benefits others, such as struggling, reluctant, and remedial readers. Large-print materials (see Figure 15.2) can make visual processing less difficult (Riviere, 1996). The larger the print, the fewer words students view on each page. This allows them to focus more easily and decreases the chance of their losing their place while reading. Larger font sizes and spacing actually cause the eyes to move more slowly while reading, allowing students to track their reading more easily (Bloodsworth, 1993), giving them more processing time. Studies have found that students in all grades make more errors with smaller text. From this, Hughes and Wilkins (2000) concluded that the reading development of some children could benefit from a larger text size and spacing than is currently the norm.

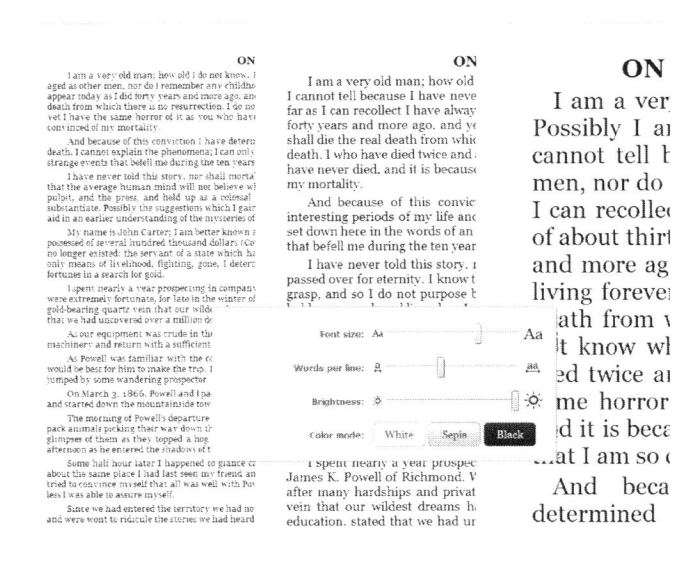

**FIGURE 15.2** The Kindle desktop program offers numerous font sizes, along with the ability to change the text or background color scheme

The type font and size used must contribute to rapid and easy reading by the student. Font sizes of 14 and 16 points are often used. eBooks often allow readers to enlarge the size of the print by sliding a text-size bar to a larger setting, so the student can find the size that best suits them.

## Interactive Features

The interactive capabilities of eBooks provide additional reading scaffolds. Most eBook programs allow you to search within the text, define words, bookmark pages, highlight text sections, and take notes (see Table 15.1). All of these features can increase a student's comprehension of a given work.

Features vary from device to device and among programs. Some features may not work depending on the format of the eBook file, and abilities may change with device platform, such as running the program on a desktop or tablet.

Using guided and active reading strategies, readers learn from their reading and about reading. As they read, they integrate information and strategies about how to read into what they are reading. Using this metacognitive structure, as students read for understanding,

**TABLE 15.1** Interactive Features for Leading eBook Devices

|  | Kindle Fire | NOOK Simple Touch | NOOK Color | Sony Reader | Kobo Touch | iRiver Story HD |
|---|---|---|---|---|---|---|
| Bookmark | Yes | Yes | Yes | Yes | Yes | Yes |
| Highlight | Yes | Yes | Yes | Yes | Yes | No |
| Margin notes | Yes | Yes | Yes | Yes | No | No |
| Drawing | No | No | No | Yes | No | No |
| Dictionary | Yes | Yes | Yes | Yes | Yes | Yes |
| Web search | Yes | Yes | Yes | No | Yes | No |
| Search within book | Yes | Yes | Yes | Yes | Yes | No |
| Sharing notes | Yes | Yes | Yes | No | Yes | No |
| Lending | Yes | Yes | Yes | No | No | No |

they need to monitor their understanding in an ongoing manner, and eBooks can help them do so. Students may do the following to monitor their understanding of what they are reading:

- interacting with the text
- highlighting or marking passages
- making notes about concepts or ideas
- answering questions from the prereading or that develop through reading
- writing about the reading

## *Highlighting*

To become effective readers, students need to be able to identify elements from a reading passage and to remember them. Both of these skills can be reinforced through highlighting. Highlighting text improves students' retention, and active highlighting is superior to passive reading of highlighted material (Fowler & Barker 1974). The act of highlighting also engages other learning modalities, and is frequently recommended for students with learning or attention issues. Highlighting is a more active process of reading because of the physical act of highlighting a word or section to identify things as important. It provides a kinesthetic element for students who need some movement. These interactions increase the chance that the material being read will be better stored in long-term memory and more easily recalled.

You can also go through an eBook and pre-highlight sections to assist readers. First, read the passage you wish to adapt, and then use the highlighter tool to identify selected text, such as vocabulary or other story elements.

## *Taking Notes*

Most eBook programs allow readers to make notes similar to margin notes in printed books. The notes do not disturb the text itself. Using a notes strategy helps maintain students'

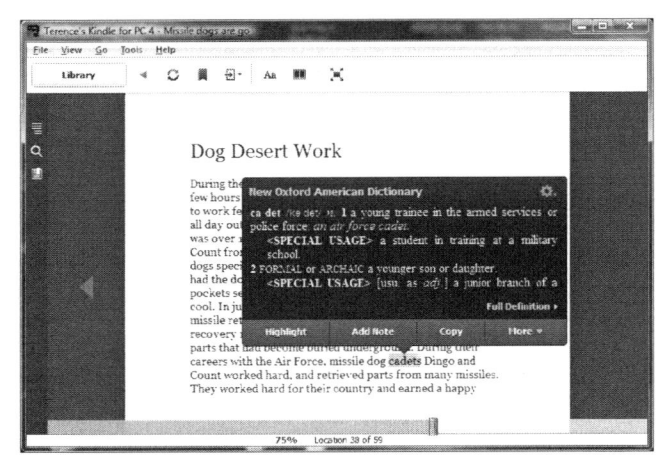

**FIGURE 15.3** The Kindle eBook program includes an interactive dictionary, highlighter, and note-taking tools

attention because students are more actively engaged in the reading process, which aids in comprehension and recall. Below are some of the ways students can use the annotations features that eBooks offer:

- writing definitions
- listing examples
- writing comments about the story
- writing out questions about the text
- summarizing sections or chapters
- making predictions based on content or structure

Using the device or program's annotation ability, you can create and embed reading guides or notes in an eBook to assist with students' reading.

### Interactive Dictionaries

Many eBook programs and devices have interactive dictionaries. These dictionaries allow users to select any word within the eBook and look up its definition instantly (see Figure 15.3). Students feel more independent when they can find the meaning of words without having to resort to additional resource materials such as a traditional paper dictionary. It can disrupt the reading process if students need to leave their desks, get a dictionary, remember the word they wish to look up, find it in the dictionary, and then return to their reading.

## Text-to-Speech and Speech Synthesis

A text-to-speech (TTS) system reads text aloud through the computer's sound card or other speech synthesis device. The text to be read is analyzed by the software, restructured to a phonetic system, and then read aloud. The computer evaluates each word and calculates its pronunciation (certain systems do this better than others). Then a speech synthesizer says the word. These systems are limited to a standard phonological structure, so foreign words, special personal pronunciations, or acronyms are often misspoken.

TTS offers users another way of receiving information, and it serves as an accommodation for various learning styles and individual differences in abilities. Studies have found advantages of using TTS with struggling readers over paper-based products (Reinking, Labbo, McKenna, & Kieffer, 1998). Research on students with reading disabilities shows that comprehension improves when text-to-speech is combined with reading (Leong, 1995; Montali and Lewandowsi, 1996; Raskind and Shaw, 2000).

Some eBook reader programs, such as Kindle and Adobe Reader (see Figure 15.4, also see Table 3.1), have text-to-speech capabilities. With some eBook applications, the text-to-speech feature is augmented by synchronized highlighting of the text being read. Two sources for such eBooks are RIF Reading Planet's Read Along Stories (www.rif.org/kids/readingplanet/bookzone/read_a-loud_stories.htm) and CAST's UDL Editions (http://udleditions.cast.org/). Having speech with synchronized highlighting can aid students in recognizing the structure of written language, and the spoken-word support has been found to improve reading comprehension for students with reading difficulties (Wise and Olson, 1994).

When text-to-speech tools are not available, the same effect can be achieved by having students read the text while listening to the audiobook version. However, simply listening to the audio without following the text does not provide the same benefits to students' comprehension and vocabulary building.

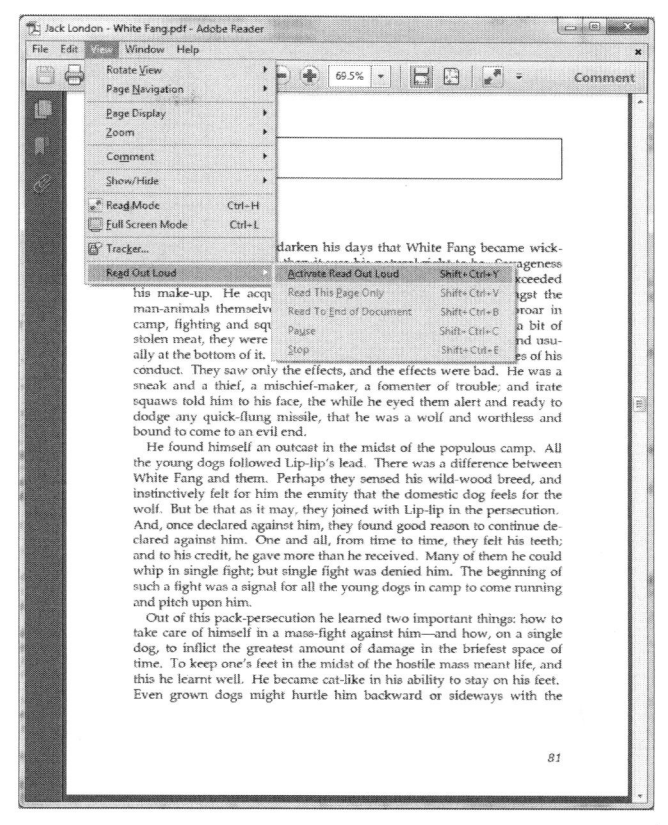

**FIGURE 15.4** Adobe Reader's read-out-loud feature is accessed from the View menu

# Simplified Text

Another form of accommodation is to shorten the text, make an abridged version of a book's text, or change text to a simpler form. For eBooks, you can use a tool such as Microsoft Word's AutoSummarize (on versions earlier than Word 2010). Selecting it from the Tools menu produces a pop-up window that lets a user determine how much of the text will be displayed in the summary. While this kind of tool will work relatively well for textbooks, it is ineffective with narratives. Online tools for summarizing text are listed in "Online Resources."

Another way to simplify text is to rewrite it to meet your students' comprehension levels. The John Hopkins University Center for Technology in Education (JHUCTE, 2012) suggests these guidelines for rewriting text:

- Retain keywords.
- Substitute synonyms that are more familiar conceptually.
- Provide contextual clues for difficult keywords.
- Write most sentences with regular sentence order (subject first, followed by verb), but avoid short, choppy sentences that sound stilted.
- Use active sentences. For example, use "The car hit the child." not "The child was hit by the car."
- Be sure every pronoun has an unmistakable antecedent.

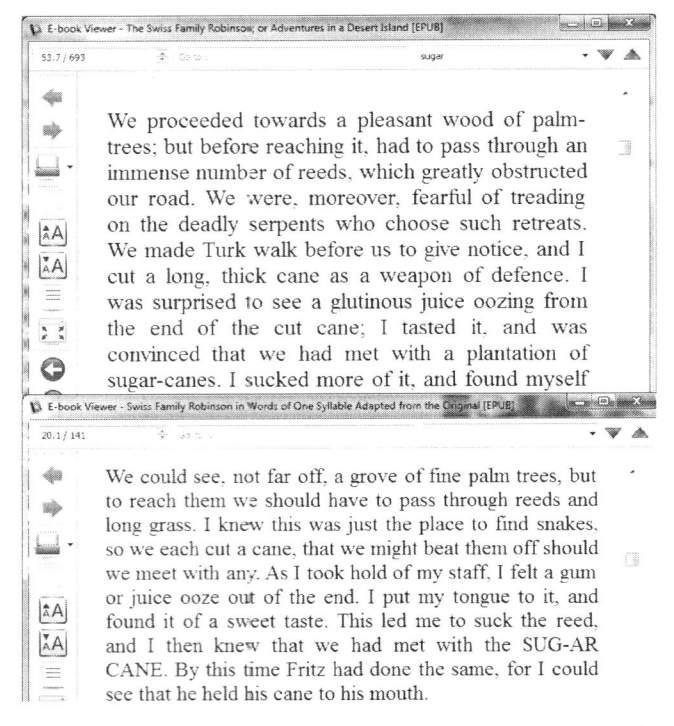

**FIGURE 15.5** At top is the original *The Swiss Family Robinson*; below is the rewritten text in words of one syllable by Mary Godolphin, as viewed on Calibre's eBook viewer (©2012, Kovid Goyal)

An example of text simplification is Mary Godolphin's conversion of classic texts such as *The Swiss Family Robinson* and *Robinson Crusoe*. In these books, she rewrote the text using only one-syllable words. These books are available for download from Project Gutenberg (www.gutenberg.org). Where it was not possible to use a one-syllable word (such as for personal names), Godolphin wrote out the word in capital letters and broke it up by syllables (such as "sug-ar cane", see Figure 15.5).

If you are rewriting an eBook, you can also include blank sections to separate parts and add images, concept maps, notes, and even extra spacing between words.

To simplify text, first create or edit the eBook using a word processor, and then save the document in RTF format. The RTF file can be converted into the desired format by using an eBook management tool such as Calibre (see chapter 5).

# SAMPLE ACCOMMODATION

As an example of how to make a book more accommodating, I will describe a recent project to adapt a book for a special-needs situation. This project involved adapting a required reading book, *The Secret Garden* (1911) by Frances Hodgson Burnett (1849–1924). This classic children's novel is often used as a multidisciplinary book for teaching language, history, science, and health.

In adapting this book, I first had to determine whether to create the eBook file or use files that already existed. Because the book is in the public domain (and therefore copyright-free), I found numerous copies available in my preferred eBook format. However, none of the eBook versions contained all the features that I wanted, so I decided to create my own version. I downloaded a text-only version and opened it in my word processor. I then added heading levels and page breaks, and bolded certain words. In each chapter, I also created guided reading questions at the beginning and summary questions and activities at the end (see Figure 15.6).

In several chapters, I added associated copyright-free public-domain pictures from a variety of sources, and I created concept maps for the characters and storyline. I saved the completed book as an RTF file, which I then added to the Calibre eBook management program. I then used this program to convert the book into the desired eBook formats (see Part III for more information on creating eBooks). Calibre also creates a "clickable" table of contents to each chapter, based on the heading levels used, allowing students to quickly jump to any chapter or subsection. With the book now in an eBook format, I transferred it to the eBook reader device.

Using the eBook reader, I developed additional accommodations. In each chapter, I highlighted passages or components that were important or potentially difficult. I added reading-guide elements as note annotations, which were indicated on the pages with nonintrusive marks. When students clicked on these marks, pop-up windows appeared with the content. Students were also able to add their own notes, questions, and answers to these windows. I added bookmarks to passages that related to specific topics, such as science. While reading the book, students were also able to add their own bookmarks to indicate pages to which they wished to return or passages for which they wanted to seek help.

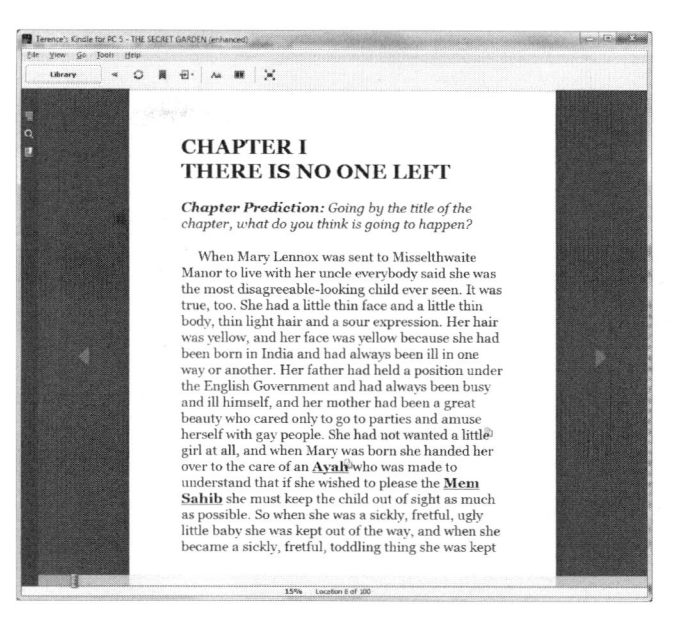

**FIGURE 15.6** Guided reading questions, reading prompts, and vocabulary marks have been added to this eBook file

This collection of annotations, both the ones created by me and the ones created by students, became an associated file on that eBook reader that other students were able to access as they read the book. I then copied that annotation file from the device, saving the file to my computer hard drive. This process allowed my students and I to keep the entire eBook with the annotation files. Now, we can share the eBook and annotation files with other students and teachers who wish to read the accommodated eBook.

# OBTAINING EBOOKS FOR STUDENTS WITH SPECIAL NEEDS

## Textbooks

If an educator is using a standard textbook with a class and needs to obtain an electronic version for a student with special needs, the first thing to do is check to see if there is a digital version of the textbook already available. Many textbook publishers publish web-based versions of their textbooks. Others, such as Houghton Mifflin Harcourt, offer downloadable versions of their textbooks in EPUB or PDF formats, which will work well with most tablets or eBook readers. If a digital version isn't already available, it can be requested from the publisher. Usually this request can be processed through the school district's office of student services or special-education department. The request can take some time and often requires special forms and permissions concerning copyright.

With an electronic textbook, students will usually be able to change the text size, use screen magnification software, integrate a text-to-speech program, use translating software, or access a print-to-Braille function. Some publishers have additional features or tools to help readers use online digital textbooks.

## Trade Books

For trade books, search the free online libraries for existing copies (see chapter xxx for lists of libraries.) Another option is for an individual or school to contract with a special-needs book subscription service such as the Accessible Book Collection (www.accessiblebook collection.org), Learning Ally (www.learningally.org), or Bookshare.org (www.bookshare.org). The Accessible Book Collection provides access to thousands of titles with features such as word counts, readability levels, and other tools for $49.95 per year. Learning Ally, previously known as Recordings for the Blind and Dyslexic, offers audiobooks. Bookshare.org (see Figure 15.7), free for all U.S. student with qualifying disabilities, has more than 140,000 eBooks in its collection (including many on the Accelerated Reader list), and makes them available in multiple formats, including Contracted Braille (BRF) or DAISY, which can be converted to other formats if needed.

Read:Outloud is a software program available for free to Bookshare users. It will read text aloud with synchronized highlighting and allows students to highlight text, take notes, and use an interactive dictionary. Read:Outloud is also available for purchase from Don Johnston (www.donjohnston.com/products/read_outloud/).

**FIGURE 15.7** Bookshare is a free eBook service for all U.S. students with qualifying disabilities (© 2012, Benetech)

Scholastic, working with Tom Snyder Productions, also has an eBook tool to assist special-needs and struggling readers, called Thinking Reader (www.tomsnyder.com). This program gives readers additional instruction, reading strategies, comprehension supports, voice narration, and synchronized highlighting.

Another type of subscription service that has been found to be effective with special-needs, second-language, and emergent readers is a weekly news service called News-2-You (http://news2you.n2y.com/). This service is a form of online newspaper, delivered through the Internet, which provides reading support through the use of symbols. By subscribing to New-2-You, a school or educator receives 38 issues a year in PDF format. Subscriptions start at $149 per year, and each publication has a regular edition, a simplified edition, and a communication board overlay.

## ACHIEVING SUCCESS WITH EBOOKS

Anderson-Inmany and Horne's (1999) studies indicated that students can access and use the scaffolding advantages of voice output, online dictionaries, and note-taking offered through electronic text to achieve success in classroom assignments. The same material in digital form offers many advantages for students with or without disabilities. With today's computer and eBook technologies, educators have tools with features valuable for learners with various abilities, language backgrounds, and special needs. eBook technologies can provide accommodations such as variable text size, text-to-speech, and interactions that many students need to be successful with text-based materials. Educators should consider using eBooks as an accommodation for students, using the abilities and functions that are already built in and creating additional supports or accommodations. The features and capabilities of eBooks can provide the accommodations or scaffolding that many students need to be successful with text-based materials.

## ONLINE RESOURCES

### Accessible Book Collection
www.accessiblebookcollection.orge
Book subscription service for special-needs readers

### Bookshare.org
www.bookshare.orge
Book subscription service for special-needs readers with print disabilities

### Calibre
http://calibre-ebook.com/
eBook management and file conversion software

### CAST's eReader

www.cast.org
Web browser with text-to-speech system

### Don Johnson's Read Outloud

www.donjohnston.com/products/read_outloud/
Reader software program that will read aloud with synchronized highlighting, allowing students to highlight text, take notes, and use an interactive dictionary

### Holt McDougal

http://holtmcdougal.hmhco.com/hm/home.htm
Digital textbooks with accommodations

### Learning Ally

www.learningally.org
Audiobooks for the blind and dyslexic

### News-2-You

http://news2you.n2y.com/
A weekly digital newspaper for special education with picture/symbol support

### Project Gutenberg

www.gutenberg.org
Online digital library

### RIF Reading Planet's Read Along Stories & Songs

www.rif.org/kids/readingplanet/bookzone/read_aloud_stories.htm
Flash-delivered stories using synchronized highlighting

### *The Secret Garden*

www.drscavanaugh.org/ebooks
Accommodated book examples for download

### Thinking Reader (Scholastic)

www.tomsnyder.com/Products/Product.asp?SKU=THITHI
<http://goo.gl/wa9X0>
eBook reader that provides reading strategies and comprehension supports

## Online Auto Summary Tools to Shorten Text

### Brevity Document Summarizer

www.lextek.com/cgi-bin/brevtest

**Great Summary**

www.greatsummary.com/highlight.html

**Summ-it Summarization Applet**

www.computing.surrey.ac.uk/SystemQ//summary/

**Text Compactor**

www.textcompactor.com

**Tools 4 Noobs Summarize**

www.tools4noobs.com/summarize/

# Appendix A: eBook Formats List

.AA – Audible audiobook format

.AU – digital audio format

.AVI – Windows video format

.AZW – Kindle ebook format based on MOBI format

.BRF – Contracted Braille

.CBR (CBZ; CBC) – comic book format that is composed of compressed JPG scanned comic book pages

.CHM – Compiled HTML file

.DAISY – Digital Accessible Information SYstem (DAISY) an open standard format for people with print disabilities

.DJVU (DJV) – Format for documents containing combination of text drawings and photographs

.DPG – Moon Shell program format for Nintendo DS or windows computer

.DOC – Microsoft Word document file

.EBO – MS Reader annotations file

.EPUB – open standard for ebooks

.EXE – an executable program file

.FB2 – Fictionbook ebook format

.GIF – image format designed for drawings

.HTM (HTML; HTMLZ) – HTML file written in hypertext markup language for web browsers reading

.JPG (JPEG) – image format designed for photographs

.LIT – Microsoft Reader format (no longer supported by Microsoft)

.LRF (LRX) – Sony proprietary ebook format

.MOV – QuickTime video

.M4A – MPEG 4 format for audio

.M4B – MPEG 4 format for audiobooks, can book mark files

.MOBI – Mobipocket ebook format (also works on Kindle)

.MP3 – digital audio format.

.MPG – MPEG – video format

.ODT – Open document standard for word processors

.OEB – Initial open ebook format (has been replaced by EPUB)

.OGG – open audio format

.PDB – Palm DOC file

.PDF – Adobe Reader file

.PML – Palm markup language

.PPS – PowerPoint show file

.PPT – PowerPoint presentation file

.PRC – Mobipocket and Palm ebook format (also works on Kindle)

.RA – real media video

.RTF – Rich Text File readable by most word processors

.SWF – Macromedia FLASH format

.TCR – Compressed ebook format

.TK3 – Files read by the TK3 reader from Nightkitchen

.TR – Tomeraider eBook files

.TXT (TXTZ) – Plain text format

.WMV – Window's media format

.OeB – formulated in compliance with Open eBook specifications

# Index

Accommodation, 30, 85, 169, 170, 172, 182, 187, 188, 189, 192, 193, 194, 197, 198
Adapt, 7, 33, 34, 38, 45, 57, 85, 89, 90, 115, 125, 132, 152, 153, 162, 188, 189, 191, 194
Assessment, ix, 17, 58, 87, 89, 90, 91, 116, 122, 124, 127, 132, 133, 134, 135, 138, 152, 167

Calibre, 36, 75, 76, 79, 108, 109, 110, 118, 194, 197
Caption, 4, 18, 20, 22, 99
Catalog, 42, 50, 59, 69, 75, 77, 78, 79, 80, 81,
Chiropractic, 7
Collaboration, 84, 88, 89, 91, 122, 125
Comic, 29, 33, 36, 41, 61, 62, 63, 100, 101, 102, 103, 104, 105
Common Core, 9, 10, 85, 86, 125, 135
Community, 41, 57, 81, 87, 154, 156, 158, 165
Comprehension, 5, 41, 61, 132, 133, 134, 152, 154, 156, 158, 167, 182, 190–93, 196, 198
Copyright, 9, 13, 27, 28, 113, 114, 117, 194, 195
Cross-platform, 18, 21, 25, 118

Differentiate, 58, 94, 167, 168, 169
DRM (Digital Rights Management), 28

eInk, 14, 15, 16
ELL (English Language Learner) ESL (English Second Language), 122, 177, 178, 179, 182, 183
Ergonomic, 8

Fluency, 41, 61, 132, 133, 135, 158

Graphic Novel, 33, 61, 63, 69

Headphone, 35, 127, 128
Highlight, 8, 94, 181, 190, 191, 196, 198

IRA (International Reading Association), 8, 41, 42, 84, 124
ISTE (International Society for Technology in Education), 8, 10, 84

Journal, 61, 172, 174

Kindle, 1, 2, 4, 5, 7, 11, 12–16, 18, 22, 26–28, 32, 43, 65–68, 70–73, 75, 76, 88, 108, 110, 117, 118, 126, 128, 159, 170, 171–73, 181, 187, 188, 190, 191, 192

Legislation, 6
Literacy, ix, 9, 38, 45, 51, 57, 83, 121, 122, 124, 125, 126, 145, 151, 156, 157, 158, 161, 179
Literature, Circle 77

Media, ix, 2, 5, 9, 32, 34, 48, 49, 54, 61, 70, 71, 76, 86, 89, 90, 92, 107, 122, 123–128, 142, 14, 145, 152, 178, 189

NCTE (National Council of Teachers of English), 8, 10, 84

POD (Print on Demand), 29
PowerPoint, 33, 34, 37, 38, 39, 45, 48, 88, 107, 110–14, 118, 181
Public Domain, x, 13, 18, 27, 29, 32, 35, 36, 37, 43, 44, 56, 62, 71, 75, 76, 116, 119, 122, 132, 145, 148, 162, 163, 194

Reader's Theater, 51, 53, 54, 57, 127, 160, 161
Rubric, 89, 91, 101, 115, 116

Search, x, 12, 13, 25, 26, 28, 44, 57, 58, 65, 68, 69, 71, 78, 81, 110, 114, 125, 139, 146, 153, 162, 171, 190, 191, 192, 196

Smartphone, 3, 17, 26, 27, 33
Standards, ix, 8, 9, 10, 85, 86, 87, 89, 125, 135, 139, 140, 142, 143, 147
Storyboard, 95, 112, 113
Strategies, ix, 86, 87, 91, 97, 122, 126, 129, 152, 190, 196, 198
Struggling, 122, 135, 151–65, 190, 192, 196

Tablet, 2, 8, 11, 15–18, 26–28, 68, 69, 83, 124, 126, 128, 190, 195
Tags, 77, 78, 79, 95
Text-to-Speech, 16, 26, 87, 127, 128, 171, 187, 188, 189, 192, 193, 196, 197

Vocabulary, 5, 138, 139, 152–54, 156–58, 164, 169, 180–82, 191, 193

# About the Author

TERENCE W. CAVANAUGH is associate professor of instructional technology in the College of Education and Human Services at University of North Florida. He has been an educator for more than 30 years at the college and secondary level. His areas of expertise include instructional technology, electronic books, assistive technology, ESOL education, and teacher education. His published works include several books on technology and education topics, such as Libraries Unlimited's *The Tech-Savvy Booktalker: A Guide for 21st-Century Educators*; *Literature Circles through Technology*; *Bookmapping: Lit Trips and Beyond*; and *Teach Science with Science Fiction Films: A Guide for Teachers and Library Media Specialists*. Cavanaugh has also written numerous chapters and articles.

# About the Contributors

KATRINA W. HALL is an associate professor of literacy at the University of North Florida. She teaches undergraduate and graduate level courses in literacy. Before coming to UNF, she taught public school at the elementary level for 10 years, earning her National Board Certification as an Early Childhood Generalist. Her area of research is framed around how children learn, with the context of literacy.

GIGI DAVID is a visiting assistant professor, Department of Childhood Education, Literacy and TESOL at the University of North Florida. Her research interests include equipping early childhood educators to facilitate the development of social competence for young children and the potential impact of enhancing the home learning environment of underserved preschool children by providing books, art materials and arts-infused activities to build readiness skills, including emergent literacy skills. As children's author and developer of arts-integration curriculum, she enriches the educational experience of elementary school children. (http://www.culturalcouncil.org/educators/k-12-art-in-public-places-lesson-plans)

LUNETTA WILLIAMS is an Associate Professor in the Department of Childhood Education, Literacy, and TESOL at the University of North Florida. Her overarching research interest is minimizing the reading achievement gap among economically disadvantaged and economically advantaged children. She has published in *Journal of Educational Research, Reading Psychology, Journal of Research in Childhood Education, Journal of Reading Education, Childhood Education, Voices from the Middle, Research in the Schools,* and *Florida Reading Journal.*

ANDREA THOERMER is a Doctoral Student in the School of Teaching and Learning at the University of Florida. She is specializing in Reading Education and Curriculum, Teaching, and Teacher Education with interests in reading comprehension, teacher expertise and professional development. She has published in The Reading Teacher and Critical Issues in Teacher Education.

CHRISTINE WEBER is an Associate Professor of Childhood Education at the University of North Florida. Her research interests include extensive work in gifted education. She was the Principal Investigator for the Working on Gifted Issues Project, a grant project funded by the Florida Department of Education for eight years. Under her leadership, the *Florida's Frameworks for K-12 Gifted Learners* was developed and disseminated to all school districts in the state.

Dr. Weber has also presented at state, national and international conferences on a wide variety of topics concerning the gifted and has published many articles which can be found in *Gifted Child Today, Gifted Education Press Quarterly,* the *Journal of Faculty Development, Gifted Child International, Florida Educational Leadership, The Florida Reading Journal and Distance Learning.*

JIN-SUK BYUN is an assistant professor of TESOL at the University of North Florida. His research interests are input, interaction, and output in second language acquisition, automaticity from SLA and psycholinguistic perspectives, the effect of TESOL/TEFL certificate program, and Classroom English.